# The Wines of the Napa Valley

# The Wines of the Napa Valley

**by Larry Walker**

**MITCHELL BEAZLEY**

First published in Great Britain in 2005
by Mitchell Beazley, an imprint of
Octopus Publishing Group Limited,
2–4 Heron Quays, London E14 4JP.

Copyright © Octopus Publishing Group Ltd 2005

Text copyright © Larry Walker 2005

Map copyright © John Flower 2005

A CIP catalogue record for this book is available from the British Library.

ISBN: 1 84000 994 2

The author and publishers will be grateful for any information which will assist them in keeping future editions up-to-date. Although all reasonable care has been taken in the preparation of this book, neither the publishers nor the author can accept any liability for any consequences arising from the use thereof, or the information contained therein.

Printed and bound in England by Mackays, Chatham.

# Contents

# Acknowledgments

Deepest thanks to the winemakers and grape-growers of Napa. Many of the questions I asked must have seemed plain dumb to those men and women, but they never once told me to get lost. I appreciate that.

This book is for the real superstars of Napa, the men and women who work long hours in the vineyard and wine cellars. Without them, there would be no Napa wine as we know it. Viva!

# Foreword

It is not the best of times to write a book about Napa. Napa wine is very much a moving target, caught up by profound changes in the vineyard and in winemaking techniques, striving to retain the exuberance of youth, while maturing into a more subtle and complex creature. There is an underlying tension between the in-your-face boldness, the fresh confidence of the early triumphs, and the mature realization that there are still miles to go. Out of that tension, that desire to excel, comes a rich and exciting approach that is still very much a work in progress, difficult to pin down on the page.

To be sure, some of the recent success carries within it the threat of taking Napa wines, Cabernet in particular, in an entirely new and perhaps undesirable direction. In today's Napa, the winemaker and the grower have achieved parity. The best winemakers know that without good grapes, they can't make good wine; the best growers know that the better the grapes they deliver, the better the wine, more money for them. But it isn't all about money. There is a lot of pride in Napa, which helps drive the whole engine.

Not long ago, Napa wine was dominated by the winemaker. Those were heady days for graduates of the University of California, Davis (UC Davis), where oenology ruled and vineyards were mostly regarded as factories producing grapes, the raw material which the winemaker then shaped into wine. When I first began writing about wine as a financial reporter for the *San Francisco Chronicle*, I needed only sit at the feet of the all-knowing winemaker, a very Californian noun, and absorb everything I needed to know. In the 1980s, there was endless talk of oak barrels, of coopers, of toast levels, and of special yeast cultures. I even remember something called "killer" yeast, murderous little organisms added to the fermenting grape juice to slaughter all indigenous yeast that might have entered the sacred temple of the winery from the vineyards without proper documentation.

That's painting with a broad brush, of course. There have always been those in Napa who recognized the importance of the vineyard. Old wine masters like Louis M Martini and Joseph Heitz, growers like Nathan Fay and Barney and Bella Rhodes, and a few others really laid the groundwork for the new Napa wines. Two things, I believe, happened in the mid-1980s and early-1990s that led Napa vintners to step outside the cellar door and walk into the vineyard. First, as Napa wines pushed into the global wine market, Napa winemakers began to taste, on a regular basis, the great wines of Europe. They began to appreciate nuance and realize that at least a part of what made those wines great was the source of the grapes. Just how important is still a matter of debate in Napa and elsewhere. Winemakers also began to question the official UC Davis line that climate was all that mattered and California had the ideal climate for growing wine grapes. (No one seemed to notice that there was not a single "climate" for Napa or California overall.) This led to the simply silly slogan that: "Every year is a vintage year in California".

The second thing that happened was the resurgence of phylloxera. Later on I'll get into why phylloxera struck again (see page 34), but its impact has been huge, especially in Napa. Growers were forced to replant vineyards that were barely twenty years old, often even younger. When the vineyards had been planted in the 1960s and 1970s, vineyard technology was driven (once more) by the UC Davis model of the vineyard as a factory, processing sunlight and agro-chemicals into grapes. Vine rows were wide-spaced – the standard model was 2.4 metres (eight feet) between vines, almost four metres (twelve feet) between rows for the convenience of machines. Any hint that the vineyard was a living thing was thoroughly debunked. The rows were bare; denuded by herbicides and/or mechanical weeders. Everything, including the vine rootstock, was designed to maximize production.

When post-phylloxera replanting began in the early 1990s, the more alert growers looked around and said, "If we have to spend all this money, let's get it right this time". Work had already been done by the Robert Mondavi Winery and others on denser planting and other techniques to reduce the yield of a single vine while concentrating more flavour in the grape. Faced with new plantings, growers took a closer look at developments in rootstock, in trellising techniques, in pruning, and shoot positioning. It became clear that vineyard technology had caught up with winemaking technology. It followed that if changes in technology made a difference in the flavour profile of the grape, the vineyard site could also make a difference. Napa discovered terroir, however reluctantly.

I believe that discovery has made Napa one of the world's most exciting wine-growing regions. Napa can truly talk about wine-growing now. It is as if one could return to the Middle Ages and report on the development of what would become the great vineyards of Burgundy. But what makes the situation very different is that Napa growers are very self-aware of the terroir mission. No one in Napa (or at least, no one that matters) is planting vineyards driven by the market or personal likes or dislikes, or because that's the way grandfather did it, or even because you have to plant Cabernet Sauvignon because that's Napa's best grape. New plantings now are based on soil samples, careful rootstock and clonal selection, and computer analysis of local weather conditions, right down to the vine row. Perhaps the most important tool a wine-grower has is a personal computer, monitoring the heartbeat of the vineyard. It's just too expensive in Napa to make a mistake in planting. And, there is also the Napa urge to be the best.

The wine-growers of Napa are listening to the dirt talk and paying attention. There's a lot to learn. The story of Napa for the twenty-first century will be the story of terroir and the continued development of the great Napa wine houses. The ideal time to write the book of Napa wine would be after this is all sorted out. However, none of us is likely to be around to lift a glass when or if that ever happens. My particular mission is to start the ball rolling on a non-technical discussion of Napa terroirs and the interaction between site and winemaking and, at the end of the day, the wine in the bottle. Napa wine is a work in progress. This book is simply a series of snapshots documenting that progress. But then, all wine really is a work in progress, a living creature, difficult to pin to the page, but certainly worth the effort.

Cheers!

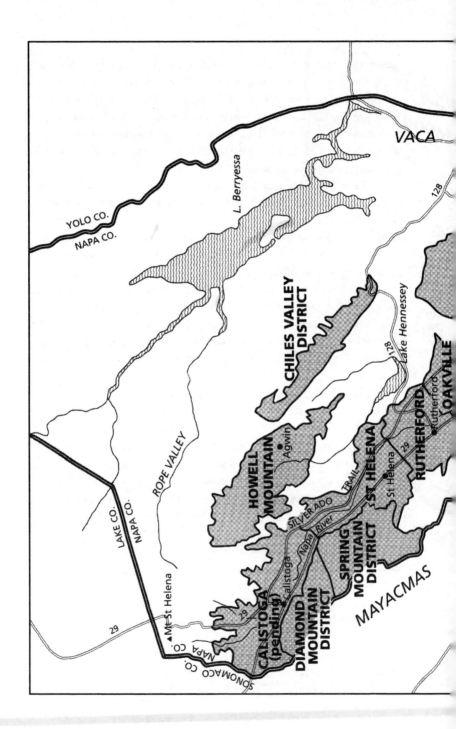

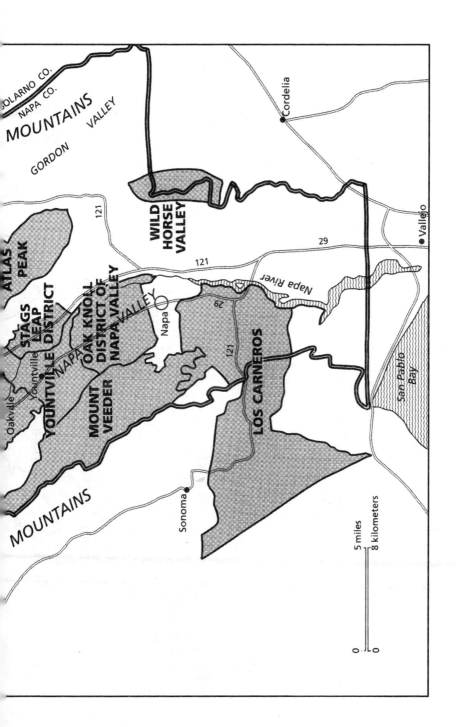

SOLARNO CO.
NAPA CO.

MOUNTAINS

GORDON VALLEY

ATLAS PEAK

STAGS LEAP DISTRICT

YOUNTVILLE DISTRICT

OAK KNOLL DISTRICT OF NAPA VALLEY

MOUNT VEEDER

NAPA VALLEY

MOUNTAINS

Oakville

Yountville

Napa

121

121

29

29

121

WILD HORSE VALLEY

Cordelia

Vallejo

Napa River

LOS CARNEROS

San Pablo Bay

Sonoma

5 miles

8 kilometers

0

0

xiii

# 1

# In the beginning

I like to think of the sunny afternoon in 1880 that Robert Louis Stevenson and Jacob Schram sat on the porch of Schram's winery, deep in a redwood canyon outside Calistoga in northern Napa, drinking wine from Schram's vineyard, as the launch of Napa wines into the world. Wine historians date the beginnings some forty or fifty years earlier, when George Yount, a kind of Jeremiah Johnson clone in his earlier days, settled down on the site of what is now Yountville in the southern part of Napa and planted vines.

What kind of place is Napa? When the Spanish established a fort over-looking the Golden Gate, where San Francisco Bay meets the Pacific Ocean, in 1776, Napa was a virtually unknown wilderness to Europeans. It was the home of roughly 5,000 Native Americans, though that number is guesswork. By the time Yount planted his vines, little more than half a century later, they were mostly gone, victims of European disease and a more or less deliberate policy of extermination.

There is no documentary evidence of where Yount got the vines, but most likely they came from the Spanish mission in Sonoma, the last of the twenty-one missions built in Alta California, which was established in 1823, only ten years before the Mexican government secularized all California missions. The vines were almost certainly what we call Mission in California, probably the same vines still cultivated in South America, called País in Chile and Criolla in Argentina. In time, DNA research may well establish the origin of the Mission grape. Some believe it is a cousin of Sardina's Monica variety. At any rate, it had already been cultivated in Mexico for more than 250 years by the time it reached Napa and could well have undergone many changes, perhaps even crossing with native Mexican grapes.

There are still about 405 hectares of Mission grapes planted in California. It makes a pleasing table grape and can also be used for raisins. No one in modern times has ever praised it as a wine grape, although there are still a few wines made, as curiosities. Traditionally it was made in both a dry and sweet style, often called Angelica in the sweet version. It was made by adding brandy to white wine that had barely begun to ferment, then ageing the wine in barrels. Old Angelica takes on a nutty somewhat sherry-like flavour.

The Mission grape had been brought to Alta California by Franciscan missionaries from Baja California, sometime in the 1770s. According to mission manuscripts, the first wine made in what is now California was probably in 1782 at Mission San Juan Capistrano, south of Santa Barbara, almost half a century before Yount arrived in northern California in 1831. Yount made himself useful in various ways to Mariano Vallejo, the last Mexican governor of California, who was then a lieutenant in charge of the Presidio in San Francisco. By the time Vallejo made colonel in 1836, he was the man in charge of handing out former mission lands. He granted Yount, the ambitious slayer of both grizzly bears and Native Americans, 4,856 hectares in Napa Valley called Rancho Caymus. At the time, there were no Europeans living in Napa Valley.

Yount's last campaign as an Indian fighter was a bloody attack on a band of Indians, probably Miwok, just south of what is now the city of Napa. Vallejo, by then a general, had accused the Indians of stealing horses. They probably had been. The Native American and European concepts of personal property were not always in agreement. Apparently Yount wiped out the entire band: men, women, and children. Yount's last battle apparently made Napa safe for the vine. He planted his vineyard in the fall of 1838 or winter of 1839. There is no record of Yount making wine until the mid-1840s. In 1857 his wine won second prize at the Napa County Fair and his brandy took first prize, although most of his energies were devoted to cattle and grain.

What did Yount's prize-winning wine taste like? The answer is, I don't want to know. As the first Napa winemaker, Yount undoubtedly followed the standard winemaking procedure as practised in the missions. The grapes were dumped into a cow skin, sewn to make a sort of bag. This was hung between two sturdy poles and the grapes were crushed by foot. The resulting mess was drained off through a small opening in the cowhide bag into large wooden tubs, which were then left to ferment for several weeks. After fermentation, the cap was put through a press and the resulting juice was distilled into brandy. The finished wine left in the tubs was then put into any kind of handy container that was reasonably airtight and the wine was consumed over the next several months. If you wanted white wine, you simply drew off some of the juice direct from the cowhide and put it in a separate fermenter. State of the art winemaking, in mid-nineteenth century Napa Valley.

By the time Stevenson and Schram shared a bottle or two, things had progressed considerably. Schram's wines, along with many other Napa wines, were already very well known by then, but it was Stevenson who first gave Napa wine its "lifestyle" spin, creating perhaps the first modern wine. In twenty-first century terms, Stevenson helped write the back story that has figured largely in the success of Napa wines. His line calling Napa wine "bottled poetry" still greets visitors on a roadside sign near Oakville. Stevenson knew the value of an image as well as Robert Mondavi did more than a century later when he took upon himself the portfolio of World Ambassador at Large for Napa Wines. Mondavi created a story line for Napa wine. He created a context, establishing that wine, at least great wine, is very much the product of a place. Mondavi was not the first to make that statement. He was just the first to make people listen.

## GEOGRAPHY AND GEOLOGY

So we come back to the question, what kind of place is Napa? First of all, there is no single Napa, at least not in a wine-growing sense. There is the political division, Napa County, and there is the American Viticultural Area (AVA), Napa Valley. In terms of defining wine character, neither bit of nomenclature is much help. There is far more variation in soils and microclimates within Napa than in all of Burgundy or Bordeaux and that within a much smaller area.

Physically, the valley proper is about forty-eight kilometres (thirty miles) long and ranges from 1.6 to 4.8 kilometres (one mile to three miles) in width, sandwiched between two arms of the California coastal mountain ranges: the Mayacamas on the west, roughly dividing Napa Valley from the more coastal Sonoma Valley; and on the east by the Vaca range, a rocky thrust of hills protecting Napa from much warmer interior valleys. Both ranges contain a number of extinct volcanoes and the many geothermal springs, in the mid and northern parts of the valley, show some lingering volcanic activity. These springs play, perhaps, a greater role in Napa wine than has previously been suspected, creating warmer zones that can have a very local impact on vineyards. More work needs to be done on that issue.

The valley runs northwest-southeast, beginning at San Pablo Bay (a shallow arm of San Francisco Bay) in the south and ending at Mount St Helena in the north, at 1,323 metres (4,343 feet), the highest mountain in the area. The elevation gain from the Bay to the base of Mount St Helena is slight, only about seventy-two metres (250 feet). However, on the west and east sides of the valley, vineyards are planted at elevations of more than 609 metres (2,000 feet) in Mount Veeder, Spring Mountain, Diamond Mountain, Howell Mountain, and Atlas Peak appellations.

It would surely surprise most visitors to Napa, who are intent on sampling as many wines as possible in between snapping pictures of the wild mustard in spring, to learn that they are sipping the current vintage while perched rather shakily on the edge of the Pacific Rim of Fire. And don't forget the less than stable San Andreas fault just a few kilometres to the west. In geological terms, Napa is still very young and is subject to unpredictable upheavals, like most teenagers. The region is the result of violent volcanic and tectonic plate action of the earth's shifting and clashing crust, played out over countless millions of years.

Today Napa is part of what geologists call the California Coastal Margin, which rose from the sea millions of years ago. Over even more millions of years the sea level rose and fell again and again, creating layers of sediment, that were punctuated by incredible fireworks displays as enormous volcanoes churned up various bit and pieces of the Pacific Ocean floor onto a landscape that is now producing $150-a-bottle cult Cabernet.

Napa Valley is somewhat unusual in the California Coastal Margin. It is called a drop and spread valley, created as two mountain ranges pulled apart. Because of the position of the Mayacamas and the Vaca ranges, Napa is a low elevation valley running north-south, rather than the more common east-west valley created by streams and rivers draining west into the Pacific. These valleys, such as the Russian River and Dry Creek Valleys in Sonoma County, also tend to be at a higher elevation.

The Napa River itself has played a key role in shaping Napa Valley and its soils and therefore the wines. It is a much tamer river today than in the past. Napa River and its short mountain-spawned adjacent streams have created alluvial fans up and down the valley, where some of Napa's best vineyards are found – think Duckhorn Three Palms Merlot. The river has also changed course several times, perhaps within historic times, because what is now the Silverado Trail was once a Native American path to San Francisco Bay, undoubtedly much closer to the river than the present highway. (An alluvial fan, roughly, is soil, gravel, and rocks dropped off by a stream or runoff from rains flowing from a higher to a lower elevation. Larger and heavier material, rocks, are dropped off first, with the flow spreading into a fan shape as the ligher gravel and soil is carried along.)

The Napa Valley you are looking at today, perhaps sitting on the terrace of Auberge de Soleil, that delightful man-made outcrop in the Vaca range, enjoying a glass of Napa's best, is little more than ten million years old, formed more or less the day before yesterday. In geological terms, the Napa Valley, indeed the entire California coast, is still in the midst of change. Only a few thousand years ago – while Native Americans were gathering mussels on its shore and putting to sea to hunt whales in fragile wooden boats – San Francisco's Golden Gate was the mouth of a huge river which drained most of California's Sierra Nevada range and Central Valley into the Pacific. A sobering thought indeed if one is contemplating planting a Pinot Noir vineyard in the Carneros region, perhaps only a few hundred metres from the Bay.

At any rate, the result of these millions upon millions of years of Mother Nature's handiwork is, quite frankly, a mess. Napa Valley is made up of a muddle of soils that have no continuity within the appellation and sub-appellations or for that matter from vineyard to vineyard. Amazingly, there are over 140 soil types and subtypes in Napa. Some of these soils, especially the alluvial fans, are very young, measured in thousands rather than millions of years and still, so to speak, being made with every tiny earthquake, with every heavy winter rain.

It's easy to see some of the more obvious changes in soil even from the Silverado Trail or Highway 29. Sometimes the division is very sharp between red soils which indicate volcanic influence and grey-brown soils which are sandy and likely marine-influenced. Clearly, if you are talking terroir, there are many, many dialects to understand.

## THE CLIMATE

The geography also has an impact on the weather pattern of Napa. Obviously the most important element in the region's climate is the Pacific Ocean. Without the ocean, Napa would be a very warm grape-growing area, roughly equivalent to La Mancha in Central Spain, hardly an ideal climate for wine production, at least premium wines. However, latitude is not the whole story. There are several factors that control the weather pattern of the San Francisco Bay Area and therefore Napa Valley. First is the Sierra Nevada range, which reaches up to 4,267 metres (14,000 feet) above sea level, less than 320 kilometres (200 miles) to the east of Napa. This range blocks moisture-laden clouds blowing off the Pacific and they dump rain and snow on the western slopes. This water flows west through a complex network of canyons and rivers into the Central Valley to form a complicated multi-river system which cuts through the coastal mountains to the sea, with the flow from the Northern Sierra moving through San Francisco Bay and the delta of the Sacramento river and associated streams, creating the gap we call the Golden Gate.

Just off the Golden Gate is a current of cold water flowing south from the Arctic called the California Current. This cold water system, which keeps the beaches of northern California way too cold for casual swimmers, causes a constant upwelling of cold water which chills the air. What happens is a classic weather pattern: warm air in the Central Valley runs up against the cold Pacific air. Cold air, being heavier, pushes toward the valley, not only through the Golden Gate with its classic cascading fog pattern, but through the coastal canyons to the north of San Francisco Bay. This cold Pacific air can reach far inland, cooling areas that would be very warm if heat were simply a product of latitude north or south.

As the fog cools the interior air, it retreats back to the sea, often in a daily cycle, creating the cool morning, warm afternoon weather pattern that wine grapes love. The fog has more impact on some areas than others. Napa itself gets some spillover fog from east-west canyons in the Mayacamas range, and southern Napa in particular, especially Carneros, gets fog from San Francisco Bay. However, even those regions in Central and Eastern Napa, such as Oakville and Stags Leap, which see very little fog, are cooled by the fog and heat weather pattern. This is painting in broad strokes. On the ground, the pattern can change in a few hundred metres, given the pattern of twisted canyons and hillsides shaped by volcanic forces.

Considering all this, the mapping of terroir in Napa is frustrating. In some vineyards, the soil profile can change almost from one row of vines to the next, as mini-alluvial fans follow the line of winter creeks down from hillsides or a fan of volcanic debris overlays a loamy soil. Add to this, the complex play of local weather conditions, called microclimates in California, and one is sometimes left feeling clueless.

Then, factor in the human element, which some would include in any terroiristic equation: what of clones? Rootstock? Trellising treatment? Organic or non organic farming? Irrigated or dry-farmed?

Still, one must make a start. After all, Napa Valley has the advantage of building on thousands of years of viticultural experience in Europe. It is not necessary to re-invent the wheel. The good news is that the best growers in Napa now realize that terroir is not just something the French invented to lock up the wine market. Where the grape grows matters. It would be wildly presumptuous at this point to even think of defining the terroir of Napa. The best that can be done is simply to try and ask the right questions. In the long run, the wine will supply the answers.

# 2

# Historic Napa: 1847–1947

I pulled the date 1847 out of the air. I'm going to pretend that it was George Yount's first commercial vintage. Why not? No one really knows, although some sources give the date as 1844. The year 1947 is, however, a different story altogether. That was the year André Tchelistcheff, the diminutive winemaker from Russia by way of France who did so much to develop the Napa Cabernet style, formed the Napa Valley Enological Research Laboratory in St Helena. The lab did various jobs for wineries involving chemical testing and other measures, that are now regarded as routine but were not so at the time. He also created the Napa Valley Technical Group, an organization that still exists. The Technical Group brought together winemakers to share information, an idea that was unheard of in Europe but had always been practiced in Napa and the rest of California.

The goal of the Technical Group was and is to make better wines. There were no trade secrets, no corporate no-go areas. It was all an open book. It was a small band, to be sure. Excluding bulk producers there were thirteen wineries operating in Napa in 1947, including Louis Martini, the Christian Brothers, Charles Krug, Beringer, Inglenook, and Beaulieu. Members knew that the success of any single Napa winery reflected on Napa wines as a whole. In the market, there was naturally intense competition, but back in the vineyards and the cellars, there was close cooperation. Incredibly, given the rise of corporate ownership in Napa, this is still the case, with a few exceptions.

Following Yount's lead, settlers started moving into Napa Valley, with the pace increasing rapidly following the discovery of gold in the Sierra foothills and the seizure of California and other territory from Mexico by the US following the Mexican-American war. Today, Napa Valley is still an attractive region, but it is difficult to imagine how spectacular the valley was to those early settlers. The valley was filled with wildlife, grizzly bear, deer, elk, and an abundance of bird life. Yount wrote that it was not unusual to see as many as fifty or sixty grizzlies in a day. They were routinely killed by settlers.

## EARLY SETTLERS

As more grapes were planted, more sophisticated winemaking techniques were used and we may assume that the cow skin fermenter was gone in a fairly short time. As grape-growing became more common, the pioneers began to realize that grapes planted on the hills above the valley floor seemed to produce better wine. This remained a pattern of development well into the twentieth century, with grain, cattle, and orchards on the valley floor and vineyards on upland sites, although some planting continued along the Napa River.

During the decade of the 1850s, planting increased dramatically. One source said vineyards grew from 50,000 vines in the mid-1850s to 200,000 vines by the end of the decade. Most of the plantings were Mission vines. However, Napa was far from being a leader in the infant California wine industry. Los Angeles took that honour. Jean Louis Vignes, a Frenchman, planted a vineyard and established the Aliso winery near the present Union Station on the banks of the Los Angeles River. His estate vineyard is now a freeway exchange. As early as the mid-1840s, Aliso wines were being shipped by sea to San Francisco and production was around 40,000 cases annually, including brandy.

Vignes did bring in some French varietals, but they did not seem to have much impact outside his own estate. However, classic *vinifera* vines were beginning to replace the Mission vine in Sonoma and Napa. In the 1850, J W Osborne, a sea captain from Massachusetts, settled in Napa and began planting vines. He bought land just north of the town of Napa in an area which he called Oak Knoll. Osborne had become interested in viticulture in the east where *vinifera* was grown under glass and sold as table grapes. One of the vines Osborne obtained from Massachusetts and planted was Zinfandel. He was a close associate of Agoston Haraszthy, who for many years was widely credited with importing Zinfandel vines from his native Hungary. After Osborne's death (he was murdered in

1863), a portion of his Oak Knoll vineyard became known as Eshcol Vineyard and is now the home of Trefethen Winery. Trefethen's second label is Eshcol and the area is now the Oak Knoll District AVA. The time line of history is beginning to firm up.

The first commercial shipment of wine from Napa occured in 1857. It was made by John Patchett, an English brewer who came to California to strike it rich in the Sierra goldfields. He didn't find any gold and settled in Napa in 1852, buying land that already had a vineyard on it, which he expanded. In 1858, he hired a German immigrant named Charles Krug (he sometimes called himself King in the early days) to make his wine. At the time, Krug was based in Sonoma. Apparently Patchett liked Krug's work. He built a stone cellar in the town of Napa to replace the adobe brick winery near Napa River.

A few years later, Krug joined forces with Yount to produce 5,000 gallons of wine on a share basis. Within a few years Yount's wines were considered to be among the best in Napa. Krug soon began making his own wine and built a small cellar which was replaced by a stone winery in 1876, near the site of the present Charles Krug Winery north of St Helena. By the time of his death in 1892, the winery had a capacity of 800,000 gallons, one of the largest in the state. More importantly, Krug was a constant advocate of better wines and openly shared information with his competitors. It could be argued that Krug, who had spent time in prison in Germany as a supporter of the liberal revolution of 1848 in that country, was responsible for the cooperative sprit that has been so important to the development of quality wines in California. Today he is probably best known as the founder of the winery that, one way or another, launched Robert Mondavi on the world.

As the pace of planting picked up in the 1860s, vine cuttings were imported from France and Germany and the Mission grape fell out of favour, a good thing all around. One of the men who sought out European vines was Jacob Schram, a barber born in the Rheinhessen wine district of Germany. He left Germany when he was a teenager, but always kept in mind that the best wines came from hillside grapes. He bought wooded hillside land on Diamond Mountain west of Calistoga and started planting in 1863. His first plantings were Mission vines – very probably nothing else was available – but as he expanded he planted Riesling, Burger, Palomino, and Zinfandel.

Like Krug, his fellow German, Schram was well respected for his hard work and his willingness to help out other growers. By the time Stevenson paid his famous visit in 1880, Schram was well known for his wines, especially the whites, which were sold in the best hotels of California. His Schramsberg whites, at least the Palomino and Sylvaner, were made with a touch of Muscat, which may have prompted Stevenson's comment about their "notable bouquet". At the time of Stevenson's visit, Schram had already had extensive tunnels dug into the hillside (by Chinese labour) and was producing about 30,000 gallons of wine a year.

Schram, who lived until 1905, had turned over the winery to his son, Herman, before his death. Herman Schram sold the winery just before Prohibition in 1920. There were a few attempts after Prohibition to revive the estate but it had been abandoned for several years when it was bought by Jack and Jamie Davies in 1965. The Davies' revived Schram's old estate and now make one of the world's great sparkling wines there.

The German influence continued with the Beringer brothers, who arrived via New York. Jacob Beringer bought a vineyard just north of the hamlet of St Helena in 1876. Using Chinese labour, Jacob – who was soon joined by his brother Fritz – excavated a winery cellar with ageing tunnels that is still a tourist attraction today. The Beringers were just part of a wave of grape-growers and vintners who settled in Napa following the Civil War.

### PHYLLOXERA AND PROHIBITION

However, just as one is about to write "and they all lived happily ever after", a tiny root louse, called then *Phylloxera vastarix* (the destroyer) turned up and ruined the happy ending for Napa vintners. The modern name for the aphid is *Dactylasphaera vitifoliae*. It is native to the Missouri and Mississippi valleys but was an unnoticed stowaway on rootstock shipped from the US to Europe, sometime in the 1850s. It found its way back to California on rootstock shipped back from Europe and from the east coast of the US. It was first spotted in Sonoma County in 1873. At about the same time, phylloxera was spreading rapidly in France. It moved a little slower in California but was present in Napa by the mid-1870s. As in France, various methods were used to counter the attack, including chemicals, flooding, and prayer. None really worked.

Finally, in both France and the US, viticulturists realized that native American vines, which had lived with phylloxera for thousands of years, were naturally resistant to the little bug. In the 1890s, California growers began grafting *vinifera* vines onto the native American roots, and the battle appeared to be won. Almost a century later, phylloxera opened a second front. More on that later (*see* page 34).

Just as Napa's vintners appeared to be in solid shape, they were slammed by something even worse than phylloxera: Prohibition. There had always been a strong anti-alcohol movement in the US: there still is for that matter. The push for Prohibition began gathering strength in the 1890s and by the outbreak of World War I, had become a national crusade, tinged with an almost hysteric streak of patriotism. In 1917 the Eighteenth Amendment to the Constitution, which created national Prohibition, was submitted to the states and was quickly approved by two-thirds of the then forty-eight states. Prohibition became the national law in October of 1919, coming into effect on 16 January 1920.

By then, most California wineries had already shut down operations, although for a time there had been false hopes that wine and beer would remain legal. However, there was a loophole that saved, but dramatically changed, the state's vineyards. The law specified that each head of household was allowed to make 200 gallons of wine a year for the family's personal use. Home winemakers pushed the price of grapes higher than it had been in years and there was a rush to plant new vineyards to meet this unexpected demand. The downside was that the grapes in demand were thick skinned red grapes, such as Alicante Bouschet, Carignane, Petite Sirah, and Zinfandel, all grapes that would stand up to shipping by rail from California to mid-western and eastern buyers. Home winemakers also liked their grapes with high sugar levels to encourage higher alcohol wines. This obsession with sugar was to haunt California growers for decades after Prohibition ended. It also led to a generation of wine drinkers with a taste for wines with some residual sugar because home winemakers without access to good yeast cultures were usually left with sweet wines when fermentation stopped.

Prior to Prohibition, the percentage of fortified or sweet wines made in California ranged between ten and thirty per cent. In 1935, eighty per cent of wine made in California was sweet. It wasn't until the mid-1960s that the production of sweet and fortified wine in California fell below half of total production. It wasn't quite that extreme in Napa, where dry table wine always exceeded sweet wines, but in any case, there were a lot of wines called dry table wines that would be considered sweet today. (Unless, of course, one were a fan of Kendall-Jackson Chardonnay.) The law also allowed wine to be made for sacramental purposes, so a few wineries with good connections to the church managed to stay open all through Prohibition, including Beaulieu and Beringer in Napa.

At any rate, as mentioned elsewhere, California as a whole, including Napa, came out of Prohibition at the end of 1933 in sad shape. Most of the wineries had been shut down for more than a decade. Equipment had not been maintained nor had any sort of sanitation been practised. It would not be wise to look closely at the various microorganisms running loose in the newly re-opened wine cellars. The vineyards were geared to high production with quality being the last thing anyone considered. The goal was just to get some wine out there because it was now legal.

## THE WAR YEARS
World War II turned out to be somewhat of a blessing for Napa wineries, especially for those wineries that had recovered enough technical expertise to fill the gap left by the loss of French and German wines in the US market. According to wine historian Charles Sullivan, the Waldorf Astoria Hotel in New York City (an icon for quality at the time) listed twenty-eight table wines from Napa producers.[1]

Also, prior to the war, it had been common practice for wine to be shipped in bulk and bottled in the local market. Obviously, this did nothing for wine quality in most cases. With the war, there was a shortage of rail cars and Napa took the lead in California for bottling on site, which became a marketing tool. The phrase, "Bottled at the Winery" on the label became a quality guarantee in the eyes of consumers.

Perhaps the most important event of the war years took place in 1943 when Louis M Martini persuaded a few fellow vintners, including the Mondavi family, to form the Napa Vintners. Initially the group was more interested in trade matters, including taxes and price controls, than improving the product. But it is significant that one of the charter members was André Tchelistcheff, the man who started the Napa

---

1. *Napa Wine: A History from Mission Days to Present,* page 237.

Technical Group four years later. In 1983, the Vintners morphed into the Napa Valley Vintners Association, easily the most successful marketing alliance in California. So, in a sense, Martini created the framework or at least the opportunity for Tchelistcheff to keep the ball rolling toward the revolution in Napa winemaking.

# 3

# Getting it right: 1947–1976

In the years following World War II, Napa wine began to take on a look that would be recognized by a time traveller from the twenty-first century. There were several familiar brands and more and more producers were turning to varietal labelling. (At the time, a wine needed to contain only 50.1 per cent of the varietal stated on the label to be called a Cabernet Sauvignon or a Chardonnay, etc.) There was some resistance to this within the larger California wine industry, especially outside of Napa where few producers made wine from a variety worth mentioning, but the more astute marketers in Napa realized the "branding" value of the varietal name.

Frank Schoonmaker, a journalist, wine merchant, and decorated spy in World War II, was a leader in the push for both varietal labelling and an appellation system for California wines. Schoonmaker first became interested in California wines at the end of Prohibition when he wrote an article for *New Yorker* magazine on the terrible conditions in California vineyards and wineries after repeal of Prohibition. He went on to write *The Complete Wine Book*, with Tom Marvel, which was published in 1934.

Unlike most journalists, Schoonmaker had a good business sense. As World War II came closer, he realized that California wine stood to reap huge profits if European wines were not available. So he formed a marketing company and lined up a number of California producers. It was his idea to use varietal labelling to distinguish the California wines from the geographical descriptions of European wines. He also argued that varietal labeling on the better California wines would distinguish them from the sea of mass-produced California "Chablis", "burgundy", "Rhine" wine, and the like that dominated California production.

When the USA entered the war near the end of 1941, Schoonmaker was sent to Spain by the government, posing as a wine merchant in order to gather information on German intelligence operations while shopping, so he said, for sherry. Following the war, Schoonmaker returned to California and continued to argue for varietal labelling. However as late as 1961, Cabernet Sauvignon, Pinot Noir, and Chardonnay accounted for only six per cent of Napa's grape production. One was more likely to find Gamay, Petite Sirah, and even French Colombard, the varietals of choice at the time.

## THE MONDAVIS

However, Napa seemed to be getting it right in the years immediately following the war. The Wine Technical Group was making a huge impact in areas such as cold fermentation, sterile filtration, barrel ageing, extended skin contact for red wines, and other bells and whistles. One of the first wineries to utilize this modern winemaking technology was a familiar Napa name, Charles Krug. The winery had been purchased during the war by Caesar Mondavi, a grape shipper and bulk wine dealer from Lodi. He set up a family company called C Mondavi & Sons. Those sons were Peter and Robert Mondavi.

The Mondavi family had the funds, the knowledge, and the energy to completely restructure the winery, which had been allowed to seriously run down. It quickly became a leader in the Napa technology revolution, with a series of award-winning table wines. Both Peter and Robert had technical as well as business training. They were graduates of the Stanford School of Business and the University of California at Berkeley, which pre-dated UC Davis as the oenology training centre in California. Robert had made wine for several years at the Sunny St Helena Winery (now Merryvale Vineyards), while Peter had been the head oenologist at the huge Acampo Winery near Lodi in the San Joaquin Valley east of San Francisco.

As they sorted out their roles at Charles Krug, it was Peter who took over winery operations and Robert who went on the road to sell the wines, though in most cases it was Robert, who held the title of general manager, who made the decisions. The Mondavis continued to bottle inexpensive but decent bulk wine at the Sunny St Helena Winery and sell it under the C K Mondavi label, while the Charles Krug label was used mostly for varietal bottlings although, inexplicably, there were a Chablis and claret as well.

The family's early success at Charles Krug centred on white wines. Peter had worked on cold fermentation at Berkeley and later he and André Tchelistcheff had discussed white wine production with the Wine Technical Group. It was Peter's knowledge of sterile fermentation and vacuum bottling that enabled the slightly sweet Charles Krug Chenin Blanc to score such a huge commercial success. The next phase focused on red wines. Early experimental work with barrel-ageing and extended skin contact and maceration once again grew out of discussions within the Wine Technical Group.

In the meantime, Robert was doing what he has always done best: he was out on the road hustling wine. He became famous for the wine tastings and dinners he hosted for both the wine trade and consumers, and he seemed to have endless energy to devote to the promotion of wine. Indeed there are those who claim that Robert was more interested in the image of wine than the wine in the bottle. Nothing could be further from the truth. It was simply that he understood the importance of image and was carrying on Robert Louis Stevenson's "bottled poetry" tradition. There is no doubt that Robert realized that all of his marketing skills would be useless without good wine in the bottle. In later years I often heard him say, "You might sell the first bottle on the image, but the wine had better be good or you won't sell a second bottle".

Robert also turned the winery itself into a marketing tool, with wine tastings on the lawn, concerts of classical, jazz, and folk music, and a well-staffed tasting room. Long before his winery had a vice-president of cultural affairs, Robert was convinced that good wine was part of the culture of the western world.

There is no doubt that Peter was just as concerned as his brother about the wines being good. There is also no doubt, according to those who were aware of the growing tensions between the brothers, that Peter resented the image that Robert was creating and believed that his brother was a little too lavish in his entertaining. While their father was alive he managed to keep the family dispute from breaking through. But after his death in 1959, the situation deteriorated, leading to the well-known story of Robert's break with his family and the establishment of his own winery (*see* page 24).

## SOUVERAIN AND INGLENOOK

Charles Krug was not the only good news coming out of Napa during and following the war. One can trace the beginnings of the often-derided "lifestyle" influx into Napa to 1943 when retired executive J Leland Stewart bought a rundown vineyard and winery on Howell Mountain at the age of forty-eight. He named the refurbished operation Souverain Cellars and began replanting the vineyards. While waiting for the vines to mature, Stewart bought grapes from elsewhere. His White Riesling was praised from the start, as was a crowd-pleasing wine made from "Green Hungarian" grapes, of all things, which won medals year after year at the California State Fair.[1] Stewart also took gold medals for his Cabernet Sauvignon, Zinfandel, and Petite Sirah. By the 1950s, Souverain was regarded as one of Napa's best wineries. Certainly, Souverain Cellars helped shape the premium wine boom of the 1960s.

(At this point, someone is certainly ready to ask how Souverain Cellars, a Napa winery, ended up in Sonoma as Château Souverain? A good question. Stewart, who was by then well into his seventies, sold Souverain to a group of investors in 1970s. They sold it to the giant food conglomerate, Pillsbury. For a time, Pillsbury operated the winery as Souverain of Rutherford. They also established a Souverain of Alexander Valley in Sonoma. Eventually, that winery was bought by Nestlé, now Beringer Blass Estates, and the name was changed to Château Souverain.)

The post-war years also saw the revival of the historic Inglenook estate, which had been founded in 1879 by Gustave Niebaum, a native of Finland, who had made a fortune in the Alaska fur trade. He remained involved in his Alaska business, but the winery was a serious hobby if not his main occupation. By the mid-1880s, Niebaum had planted over 405 hectares of vines. Wine production began in 1884 and Inglenook was one of the first to offer estate-bottled wines. When Niebaum died in 1908, the winery was closed for three years. It reopened for a few years before Prohibition closed it. It reopened again in 1933 and in 1939 it passed into the hands of John Daniel Junior, who was related to Niebaum's widow, Susanne. Daniel had grown up on the estate. He restored Inglenook's reputation for both white and red wines, all based on estate vineyards.

---

1. It isn't clear to this day just what "Green Hungarian" might be. *See* Appendix IV, pages 249–50.

Daniel followed in Niebaum's tradition by focusing on varietals and vintage dating, something not at all common in California at the time. Inglenook Cabernets from the 1940s and 1950s are legendary: some believe they may be the best Napa Cabernets ever produced. I've been lucky enough to taste Inglenook Cabernets going back to the early 1930s and I must say that if not the best, they certainly stand beside Beaulieu and the great Louis M Martini Cabernets of the 1950s and early 1960s as iconic expressions of Napa Cabernet.

It is more the pity that of those three estates, only Beaulieu remains committed to fine Cabernet, and even then there were several years of stumbling around. Louis M Martini is now rather in limbo. It was bought by E & J Gallo, following decades of aimless threshing about, and its future is uncertain. Inglenook, after years of greatness, was sold to United Vintners in 1964, then to Heublein in 1969. Heublein stopped making wine at Inglenook in 1992 and in 1994 sold the brand to Canandaigua where it now languishes as a much-debased label having no connection at all to Napa. The good news is that Francis Ford Coppola has brought most of the estate under his ownership and is once more making wine in the historic building.

## ICONIC NAPA CABERNETS

It is interesting to contrast the Inglenook Cabernets of the time with Beaulieu Cabernets, made by André Tchelistcheff. Tchelistcheff was a great champion of small oak barrels, while the Inglenook wines were made in huge oak casks. Inglenook Cabernets came from three estate vineyards, all on what are now called benchlands and were blended for stylistic consistency. Tchelistcheff argued that the vineyards, as well as ageing in large casks, made Inglenook Cabernets true Napa Cabernets while his own Beaulieu Cabernets were more in the French style. At this distance in time it is impossible to offer any opinion on that point, although having tasted both within the past few years, I can only say that there is a sharp difference in style. However, that may be related more to terroir, as Tchelistcheff said, than any deliberate attempt to make a "Napa"- or a "French"-style wine. The older Beaulieu Cabernets – and I'm speaking of the Georges Latour Private Reserve – while very good, seem to have lost more with time than the older Inglenooks. It isn't quite an "angels on the head of a pin" debate, but it is close. In the end, one would be quite fortunate to have a glass of either in hand.

The Louis M Martini Cabernets of the1950s through to the early 1970s represent a kind of quintessential California Cabernet that simply doesn't exist any longer. Louis M Martini arrived in San Francisco from Italy in 1900. A few years later, he returned to Italy and studied oenology in Alba, making his first California wine at the family home in San Francisco in 1907. In 1923, while Prohibition was still the law of the land, he bought a winery near Fresno and established the Louis M Martini Grape Products Co, which shipped grapes to home winemakers.

Martini had his heart set on making fine wine, however, and knew that Napa was the place to do that. He started building the Louis M Martini winery in St Helena as soon as Prohibition was repealed. For a few years he made and sold bulk wine, but began selling wine under his own label in 1940. His great genius was in selecting vineyard sites, then making a flawless, balanced, and elegant blend. I'm not sure if he learned how to blend wine in Alba, but if he did I only wish more California winemakers had trained there. His son, Louis P Martini, who took over winemaking in the early 1950s, was also a master blender.

The Martinis resisted the trend toward regional labelling, preferring to label their bottles as "California" wines. This was partly because a few of the Martini vineyards were outside of Napa; the Martini Monte Rosso Vineyard in Sonoma is one of California's outstanding sources of old-vine Zinfandel and Cabernet Sauvignon. Chiefly, though, it was a winemaking decision: the Martinis wanted the freedom to blend for the best wine possible without being concerned about grape origins.

The best Martini wines were Cabernet Sauvignon and Zinfandel with the top of the line labelled as Private Selection or Reserve. Occasionally, these wines still turn up in auctions and are almost always incredible bargains since the Martini name doesn't command the respect it once had. At the same time, the wines that didn't make the cut into the top of the line bottles, were bottled and sold as Mountain Red or Mountain Cabernet or Zinfandel. The mountain may have been somewhat notional, but the wines were always solid and reasonably priced.

There isn't much point in this context in looking in depth at why the quality of Martini wines started to decline in the 1980s. This was surely due to a combination of things, including poor marketing decisions that left the winery short of cash and unable to keep up with the competition in terms of oenological or viticultural advances. Mind you, the wines continued to be good, sometimes very good, but I have the feeling that Louis M would have bulked out most of them without hesitation. It is certainly possible that E & J Gallo, which bought Martini in 2002, will revive the winery, restoring some of its past grace.

## THE SIXTIES, SEVENTIES, AND SPARKLING WINE

By the 1960s Napa was well on its way. The big five – Beaulieu, Beringer Brothers, Charles Krug, Inglenook, and Louis M Martini – were still humming along and some new kids had come out to play as well. These included Mayacamas, Stony Hill, Hanns Kornell Cellars, and Christian Brothers. Before the end of the decade, Heitz Cellars, Schramsberg, Robert Mondavi, Chappellet, Spring Mountain, Sterling, and Chateau Montelena were also making wine. Freemark Abbey, which had a history reaching back into the nineteenth century, had been revived in 1967 as well.

Then, in the 1970s, came the deluge. Between 1970 and 1975, about thirty-five wineries opened the cellar door in Napa. The names become more familiar. Cuvaison opened in 1970, while 1972 saw the beginnings of Burgess Cellars, Mount Veeder Vineyards, Caymus Vineyards, Diamond Creek Vineyards, Stag's Leap Wine Cellars, and Carneros Creek Vineyards. A very good year indeed. Other auspicious beginnings at this time included: Franciscan Vineyards, Silver Oak Cellars, Trefethen Vineyards, Clos du Val, Joseph Phelps, and Domaine Chandon.

The opening of the Chandon winery in 1973 marked the first move by a Champagne house into California and, in a sense, gave a certain legitimacy to the pioneering sparkling wine work of Jack and Jamie Davies at Schramsberg – although contrary to true believers in California wine, the decision to come to California was probably made before anyone involved in France had tasted the early Schramsberg vintages. The owners of Moët Hennessey realized in the 1960s that growing world demand for Champagne could not be met in France alone and began looking elsewhere to plant vineyards. The price of Napa land was then still relatively low, another consideration that must have been a factor, but there was also a firm belief that good sparkling wine could be made from California grapes.

The first Chandon vineyards were planted in 1973 on Mount Veeder and in Carneros and the first wines were made at Mount Veeder Winery from purchased Pope Valley grapes that same year. The first crush of any size was 1974 and the winery doors opened in 1977 just south of the town of Yountville, not far from George Yount's first vineyard.

There was never a thought of putting the word Champagne on the Chandon label. At the time, almost all producers of California sparkling wine did use the word "Champagne", even those who made their bubbly by the bulk Charmat process. Even Schramsberg labelled its sparkling wine "Champagne", a practice which continued into the 1990s. Korbel Cellars in Sonoma, the largest producer of méthode champenoise wine in California, has continued to use the word "Champagne" on its label.

The decision was also made early on not to vintage date Domaine Chandon wines, but to have a fairly high percentage of reserve wine in the bottling. The non-vintage approach may have been designed to side-step any direct comparison with Moët & Chandon, at least on a vintage basis.

By whatever name, the Chandon sparklers were a critical and financial success, which must have influenced later moves by French and Spanish Champagne and cava houses to head west. Three ended in Napa. Taittinger planted vineyards in Carneros in 1982 and opened Domaine Carneros in 1990. In 1983, the Mumm Champagne house and Seagram Classic Wines entered into a joint venture to produce sparkling wine in Napa. In 1986, the first bottling of Domaine Mumm (as it was called then) came to market. The winery, now owned by Diageo, is on the Silverado Trail and the bubbly is now called Mumm Napa. Codorníu, the giant Spanish cava producer, also settled in Carneros and started planting vines in 1985, opening an impressive winery in 1991. A few years ago, Codorníu virtually ceased production of sparkling wine to concentrate on table wine and changed the name of the winery to Artesa, moving smoothly from one difficult-to-pronounce Catalan name, to another. Interestingly, Codorníu's major competitor in the world of cava, Freixenet, established its own outpost in California a few kilometres away on the Sonoma side of Carneros, calling the winery Gloria Ferrer, after the wife of the owner. Gloria Ferrer has a very successful sparkling wine and an expanding still wine programme as well.

There was a surge in sparkling wine production in Napa in the 1950s.

The theory is that more Americans were travelling to Europe at this time, having been exposed to the continent's charms as soldiers in World War II and discovered that sparkling wine was a Good Thing. Hanns Kornell, who had fled Germany before the war, was making méthode champenoise wines at the old Larkmead Winery (now Rombauer). Kornell had trained in sparkling wine production in Germany. Kornell continued to make sparkling wine, using grapes such as Riesling and Green Hungarian (see page 18), until his death in 1994. Sadly, the winery has now passed out of the family hands.

The Christian Brothers also produced méthode champenoise wines, turning their Greystone winery north of St Helena into a sparkling wine facility. Greystone is now the western home of the Culinary Institute of America. Although Kornell's bubblies passed muster as Wednesday kind of wines, Napa had to wait until 1965, when Jack and Jamie Davies took over Jacob Schram's old winery on Diamond Mountain and revived Schramsberg Vineyards, for a truly fine sparkling wine.

## URBAN INVASION

At about the same time that Robert Mondavi was famously feuding with his family (see page 24) and getting ready to build his own winery on Highway 29 near Oakville, the state of California announced plans to push a four-lane expressway north from the town of Napa through the heart of the valley perhaps as far north as Calistoga. The plan would have taken many hectares of vines out of production but more importantly, such a limited access freeway would have encouraged the sprawl of Napa city to the north, with its tacky shopping strip malls and even tackier houses.

One such plan involved creating an up-market "tasteful" housing project on a good-sized portion of the To Kalon vineyard, an historic vineyard that remains one of the standards of Napa vine quality. It took a bold approach to stop the plan. The rallying point for conservationists and most vintners was a proposal calling for the creation of a National Vineyard which would be made part of the National Park System. That plan would certainly never have flown, but it did thrust the issue into the news and helped to bring about basic changes in zoning that made eight hectares the minimum parcel size in 1968. Later, this was raised to sixteen hectares by the Napa County Planning Commission.

The only flaw in the plan, which has survived law suits by pro-growth forces, is that what the planning commission gives, it can also take away. There has certainly been vineyard land lost since 1968. But by and large Napa has escaped the surge of growth that has mostly wiped out the vineyards in Santa Clara County south of San Francisco and vastly reduced those in the Livermore Valley east of San Francisco (the site of a number of historic vineyards). In Livermore, only the leadership of the Wente family has stopped the bulldozers. Among Napa wine-growers, Jack and Jamie Davies and the Martini family led the charge.

## THE CURIOUS INCIDENT OF THE MINK COAT

While few wine drinkers are familiar with the idea of a National Vineyard, there's hardly a person capable of using a corkscrew who doesn't know about the feud that split the Mondavi family and sent Robert Mondavi off on his own. But perhaps few know that, while the feud between Robert and his brother Peter was deep and in the end disastrous (at least for the latter) what brought it to an open split was a mink coat.

Robert tells the story in his book, *Harvests of Joy*. He and his first wife, Marge, were invited by President John F Kennedy to attend a White House dinner in honour of the president of Italy. Marge thought she needed a new coat for the occasion and went shopping at I Magnin, an up-market but hardly lap-of-luxury store in San Francisco. After trying several coats, Marge found just the one she wanted. It was a mink coat and it was priced at $5,000. As Robert writes: "... the coat fit perfectly and Marge looked smashing." Still, they had set a limit of $1,500 to spend for the coat and that, it seems, was that. A few weeks passed and Marge was still shopping for a coat. Back at I Magnin, she found that the mink was on sale for $2,500. After much discussion, the couple decided they would cut back on their spending over the next year so Marge could wear mink to the White House.

Two years later, Peter still remembered that expensive mink coat. Perhaps his wife whispered in his ear? Here's how Robert tells it in *Harvests of Joy*:

*That fuse kept burning though, through the next two years of simmering tensions and sometimes open conflict. Then one day in November 1965, all the Mondavis assembled at one of our big family gatherings at the winery for what was supposed to be a happy, festive occasion. It turned out to be anything but. I don't remember exactly how it started, but at some point, Peter and I started to squabble. Tempers flared and Peter accused me of spending too much company money on travel and promotion. Then he really lost his temper and accused me of taking money from the winery. How else could I afford to buy that mink coat? In essence, I felt my own brother was accusing me of being a thief and a swindler. "Say that again and I'll hit you," I warned him. He said it again. Then I gave him a third chance: "Take it back." "No." So I smacked him, hard. Twice.*

Those two smacks led to years of legal battles. Robert claimed he had been unlawfully kicked out of the Charles Krug winery and asked the court to dissolve the partnership that his father had established, which would lead to a forced sale of the winery. He asked for twenty per cent of the winery value. In 1976 the court ruled in favour of Robert and in 1978 Robert and Peter reached a settlement which gave Robert the money he wanted and left the Charles Krug winery to Peter, heavily in debt.

And incidentally, Marge never got to wear her mink to the White House. Kennedy was murdered in Dallas before the dinner took place.

What led Robert to take the sort of stands that angered Peter so much? After all, he had been making and/or selling California wine for about three decades. What was the turning point that focused him on quality? Looking again at *Harvests of Joy*, there is little doubt that it was a visit to France in 1962, the first time Robert had been in Europe. He was blown away, or as he puts it, "much of what I saw was a revelation". He realized for the first time the difference between wine as a business and wine as an artisan undertaking, or that was his take on it, at any rate. He wrote: "We were a big, young country, oriented toward mass production and scientific research, and in our winemaking we emphasized crop yields, sugar levels and profit margins. The great European wineries, with centuries of tradition and craft behind them, put their emphasis on less tangible qualities such as style, character, and bouquet".

It all came together for Mondavi over lunch at La Pyramide, a three-star restaurant in the town of Vienne in Provence:

*What really dazzled me was how each dish complemented and enhanced the other, the way the sounds of different instruments meld into a symphony. The wines we tasted during the meal were not big and bold like ours in California; they were gentle and complex, and they artfully accentuated the many sensations and feelings that the cuisine inspired. I'd go so far as to say that the food and the wine transported us into a world of gentleness and balance, of grace and harmony. "This is the kind of wine I want to create," I told Marge.*

It was after the fight with his brother in November of 1965 that Robert earned the nickname of "Rapid Robert". Operating on borrowed money, he had a winery built in time for the 1966 harvest. It didn't have a roof, but there was a crush pad and Rapid Robert was off and running.

In the years since that first harvest, some very good wines and even a few great wines have come out of the Robert Mondavi Winery. But contrary to popular mythology, Robert was not a pioneer in making fine wine in Napa. That had been going on for some time. Nor was he the first in Napa to understand the power of promotion. What Robert did was realize that the market for fine wines was about to reach critical mass and Napa had a role to play in that market. He shrewdly linked his fledgling winery and the image of Napa and, in the end, both benefited.

Robert became the face of Napa in the world. He had a true passion for quality. He really believed that the finest wine in the world came from Napa and he took that message around the globe. It may have been the so-called "Judgment of Paris" that first put the spotlight on Napa, but it was Robert Mondavi who kept it there.

## THE JUDGMENT OF PARIS

In 1976, the 200th birthday year of the USA, Steven Spurrier, a wine merchant, educator, and writer, conceived the idea of a grand shoot-out between ten French wines and ten California wines. The contest would match the best of California against the best of France. It was a neat idea for a publicity coup, but what did it really mean in terms of the wine in the bottle?

For openers, the vintages ranged from 1969 (Freemark Abbey Cabernet Sauvignon) to 1974 (Chalone Vineyard Chardonnay). This immediately put the French at a disadvantage since (at least in those days) Bordeaux and burgundy vintages were less user-friendly in their youth than the more fruity and lively California wines. Also, perhaps a minor point, but it is usually reported that all the judges were French. In fact, while nine of the eleven judges were French, Spurrier and his associate Dorothy Gallagher took part in the judging as well.

In addition, Spurrier's statistical analysis of results was meaningless. The wines were judged on a twenty-point basis, with each judge's score tabulated as part of the average. As an example, if wine A were given an eighteen-point rating by one judge and a two-point rating by another, the average score would be ten. But if the same wine A had been rated eighteen and sixteen, the average score would have been seventeen. Factor the ratings of eleven judges into that and you can see the possibility of statistical confusion. Apparently, it would not have changed the rankings of the first place wines, Stag's Leap Wine Cellars 1973 Cabernet Sauvignon and Chateau Montelena 1973 Chardonnay, but if applied to the overall rating, the French red wines came in first and the French and California white wines tied.

The California wine historian Charles Sullivan in his remarkably informative book *Napa Wine: A History from Mission Days to Present* said the outcome of the tasting was clear. No "whining French apologist or cleverly dodging Francophile East Coast wine writer could obscure the fact that the winners, red and white, were both Californians, both from the Napa Valley."[2] Well, I would hate to be lumped in with those cleverly dodging Francophiles, but one problem with the Spurrier tasting is that it is really only a snapshot of a dozen or so wines at a point in time. In later years, the tasting has been repeated time and time again and usually California still came out tops, but all that adds up to a series of snapshots through time. It says nothing about the overall quality of French compared with California wine. I have been to tastings that clearly showed the superiority of New York's Long Island wines to Napa wines. I have been to tastings establishing the supremacy of California sparkling wine over Champagne. Neither of those tastings were covered in depth by *Time Magazine* as was the Spurrier tasting.

In the long run, one result of the Spurrier tasting may well have been a collective hubris on the part of California wine producers that has never quite worn off and is in many cases not entirely justified. Still, the outcome was remarkable and gave California and especially Napa an

---

2. *Napa Wine: A History from Mission Days to Present*, page 314.

incredible boost (only three non-Napa wines were in the tasting: Chalone, then based entirely at the namesake estate in Monterey, Ridge Vineyards, and David Bruce).

## NEW KIDS ON THE BLOCK

It is interesting that of the ranking Napa wineries in the Paris tasting, only Freemark Abbey existed before 1947 – and it had actually closed for a number of years before reopening in 1967. Heitz Cellars was founded in 1961, followed by Spring Mountain in 1968, and Montelena in 1969. Stag's Leap and Veedercrest were founded in 1972 (though the latter closed in 1982) and Clos du Val opened its doors in 1973. Clearly, Spurrier tilted toward the new Napa.

So what of the old Napa? By the time of the Paris tasting, the Louis M Martini Winery was past its prime. Inglenook, Beaulieu, and Christian Brothers were more or less trapped in a corporate time warp, although Beaulieu was still capable of coming up with the goods. How could they miss with the outstanding vineyards they owned? Charles Krug was suffering from the legal struggle between the Mondavis. Of the old guard, only Beringer, owned at that point by the Swiss company Nestlé, was producing wine of quality, thanks to an influx of cash that made possible the purchase of several top vineyards.

There were also new names in the valley. Besides the Paris winners, Joe Heitz was making a name for his Martha's Vineyard Cabernet. Freemark Abbey was going through a revival. Donn Chapplett started his winery in 1969 and Michael Robbins began the wine renaissance at Spring Mountain.

In that same year, Peter Newton, an Englishman with international business interests, and his partners built Sterling Vineyards, a faux monastery atop a small hill just south of Calistoga. Newton and his associates had the audacity to install an aerial tramcar to bring visitors to taste wine, while also charging them a fee, which was unheard of at the time. Even more important than the tramcar, the partners hired Ric Forman, a twenty-four-year-old graduate of UC Davis who had worked exactly two vintages in Napa, one at Stony Hill and one with Robert Mondavi, as the inaugural winemaker. Before the first grapes were crushed, they sent Forman off to France to get a firsthand look at the winemaking in Bordeaux and Burgundy.

That may well have been the most important thing to happen to Napa wines since Robert Louis Stevenson trudged up Diamond Mountain to drink wine with Jacob Schram, although it certainly didn't make the headlines like the Paris tasting or the Mondavi family feud. Forman was one of the key winemakers in the shaping of the new Napa. When he left for France, he was a thorough disciple of UC Davis. France changed him, as it had changed Robert Mondavi a few years earlier. Forman said later that in France he came to realize that wine could not be made by a recipe or any sort of formula. Wine was a product of a place.

# 4

# Napa defines itself: the 1980s

"Build it and they will come" might well have been Napa's theme for the 1980s. Despite some economic ups and downs, wineries were springing up all over Napa, and the tourists arrived in short order. It was estimated that at least three million visitors a year were coming to Napa by the mid-1980s to belly up to what was described then as the world's longest "free bar". That would be Highway 29, from the city of Napa in the south, north to Calistoga at the foot of Mount St Helena.

Astute winery owners soon saw the cash flow possibilities of T-shirts, coffee mugs, and dozens of other tourist baubles that had very little to do with wine. One of the most popular tourist stops on Highway 29 was Sattui Winery, which opened in 1976, just south of St Helena. Owner Daryl Sattui said his great-grandfather had operated a winery in San Francisco in the late-nineteenth century. Tugged by this ancestral urge, Sattui decided he wanted a winery and although he admitted he knew very little about winemaking, he was an ace entrepreneur.

He spent a little time working at Carneros Creek and Christian Brothers and then opened his "winery" where, as he cheerfully admitted, no wine was made. Sattui wine was bought in bulk, bottled elsewhere and sold on the site, where most day-trippers were more interested in the deli treats and the picnic tables than the provenance of Sattui wines. Sattui did eventually build a working winery – which he opened with much fanfare in 1989 – although a lot of wine was still bought in bulk.

But by that time Sattui had focused Napa on a very Californian question: What is a winery? By 1990 over 200,000 visitors, by winery count, would have answered: Sattui. But the question seems like a no-brainer, right? A winery is a place where wine is made. Well, not in

California where tourism is a way of life. Keep in mind that California was the birthplace of drive-in restaurants and fast food, why not wineries that do not make wine?

## THE WHITE ZINFANDEL PHENOMENON

Aside from Sattui's family fantasy, a development at Sutter Home Winery in St Helena raised more questions about Napa authenticity. Sutter Home was well-established, dating back to the 1890s when a cousin of Captain John Sutter, the man who kicked off the Gold Rush in 1849, built a winery on Howell Mountain. In 1906, the winery was re-established in St Helena and it was purchased by the Trinchero family in 1947. Sutter Home had a solid reputation, although it was never especially distinguished.

In the mid-1970s, owner Bob Trinchero, on a tip from a California wine merchant, Daryl Corti – who had found some excellent Zinfandel grapes in Amador County in the Sierra foothills – began producing Amador Zinfandel. Zinfandel had been planted in the lower ranges of the Sierra in the mid-nineteenth century by Gold Rush pioneers who discovered that they could make more money selling wine to miners than taking to the mountains to search for gold. It was Corti's message to Trinchero that many of those century-old vineyards were still producing and the wine was excellent. Others were quick to follow Trinchero's lead, including Louis M Martini and Paul Draper at Ridge Vineyards.

Wine consumers took to Sutter Home's Amador Zinfandel and Trinchero started cutting other wines out of production to concentrate on Zinfandel. In the early 1970s, Trinchero began making a rosé from some of those grapes and in the mid-1970s, one batch of his Zinfandel rosé was put on the market with a pinch of sugar on the finish. The public lapped it up and the craze for white Zinfandel and blush wine was born. By 1987, Sutter Home was selling more than two million cases of sweet White Zinfandel. Not a single one of the grapes which made that wine was grown in Napa County. On the other hand it was common knowledge that there was nothing new about Napa wineries buying grapes from outside the valley to make wine.

Sutter Home's success with White Zinfandel, coupled with the growth of Napa "picnic" wineries, sparked the debate on what was a winery and, more specifically, what was a Napa winery? It also led to the near death of Zinfandel as a serious wine grape in California. The defenders of White

Zinfandel are fond of saying that only the market success of blush wine "saved" Zinfandel grapes all over the state from being pulled out and replanted to Chardonnay and Cabernet Sauvignon. That is hardly true. What it did was lead growers of Zinfandel to switch to tailoring their grape production to the White Zinfandel market. Growers could harvest the crop early and not be bothered with possible vintage rain as the quality of the crop was a matter of indifference to producers of White Zin. Production of red Zinfandel declined and it became necessary when ordering a glass of wine in a restaurant to specify "red" Zinfandel.

## GROWERS VERSUS VINTNERS

But the key issue for Napa was not whither Zinfandel, but the basic, almost existential question, what is a winery? By the mid-1980s, there were about 150 wineries in Napa, with new ones appearing almost daily. A decade earlier there had been perhaps fifty. The question being debated in Napa was how many were "real" wineries and how many were merely another roadside attraction, depending on gift-shop sales and a lively picnic business for profits.

The debate opened a chasm between growers and vintners, never on the most friendly of terms anyway. Vintners pushed for a definition that would encourage a continued flood of tourists and expanding sales of merchandise not related to wines and events, such as art shows and concerts. They were also strongly in favour of having no restrictions on grapes being trucked in from outside Napa to be used in "Napa Valley" wines. Growers, not surprisingly, were especially against that particular point. In fact, it was only after bitter debate that vintners finally agreed in 1987 that a winery was, indeed, a place where wine should be made. Before that, they had argued that a facility where bulk wine could be brought in and bottled, with no further processing, should qualify as a winery, a fairly astonishing position, but one reflecting the California view of wine as an industrial product.

Led by Andy Beckstoffer, a Hueblein marketing executive turned vineyard owner and manager, the growers countered with the proposal that seventy-five per cent of grapes processed by new Napa wineries had to be grown in Napa Valley. They also urged that the seventy-five per cent be applied to future expansions by existing wineries. Vintners were stunned. They claimed it was a scheme by the growers to boost grape prices.

Perhaps the key to understanding this issue for those outside the Napa/California wine experience is that California lacked any meaningful appellation system – and still does in many respects. The growers' demands would not even have been necessary under an appellation system that was recognized by the general wine consumer. Large wineries realized that they could put a "California" appellation on their wines and not suffer in the market as the bulk of consumers were not educated to care about grape origin. After all, until very recently, the California wine story had never focused on origin as a key element of the plot line.

It is quite telling that while this battle was raging, Beringer introduced a winery brand called Napa Ridge in 1985. The wines were bottled at the historic Italian Swiss Colony Winery in northern Sonoma County. Very few of the grapes that went into Napa Ridge came from Napa County. The wines were certainly good "value for money" bottlings and sales soared, reaching more than a million cases by the mid-1990s. One would have to be naive to believe that Beringer wasn't trading on the Napa appellation with its Napa Ridge wines. What would the average consumer in Kansas City believe? If the label says Napa, the wine must be from Napa, right? It was a good indication that wine marketers believed that the public was beginning to grasp that Napa wine was something to care about. In the meantime, Napa vintners looked the other way while Beringer rolled up tidy profits on Napa Ridge. It was only when the giant Central Valley producer Bronco bought the brand from Beringer, that a hue and cry was raised about protecting the "integrity" of Napa wines. (Bear in mind that Napa is a fairly small place compared to some other major world wine regions. It is very difficult to hide those trucks bringing in Central Valley grapes.) That issue is still being debated in the courts.

At this same time, there was a growing feeling among Napa County regulators that the whole winery thing was getting out of hand. There were something like 200 wineries by 1988 and applications were on the books for dozens more. Since the actual area of wine-growing in Napa is about 620 square kilometres (240 square miles), that means almost one winery to every 2.6 square kilometres (one square mile). Not a problem, perhaps, in Bordeaux, but then you don't find many Bordeaux wineries selling croquet sets and monogrammed wine glasses. To no one's surprise, Napa planners imposed a moratorium on new wineries and the vintners and growers retired to opposite corners to snarl and sulk.

After two more years of debate – and a county election which saw vintners supporting pro-growth candidates to the board of supervisors (they won) – a compromise was reached in early 1990 that gave the growers their seventy-five per cent rule. Also, new wineries could not offer public tours or tastings except by appointment. In some cases, the number of visitors is restricted. However, in order to get an appointment, all you need do is whip out your mobile phone and call from the cellar door. There always seems to be a slot open. Vintners got to keep most non-wine-related activities. In the end, a winery in Napa was defined as a place where wine is actually made, but selling over-priced trinkets to tourists remained an important part of the picture in some quarters.

## PHYLLOXERA STRIKES AGAIN

By the time Napa had solved its identity crisis, a new problem appeared that brought the growers and vintners back together: the return of phylloxera. The root-munching insect had first hit California (and most other wine-growing regions) in the nineteenth century (*see* page 11). At that time the use of rootstocks derived from native North American vines saved Napa's vineyards and most believed phylloxera was a thing of the past. In the 1890s, two rootstocks vied for favour in Napa: the St George and the AxR-1. Both had been developed in France and both seemed resistant to phylloxera. Eventually, St George carried the day as growers thought it performed well in a great number of soils.

However, during the years of Prohibition in the US, wine grape research came to a halt. While Europeans continued to develop new rootstocks, Californians were idle. With the repeal of Prohibition in 1933, and the dominance of UC Davis in vine research, growers bought into the Davis approach of thinking of the vine as a grape-producing factory, with the emphasis, as noted before, on maximum production.

The rootstock debate of the 1890s was reopened and this time the vine experts came down on the side of AxR-1 because it was a more efficient factory worker, producing more grapes than St George. It was presented as a one-size-fits-all rootstock, suitable to any soil and climate – off the rack viticulture. By the 1960s, most vineyards in California were planted on AxR-1. But what wasn't widely known in California was that research in France demonstrated that AxR-1 was, in fact, not all that resistant to phylloxera. There were even warning voices raised in

California, but few listened. In the mid-1980s, the phylloxera louse was discovered in North Coast vineyards, dining very well on AxR-1 roots. Those vines that were planted on St George, mostly older vineyards, were not hit by the infestations.

Those who had recommended AxR-1 claimed that this was a new "mutant" biotype of phylloxera. It did seem to move faster and kill quicker than its nineteenth-century ancestor; nevertheless, St George had remained resistant, while AxR-1 went down. Who was to blame? The truth is, the entire factory farming California approach was to blame. It had created a virtually monoculture rootstock and monocultures are always more susceptible to pest and disease. It could be that the mutant biotype (if it was such) spread faster simply because it found the table set for it in vineyard after vineyard.

The economic impact was enormous for both growers and vintners as vineyard after vineyard was ripped out and replanted in Napa, Sonoma, and Mendocino. (The sandy soils of the Central Valley largely protected those vines from phylloxera.) But beyond the financial cost, there is another factor that is harder to quantify: a lot of Napa wine from the 1990s was made from young vines. Although replanting could take place over three or four years, leaving old vines in place for a time, there is a young vine factor in those vintages. Exactly how this played out in the wine itself is difficult to assess. There are certainly outstanding vintages from the 1990s, but would they have been different in the absence of phylloxera? That may be a question to ponder late at night over a second bottle of Napa Cabernet.

After all the finger-pointing and the "I told you so" pronouncements, there is one undisputable fact: the return of phylloxera has had a positive impact on Napa viticulture. It gave growers a rare opportunity to replant vineyards, taking advantage of the latest clonal and rootstock research. If they had to spend all that money, the general feeling was that they had better do it right.

Replanting also cleared away the last of the debris from the factory farming approach. If growers were taking pains to match rootstock and clones to soils and climate – even trellis systems and row direction – then production was no longer the chief consideration. Sure, production was still a factor, but no longer the dominant factor. There was a dramatic shift in the kind of questions Napa growers (and vintners, too) were asking. The old questions – how many tonnes per hectare can I get and what does the market want? – were much less important. New questions were, by their nature, terroir-centric. What variety will do best on this site? What yield will best express the flavour profile of the grapes?

Of course, there are still plenty of grapes planted in the wrong place, chasing after the market. Merlot leaps to mind. And there are still too many growers who go for tonnage, rather than quality, but it's a lot fewer than twenty or thirty years ago. Wineries have come up with more creative ways to pay the growers, in many cases paying them by how many hectares of grapes are grown, rather than how many tonnes per hectare. The best growers are more concerned with kilogrammes per vine than tonnes per hectare.

All of these factors have come together to create a real awareness of terroir, but the concept has taken a distinctly Californian twist. Beckstoffer gives more or less the standard textbook definition, but adds, "I think in Napa, you have to add attitude as an element of terroir. In Napa, we have a history of doing things well, of doing it right. Maybe not every time, but often. That attitude means that we will not settle for second best, so whatever has to be done, we will do it." Terroir with attitude. That's Napa style all right.

# 5

# Paint it green: the 1990s

The new concern for terroir played nicely into the green viticultural movement that developed in the early 1990s. There was also considerable public pressure for vineyards to go green as the suburbs spilled farther afield. New ex-urban homeowners who bought their dream estate next door to a vineyard were outraged when vines were sprayed to prevent mildew or a tractor fired up at 5am in the morning.

Napa has a "right-to-farm" regulation that is part of every purchase agreement for homes in agricultural areas of the county, but that didn't stop people complaining. There was also concern from environmentalists about hillside planting which, if not done properly, led to severe erosion and silting and the degradation of streams and the Napa River itself. This led to strict hillside planting regulations which other California wine country communities have adopted.

The protests against new vineyard planting never reached the intensity in Napa that they did elsewhere. In neighbouring Sonoma County, for example, it was charged that redwoods were being cut down to make way for vines, which certainly may have happened now and again, but was a very small threat to the coastal redwood forest compared to new housing and commercial development.

At any rate, the California wine industry responded by launching a "sustainable agriculture" counter-attack. No matter how much green paint was applied, the move was frankly centred on the primary need to put up at least the appearance of being environmentally friendly. The sustainable drive was led by the California Wine Institute and the California Association of Winegrape Growers (CAWG). There was the clear realization that if the wine industry was going to survive in an increasingly urban environment, it would have to learn to live with its neighbours and pay more than lip service to environmental concerns.

## SUSTAINABLE WINEMAKING

By the mid-1990s, sustainable was the new buzz word and green was the colour of choice. This raises the question: just what does sustainable mean? A good starting point would be the definition of the Central Coast Vineyard Group, a collection of winemakers and growers who had been wrestling for some time with issues of ex-urban incursion into vineyard areas. The group's definition of sustainability follows: "Sustainability rests on the principle that we must meet the needs of the present without compromising the ability of future generations to meet their own needs."

The longer you look at that sentence the more questions come up. One example: the use of fossil fuel (in the form of petrol or electricity) could compromise "the ability of future generations to meet their own needs." Yet no one seems to be farming with mules in California or making wine by candlelight without refrigeration units.

There is no doubt that sustainable agriculture is better than the slash and burn system but just how green is it really? That depends on who you talk to. It is pretty clear that the interest in sustainable farming in the beginning had to do with the pressure on wineries and growers to get along with their neighbours.

The Code of Sustainable Wine-growing Practices was finally issued by the California Wine Institute and CAWG in 2002. It is voluntary, but it does set clear goals and there is considerable peer pressure to meet those goals. In a joint statement, the two groups said: "The intent of the code is to promote farming and winemaking practices that are sensitive to the environment, responsive to the needs and interest of society-at-large, and economically feasible in practice."

Dennis Groth, the owner of Groth Vineyards in Napa, was involved in framing the code. He claims the goal was to produce a practical handbook that could be used as a guide. "It is a very active project," he says. "There was a lot of interest and a lot of groups had already been working on some kind of sustainable approach. We really wanted to take a positive approach," he adds. "And we wanted something that will really work. We want people to be able to measure results, to be able to check references and find source materials."

Even while the Code of Sustainable Wine-growing Practices was being written, Groth made it clear that there was a distinction in his mind between organic and sustainable. "We can't promise to eliminate all chemicals," he said at the time. "For example, we will set up guidelines to monitor insect counts and only intervene when we have to."

Michael Honig, of Honig Winery in Napa, was the chairman of the group that prepared the code. "From my point of view, it just makes good sense to farm this way. It's better for the grapes and it helps to sell the wines," he said. A key point that. Honig was quite frank in addressing the public relations aspects of the code: "If you look at what has been going on in the way of protests against vineyards, this is something that we had to deal with." As the code was being shaped and debated, the California Wine Institute noted:

> It has become apparent that on an international scale, regulatory and governmental bodies are willing to make more sweeping environmental decisions. Many businesses are moving ahead of the curve, and are now set to adopt the environmental practices being outlined through the ISO 14001 standards (International Standards Organization). These standards will require businesses, throughout a supply chain, to conform to environmental management system applications in their business practices.

For example, the Wine Institute cited the decision by Home Depot, the giant US home supply chain, to buy lumber only from suppliers that were practising sustainable forestry as defined in the ISO standards. According to the Wine Institute, this decision had a major impact on the New Zealand timber industry as Home Depot is the largest single buyer of that country's timber products. (Later, Home Depot appointed its own environmental affairs director who has put pressure on timber interests around the globe.) The Wine Institute stated:

> Such actions are likely to become more and more common as retailers attempt to put on a green face in order to meet market pressure. The consumer trend of seeking out eco-friendly products is projected to continue into the future. As California's population explodes, land will become an increasingly precious commodity. We need to communicate now that we are stewards of the land, striving to sustain our industry for generations to come. Sustainable wine-growing not only improves wine

*quality, but helps us compete in the global marketplace where consumers*
*are increasingly interested in knowing that the foods and wines they enjoy*
*are produced in an environmentally friendly manner.*

Is this merely public relations or a sincere interest in protecting the environment? In a sense, it really doesn't matter. It's what is accomplished that makes a difference and if the results are positive, in this case, motive may well be beside the point.

## THE NAPA RIVER

Some environmentally aware growers and vintners looked beyond the vines toward the Napa River. The Napa River does not loom large when wine buffs turn their thoughts to Napa. As rivers go, it doesn't appear especially spectacular. It runs about sixty-seven kilometres (forty miles) from where it rises on Mount St Helena to the San Francisco Bay. It drains a watershed of about 109,265 hectares, of which about 6,550 hecatres are planted to vines. Napa planning officials are not expecting a great expansion of that area, perhaps about 4,000 hectares by 2010.

Historically, the Napa River watershed has supported a rich riparian forest system with significant wetlands. Since the arrival of Europeans, the river system has been hugely degraded, which comes as no surprise. It has been estimated that since 1800, 2,630 hectares of wetlands have been drained or filled and almost 810 hectares of the original watershed is now covered by pavement or housing. In addition, channels have been straightened, levees have been constructed, and a number of other measures taken to control flooding. None of that works, of course, because the more a river is channelled and controlled, the more severe the floods are when they come, something that has been slowly and painfully learned by those agencies in charge of river use.

Despite all this, a small population of endangered Chinook salmon and Steelhead trout spawn in the river and in its many tributaries. The Steelhead run has been reduced from historical levels of 6,000 adults to only a few hundred fish. Nonetheless, the river still supports an active recreational fishery. Bird species dependent on the river include herons, egrets, kingfishers, rails, and grebes, as well as: Mallard, Merganser, and Wood ducks, Green-winged teals, and the endangered California Clapper Rail. There are also deer, foxes, coyotes, bobcats, and mountain lions that depend on the river.

Many of the world's great wine regions grew up around a river. There's the Rhône, the Ebro, and the Rhine, for example. But in truth, it would be hard to claim that the Napa River played a key role in the development of Napa as a modern wine region. It is navigable up to the city of Napa from San Francisco Bay, but in the economic development of Napa Valley, the railroad played a more important role than the river.

However, the river's role in forming the look and terroir of Napa can't be denied. Today the river seems stable. But in the past, it has been a gypsy river, wandering around the valley floor, dropping drifts of alluvial debris and deep gravel deposits here and there, creating a mixed jumble of soils, doing its part in adding to the productive patchwork of Napa soils and sites.

As the movement toward sustainable agriculture took hold in Napa, a coalition of wineries, government agencies, and environmental groups came together in the mid-1990s not only to save what was left of the Napa River, but to restore it to some degree.

Paul Wagner, a Napa marketing consultant who has been active in the Napa River movement says there was a realization by the people of Napa that they wanted a living river. "The river is not our enemy. What we have to do is work to make the river happy. We are tearing down levees, restoring wetlands, and widening the flood planes, essentially creating no-go areas for humans to give the river some space," he explains.

In October of 2000, the various groups involved – which included almost 200 Napa wineries – reached an agreement that has served as a model in other areas of California for cooperation between wineries and environmentalists in saving and restoring local rivers. The basic terms of the agreement involve banning new vineyard plantings within fifteen metres (fifty feet) of stream banks to prevent soil erosion, the protection of oak trees and other vegetation along streams, and the restoration of riparian habitat. It is worth noting that these agreements were reached before the voluntary Code of Sustainable Wine-growing Practices was endorsed by the Wine Institute and the CAWG.

Does the greening of Napa (and California) viticulture have any impact on wine quality? I would argue that there is a rub off. It simply makes sense that if growers and vintners are paying more attention to the world around them, they are paying more attention to the grape vines as well. Vines are, after all, part of the natural world. If a grower starts thinking about, say, the water level of the Napa River, his or her thoughts are likely to turn to how much water is lavished on the vines. If he or she is a first-rate grower, thought will be given to the effect of water use on grape quality and wine quality. If water comes to be regarded – as it should be – as a finite resource, the role of water in growing vines becomes more critical and the grower (again, the thoughtful one) stops thinking of a grape vine as a mini-factory, churning out raw material for the production of featureless commodity wines.

# 6

# The new century

At the beginning of the twenty-first century, the number of wineries in Napa was exploding, even as the regulatory agencies made it ever more tedious and time consuming to open the cellar doors. By the year 2000, it was almost impossible to put a definite number on the existing wineries, including those somewhere in the permit process or being planned. Each winery must receive both state and federal operating permits, but reports on these permits often lag reality. Also, most wineries don't receive final permits until they are almost ready for first crush. The best estimate as of 2000 is that there were about 300 wineries in Napa in operation or very close to operation. The pace may have slowed somewhat, but it certainly has not stopped. Early in 2004, there were forty applications for new wineries before Napa planners.

What will eventually put a cap on new wineries is the sheer lack of plantable vineyard land. With the regulation requiring Napa wineries to use at least seventy-five per cent Napa grapes, and plantable land becoming harder to find, Napa may top out at something like 325 to 350 wineries.

Obviously, the wine being produced is of more importance than playing hide-and-seek with the numbers. From 1990 forward, I doubt if a single winery (outside Carneros) has been established dedicated to any wine other than Cabernet Sauvignon and its Bordeaux kin, with the possible exception of a few brave rebels opting for Zinfandel. Many of Napa's new producers make Chardonnay and even Sauvignon Blanc. Chardonnay because the market demands it, Sauvignon Blanc because it does reasonably well, sometimes very well, in Napa. But no one has put up their shingle in Napa recently with the intent of making great Chardonnay. (Having said that, I'm sure that somewhere in Napa someone is planning or trying to do just that.) Beyond Cab and a little Zinfandel, there is some interest in Syrah and Sangiovese, at least in certain areas. However, as operating costs continue to rise, growers and vintners are more likely to turn to the wine that brings in the most cash: Cabernet. Even the best non-Cabernet wines can't command the prices paid for King Cab. But it is to be hoped, for the sake of diversity that not everyone will follow the Cabernet road. Alternatives include:

## SAUVIGNON BLANC

It isn't clear exactly when the grape arrived in California, but by the 1890s, it was being grown in Napa. One of the most important selections of cuttings was imported by Louis Mel and Charles Wetmore from Château d'Yquem to the Livermore Valley east of San Francisco Bay in 1878 and was later planted on the Wente family estate. (Jean Wente, writing in *The University of California/Sotheby Book of California Wine*, notes: "California Sauvignon Blanc is always being discovered, a forlorn luxury ...") Cuttings of Semillon were brought in at the same time. UC Davis researchers and professors have historically held the varietal at arm's length. Following Prohibition, growers and vintners were advised that the flavours were too strong for the "average consumer". Happily for the "average consumer" that advice was ignored.

In the early days, influenced by the d'Yquem connection, most California (and Napa) Sauvignon Blanc was called Sauterne (note the absence of the terminal "s"). If one looks carefully through the clutter and ruin of California jug and box wines today, it is still possible to find California Sauterne, though thankfully none from Napa.

Sauvignon Blanc is Napa's best white wine grape overall. Underrated everywhere, it can produce stunning wines when grown in well-drained gravelly soils, which are found most often close to the Napa River. (No doubt there are also mountain and hillside sites that would be suitable to Sauvignon Blanc, but they are simply too valuable for Cabernet to be used for Sauvignon Blanc, with a few notable exceptions.) Overall, Napa Sauvignon Blanc gets enough heat to mature, but holds good acidity due to the temperature swing between night and day.

As elsewhere in California, Napa Sauvignon Blanc is made in a variety of styles. The best in Napa approach the Graves style and the worst try to be mini-Chardonnays. Most Napa winemakers shun the "cat's piss" New

Zealand style, which is most likely a good thing in the long run. That style can be refreshing and it certainly grabs the palate, but in the end it can be something of a one-trick pony.

There is an honorable tradition of Sauvignon Blanc in Napa, going back at least to Robert Mondavi's innovative bottling of a Fumé Blanc in 1966. There were also several marvellous vintages of Sauvignon Blanc from Sterling Vineyards when Ric Forman was the winemaker there in the late 1960s and early 1970s.

The unexpected thing about Napa Sauvignon Blanc is its ability to age, especially those early Sterling wines, which develop a remarkable complexity and richness after ten to fifteen years in bottle. Also, the Robert Mondavi To Kalon Vineyard Reserve Sauvignon Blanc can be a stunning wine with several years of bottle age. They rarely come up for auction, of course – who cellars California Sauvignon Blanc after all? But should the opportunity come up, do look for older Napa varietals.

While researching this book, I tasted over 100 California Sauvignon Blancs, and found eighteen worth an enthusiastic thumbs up. Of those, ten were made by Napa wineries from Napa grapes and another was made by a Napa winery from Monterey County grapes – Cain Musque. Several of Napa's best Sauvignon Blancs are bottled as "Meritage" blends (*see* footnote on page 111). Napa's top Sauvignon Blancs include: Beringer, Cakebread Cellars, Chateau Potelle, Duckhorn, Flora Springs, Grgich Hills, Groth, Honig, Merryvale, Origin, Robert Pecota, Joseph Phelps, St Clement, St Supéry, Selene, Signorello, Spottswoode, and Spring Mountain Vineyards.

## ZINFANDEL
The roots of Zinfandel reach deep into Napa's viticultural history. It was first grown by Joseph Osborne in what is now the Oak Knoll appellation in the 1860s. It was the standard Napa red grape during the period that Napa growers were taking the Mission grape out of production. Zinfandel was the most widely planted red grape in California by the beginning of the twentieth century and still held that position at the beginning of the twenty-first century.

Zinfandel was once known as California's mystery grape but recent DNA tests indicate that it is a clone of the Italian grape Primitivo, or perhaps the other way around. It is also related to the Plavac Mali grape found in Croatia. One intriguing theory is that Zinfandel did, in fact, come to the US from Central Europe in the 1820s but was taken back to Italy by Italian immigrants to California who liked the grape and returned it to the homeland with them. There are indications that Primitivo is regarded in southern Italy as a "new" grape. I like that story and would be sorry to learn of any facts that get in the way.

One Zinfandel myth that has been laid to rest is the old story that Agoston Haraszthy was the first to bring Zinfandel to the US, importing it with a number of other vines from Hungary in the 1850s. He never made that claim himself but it was put forward by his son, Arpad Haraszthy years after Agoston's death. The Zinfandel claim was taken seriously for decades, but has finally been laid to rest thanks to the careful work of wine historians like Charles Sullivan.

Zinfandel in California is made in a sometimes bewildering number of styles, ranging from the faux-rosé white Zinfandel to late-harvest and port styles. Paul Draper of Ridge Vineyards, who knows a thing or two about Zinfandel, has identified seven different styles. He calls the style he makes "claret", identifying a claret-style Zinfandel as one grown in a fairly cool climate, not over-cropped, and not overripe. The best will age at least six years and often longer. The top Napa Zinfandels fit that description.

It's a safe bet that if it were not for the worldwide sweep of Cabernet Sauvignon, Zinfandel would undoubtedly be Napa's premier red wine. Napa Zinfandels, at their best, are balanced and luscious wines, featuring dark fruit and a long finish. The best vineyards are above the valley floor on rocky hillsides, more often than not on volcanic soils.

Napa's best Zinfandels include: Biale, Buehler, Burgess Cellars, Château Potelle, Edizone Pennino (Niebaum-Coppola), Elyse, Green & Red Vineyard, Markham, Storybook Mountain, and The Terraces.

## THE REST

Syrah and other Rhône varieties have had a lot of play in California, starting in the mid-1970s when the Rhône Rangers came on the scene, with Randal Grahm of Bonny Doon bearing the standard. Today, Syrah is planted up and down the state, most often bottled as a gulpable sort of wine and likely to be labelled Shiraz, following in both name and style the Australian model.

There is some evidence that true Syrah was planted in Napa in the nineteenth century at Charles Krug, though no one paid much attention to it. In modern times, Joseph Phelps planted Syrah in the early 1970s and was most likely the first Napa winery to make a Syrah since Prohibition ended. Syrah has its fans in Napa, to be sure, but it does not play a significant role in the Napa picture. Joseph Phelps still makes a Syrah under the Vin du Mistral label, in a style suitable for early drinking. Phelps also produces a Viognier, a Grenache Rosé, and a blend of Grenache, Mourvèdre, and Syrah which is bottled as Le Mistral. The line has become very popular and the wines are consistently first rate. Shafer's Relentless is a delicious blend of Syrah and Petite Sirah, while Truchard Winery also makes an attractive Syrah.

Sangiovese has received more attention in Napa, perhaps because of the involvement of Italian Piero Antinori at Atlas Peak. Other noteworthy producers include Shafer with its Firebreak bottling, Benessere, and Swanson, which also makes an attractive rosé from Sangiovese that is worth looking out for.

Before the Cabernet boom, Charbono enjoyed a limited success in Napa. Inglenook was one of the leading producers of the varietal, although it was dropped from the line-up long ago. There is still some Charbono grown in the warmer northern part of Napa around Calistoga, where Summers Winery is the only Napa producer of Charbono as far as I can discover. Duxoup, an artisan Sonoma winery, makes a Charbono from Napa grapes grown near Calistoga.

Petite Sirah was widely planted in the nineteenth century, but very little is made today. Historically, there has been considerable confusion in Napa and elsewhere in California over Petite Sirah, Syrah, and Durif. Stags' Leap (owned by Beringer Blass) makes an outstanding Petite Sirah, partially from old vines, which ages very well, or at any rate its fans believe so.

Riesling also has a long history in Napa, which isn't surprising when you consider the number of immigrants from Germany who were planting vineyards in the mid-nineteenth century, including Jacob Schram. The first Rieslings arrived in the 1850s and the variety remained well established until Prohibition. A cool location is the key to quality Riesling in Napa, like Smith Madrone's Spring Mountain Riesling and Trefethen in the Oak Knoll District. Joseph Phelps is a serious and well-respected producer of Riesling. In fact, the first Phelps wine, released in 1973, was a Riesling made by Walter Schug who trained in Germany.

Chenin Blanc is made by a few wineries, including Casa Nuestra and Milat, which both produce pleasing Chenin in an off-dry style. Pine Ridge and Chapplett also make very good dry Chenins. The variety is not mentioned before Prohibition but came into its own after World War II. It became an important wine in the 1950s when Charles Krug started using cold fermentation to produce an off-dry Chenin. When Robert Mondavi started his own winery he also produced a reasonably good, slightly sweet Chenin Blanc. It is odd, considering past success with the varietal in Napa, that so few vintners make the wine. It is a very versatile grape and the Napa weather and soils seem to suit it. David Duckhorn, co-owner of Milat Vineyards in the St Helena AVA, believes Chenin's poor reputation in California "is a function of being in the wrong place at the wrong time". He says: "Like many varietals planted in California, American farmers tended to disregard European knowledge of site specificity and plant varietals where they thought they would yield the most at the highest price. Now we are learning that Chenin Blanc makes spectacular wine when grown in the right areas."

In the end, however, it seems that Cabernet Sauvignon will continue to dominate Napa vineyards in the new century, probably to an even greater extent than now.

# 7

# Beware, the cults are coming

In sorting out Napa for the twenty-first century, the cult wines loom large. The Napa cult Cabernets are trophy wines born in the "if you've got it flaunt it" days of the early 1990s. (It would be interesting to see a political analyst try to put the Napa cult wines in the context of the growing disparity of income in the USA.) They are wines of very limited production, mostly well under 1,000 cases. The starting price is up from $150 and they are invariably in the upper nineties on the 100-point scale rating system.

Besides the high scores, high prices, and limited availability, the cult wines – painting with a broad brush – have in common huge, explosive up-front flavours and a massive structure. They are commonly overripe, over-concentrated, and generally over-the-top. They are also undrinkable when young and of questionable ageability. But that doesn't matter to the people who buy them because they are only interested in bragging rights, not the wine in the glass. A large part of the allure of these wines is the difficulty in buying them. They are mostly sold directly to consumers from a mailing list and there is a long wait to get on the mailing list. I believe that these cult favourites will, in time, be simply a curious footnote in the story of Napa wines. But, in the meantime, there they are and what to do about them? They attract way more attention that they deserve.

## THE ORIGINS OF CULT
The roots of cult wines go all the way back to the 1960s and a marvellous Chablis-like Chardonnay from Stony Hill, a winery at the foot of Spring Mountain. It sold for $6 a bottle, at that time a high price for a California wine. Like today's cults, it was sold almost entirely to a privileged few on

a mailing list. Stony Hill still exists and is still sold almost entirely to a customer mailing list. It is an exceptionally good Chardonnay.

In the 1970s, Heitz Martha's Vineyard was an early cult hit. It cost $12.75 at the beginning of the decade and was selling for $25 at the end of it, an unheard of price in California. Customers on a mailing list would get a postcard telling them of the release date and line up outside the tasting room in St Helena to buy the wine.

During the 1980s, Randy Dunn became a proto-cult figure with his eponymous Howell Mountain Cabernets. Dunn also made the Caymus Special Selection, which has always been an "almost cult" and the Grace Family Cabernets. If Dunn had sought it out, he could probably have competed in the cult sweepstakes, but he decided that there were more important things in life. Now he makes about 2,000 cases a year of Cabernet which sells in the $50 range.

But the real cult madness came in the 1990s, with the runaway prices and the tiny production that signalled the true birth of the California cult wines. Many of the cult wines of the 1990s didn't exist when the decade started. Karen McNeil, who is director of wine education at the Culinary Institute of America in Napa and winner of a James Beard award for wine education, says the focus on cult wines has skewed the overall appreciation of wine, especially among the younger consumers:

*I'll be working with a class of, say, fifty students. We'll be talking about Cabernet Sauvignon and I can tell by their comments that unless I am about to serve them a Harlan Estate, they feel they are missing something. People feel they haven't really experienced wine unless they have tasted Screaming Eagle. I don't want my students to taste those wines. I want them to have a more organic experience. I want them to find a producer, and it can be from anywhere in the world, and get to know that wine, get to know the piece of ground the wines comes from. I don't begrudge any of the cult wine producers being famous or getting the prices they get. But there are more wines in the world.*

McNeil adds that the whole cult experience puts too much emphasis on the ego of the brand or the winemaker. "Over time, what you should respect is a piece of ground. The miraculous phenomena that a piece of ground can give to the wine year after year. The cult wines are a pop culture thing. It takes away the ties to the land, to the place. All it takes to be successful is enough money, ego, and the skill to manipulate the media. It divorces wine from what makes it great, which is the land," she says.

So who are the leading cultists in Napa? The following is my short list.

## Araujo Estate Wines

The attraction here is Eisele Vineyard, which was the source of the great Joseph Phelps Cabernets of the mid-1970s. The Araujo family bought the estate in 1990. They produce about 1,500 cases of wine each year, with half of that going to a few restaurants and half to a mailing list. The wine sells on release at $150 a bottle.

## Bryant Family Vineyard

Cabernet Sauvignon is produced in the hills of eastern Napa (outside the valley proper) near Lake Hennessey. The Cabernet is huge and extracted. Production is about 500 cases. The style, which was established early on by winemaker Helen Turley, was to ferment with wild yeast, pick highly extracted fruit – yummy, grape jam! – and bottle without filtration. I am told Turley uses that technique with all Cabernet Sauvignon she produces. Regardless of site, so it would seem. Turley has now left the winery.

## Colgin Cellars

Cabernet Sauvignon is made from the Herb Lamb vineyard from the St Helena appellation. Fewer than 500 cases are made annually. The wine, in common with the other cults, is intense and concentrated, but is perhaps more balanced that the general run of these trophy wines.

## Dalla Valle Vineyards

A blend of Cabernet Sauvignon and Cabernet Franc, Dalla Valle Maya is one of the few exceptions to the "don't go there" cult rule number one. The hillside vineyard in the Oakville district above the Silverado Trail produces deeply tannic wine with rich intensity but also attractive understated fruit that doesn't entirely wipe out the palate. Dalla Valle also has an attractive if rather overstated Sangiovese called Pietro Rosso.

## Grace Family Vineyards

Dick and Ann Grace started out as home winemakers with 0.4 hectares of Cabernet Sauvignon they planted in 1976. Charlie Wagner, the owner of Caymus Vineyards, tasted the wine and featured it as a vineyard-designated wine in 1978. In 1983, the family made wine on its own and the critics lapped it up. To be fair, it can be an amazing wine, all 350 cases of it. Does it justify the price or deserve the reputation? No.

## Harlan Estate

It sets my teeth on edge when I see Harlan Estate described as a California "First Growth". First growth is about centuries of winemaking, matching house style to terroir. It is not about scores in the high nineties. I recently read a review by an American wine critic (not Robert Parker) that described Harlan Estate as follows: "Liqueur-like superripe nose … Valrona chocolate; distinctly port-like notes … explosive fruit bordering on confectionary … freakishly ripe wine". The critic gave the wine ninety-seven points. A "port-like" Cabernet Sauvignon is not my idea of any sort of first growth. "Freakishly ripe" says it all, really.

## Screaming Eagle

The grapes come from a rocky hillside in the Oakville district, but really they could be from anywhere. This over-extracted, super-tannic wine simply wipes out all traces of origin. It sells for about $400 on release and commands incredible prices in charity wine auctions. Of course, things do get kind of nutty at those auctions, but at the 2004 Napa Valley Wine Auction, a trio of three-litre bottles of Screaming Eagle fetched a tidy $220,000. The winning bidder from Hong Kong had clearly found the trophy he was after.

Some cult lists vary but these seven seem to be the core. Sometimes Shafer's Hillside Select Cabernet Sauvignon makes the cult cut, but it isn't. The Hillside Select reflects a specific site, and is not overripe or over-extracted. Doug Shafer claims the key to the wine is the vineyard. He is uncomfortable with the wine being given cult status. "It's all about the vineyard. I don't want to take anything away from the guys in the cellar, but that wine is vineyard-driven," he says. In the end, cult wines have little to do with putting the best wine in the bottle and everything to do with media-driven image, ego, and the 100-point sweepstakes.

# 8

# Napa dirt

In 1977 the federal Bureau of Alcohol, Tobacco, and Firearms (BATF) – at that time the agency that regulated wine in the US – issued the rules regarding the establishment of an appellation of origins system for wine in the US. The appellations were to be known as American Viticultural Areas (AVAs) and they differ sharply from the European appellation systems. There are two levels of AVAs in the US. First, there is a simple political statement applying to individual states and counties within a state. That is, a wine made in California can state that fact on the label. Likewise, a wine made in Napa can also carry that name on the label. The second level requires some sort of geographical designations, Napa Valley for example. Unlike the European system, there is no implied claim of wine quality for AVAs, nor are there any regulations at all regarding grape variety or yield. It is simply a statement of geographic origin. In general, AVAs tend to be inclusive rather than exclusive.

## MAPPING NAPA

That is certainly the case for the Napa Valley AVA, which was approved in 1981. The original proposal, which had been created by a committee of vintners and growers, would have limited the AVA to the area in the drainage system of the Napa River. That would have included hillside and mountain vineyards but would have excluded Pope Valley, Chiles Valley, Wooden Valley, and a few other vineyards in the Vaca range on the eastern side of Napa County.

The issue became controversial, as these areas had traditionally produced "Napa" wines. Influential vintners like Robert Mondavi and Louis M Martini supported the excluded portions, but when the issue was put to a vote of the Napa Vintners and Growers Association, the vote favoured the original Napa River drainage AVA, which was duly submitted to the BATF. A few months later the BATF approved a Napa Valley AVA that included virtually the whole of Napa County, even areas outside the Napa River watershed. Nothing was excluded. That decision set the pattern for almost every decision that followed involving sub-appellations within Napa. While lip-service is paid to such things as soil type and weather pattern, in the end, the decisions are more likely to be based on past usage or even marketing issues.

## THE STORY OF STAGS LEAP

A good example is the Stags Leap District AVA. Historically, the area had never been especially important for wines. It was grazing land, with a few orchards and small plantings of grapes like Petite Sirah, Carignane, and Zinfandel, a typical nineteenth-century California "field mix". In 1961, Nathan Fay planted Cabernet in an old orchard. A few winemakers – including Mondavi – noticed that the grapes were excellent. Others followed and when Warren Winiarski's Stag's Leap Cabernet Sauvignon took top honours at the Steven Spurrier Paris tasting of 1976 (*see* page 26), the name suddenly became an issue.

A few years before the Paris tasting, Carl Doumani had bought an old property in the Stags Leap area just off the Silverado Trail. There were a few beaten-up Petite Sirah vines on the land which Doumani coaxed back into productivity and made into a wine which he called Stags' Leap, making the placement of the apostrophe the only thing that distinguished it from Winiarski's brand. Doumani and Winiarski went to court and eventually, Doumani won the right to use the name. But the plot thickens. Gary Andrus produced a Stag's Leap Cuvée Cabernet for his Pine Ridge label. Doumani and Winiarski forgot their differences and went back to court, this time to block the use of the Stag's Leap name by Andrus. They lost. The court ruled that Stag's Leap was a geographic name dating back to the 1880s or earlier (true) and that it belonged to no one and everyone.

It was against this background that other Stags Leap district vintners such as John Shafer began the push for a Stags Leap AVA. At first, Winiarski was dead against it, fearing that the appellation would dilute the value of his brand name. However, after the court granted Andrus the right to use the name, Winiarski changed his mind.

The original proposal for a Stags Leap AVA (note that the apostrophe is missing altogether in the AVA name) called for a fairly small area, around 200 hectares in size, on volcanic soils east of the Silverado Trail. It could have served as a model for what an AVA should be. Then, market forces kicked in. The Stags Leap name had consumer cachet, with or without the apostrophe, and no one with any possible claim to it wanted to be left out.

The Robert Mondavi family and Silverado Vineyards, owned by the Disney family (as in Walt), owned property west of the Silverado Trail. They convinced the original Stags Leap group that they should be included, which doubled the size of vineyard hectareage and extended the proposed AVA west to the Napa River. This completely changed the soil profile of the AVA. Rather than the rocky volcanic soils east of the Trail, the expansion was on deep alluvial and loamy soil, common on the valley floor from north to south. The Mondavi-Disney extension also moved the original boundary south of Clos du Val, following the bed of a curiously straight wet-weather creek.

When Stanley Anderson, owner of S Anderson Vineyards on the Yountville crossroad, learned of the expansion, he didn't see why he should be locked out. So he got together other growers along the road and asked to be included, adding another sixty-one hectares to the pie. When the BATF held hearings in late 1987, still another grower turned up. He argued that the wet-weather creek that marked the southern boundary was actually an irrigation ditch that his father had dug. His vineyards were just south of that ditch and he claimed a right to share in the benefits of Stags Leap.

The bureaucrats gathered up many thousands of dollars worth of historical and geological reports and position papers filed by a raft of expensive lawyers, and returned to Washington. Early in 1988 they gave the right to use Stags Leap District to everyone who had asked.

## CREATING THE SUB-APPELLATIONS

From the beginning of the appellation discussion, there was resistance to creating sub-appellations. It was felt that the patchwork of smaller appellations would detract from the larger Napa AVA. The argument ran that Napa had done a remarkable job of presenting a unified front to the consumer (and the trade) and the fragmentation of appellations could be confusing. Is a Howell Mountain Cabernet superior to a plain Napa Valley Cabernet? That debate still continues in Napa, but it is rather a moot point, since at the last count there were foureen sub-appellations existing and at least one pending.

None of the Napa sub-appellations are textbook cases of matching terroir/site and wine profile to a growing area. But I have to wonder how many European appellations get that job done either? At least some of the failings in Napa can be laid on the table of the bureaucrats who established the original ground rules and are responsible for how they have been put in place. As you can see, in the case of Stags Leap, the original proposal made sense, as it was handed down it is laughable.

I think, on the whole, Napa is trying to do the right thing. In this case, reserve the Napa Valley appellation as a kind of brand mark, a marketing tool, and refine and define the terroir in the sub-appellations. It doesn't always work. In fact, it could be argued that it hasn't worked very well at all: that it has in common with many other human enterprises.

The fourteen existing Napa sub-appellations are covered in some detail below, along with producers within each AVA which seem to represent that particular AVA. There is no intention of mentioning every winery in the appellation, as every winery is not worth mentioning. There is obviously some overlap in descriptions of soils and climate, as would only be expected in such localized sub-divisions.

## ATLAS PEAK
In any discussion of Napa mountain grapes, the names of Mount Veeder, Howell Mountain, and Spring Mountain inevitably come up. Atlas Peak is often overlooked. The sub-appellation, which was created in 1992, takes its name from the highest peak in the Vaca range on the east side of Napa. It includes about 4,450 hectares of land of which some 1,011 hectares are planted to vines, with Cabernet Sauvignon the dominant varietal. Atlas Peak soils are almost entirely volcanic in origin, fairly shallow, well-drained, and infertile, leading to a loss of vigour in the vines.

Most of the planted area is well above the fog, so there is no lack of sunshine, although nights can be chilly, with a drastic fall in temperature following sunset. Temperatures can drop by 16°C (30°F) in two hours. The area gets seventy-six to ninety centimetres (thirty to thirty-six inches) of rain annually.

There were vineyards planted in the area as early as 1870, with additional plantings in the 1890s. However, it is estimated that by 1900, there were only about forty hectares of vines on Atlas Peak. None survived Prohibition. The modern era began in 1986 when 445 hectares were purchased by an investment group including Bollinger of France, Whitbread of the UK, and Antinori of Italy. The owners took the name of Atlas Peak for the new vineyards and winery. Some 186 hectares were planted over the next few years. Ownership changed in the early 1990s and the winery and brand are now owned by Allied-Domecq (which also owns Clos du Bois in Sonoma County and Callaway Winery in southern California as well as William Hill Winery in Napa) while the vineyards are owned by Antinori. There are just under 200 hectares now planted by Atlas Peak, by far the largest single planting in the AVA.

The most planted grapes, after Cabernet Sauvignon, are Sangiovese, Merlot, Zinfandel, and Chardonnay. At this point, Cabernet is performing very well and is the single best variety in the AVA. Typically, Atlas Peak AVA Cabernet has a bright and lively character with good acidity and mouthfeel. It is uncertain how it might age because it has very little track record. As the Sangiovese vines mature, the wines are taking on a richness and depth of flavour not commonly found in Italian Sangiovese. At its best, Chardonnay from the AVA has a minerally quality that can be quite attractive.

There are only a handful of wineries in the district, with most Atlas Peak AVA grapes sold to vintners outside the AVA, including Caymus, Joseph Phelps, Rutherford Grove, Stag's Leap Winery, Storybook, Villa Mount Eden, and V Sattui. The demand for Atlas Peak Cabernet Sauvignon has been strong and it appears to be an important element in Cabernet blends. At this point, the Atlas Peak AVA has to take a backseat to the other mountain appellations in Napa. However, with new plantings coming on line and as already planted vineyards mature, it is likely that the AVA will take on more importance. Only time will tell.

## The Best of Atlas Peak

**ATLAS PEAK VINEYARDS**
3700 Soda Canyon Road, Napa, CA 94558. Tel: 707 252 7971;
Fax: 707 252 7974; Email: info@atlaspeak.com; Website: www.atlaspeak.com
Vineyards: 202ha

At this point, the only winery in the AVA to have produced consistently high quality wines reflecting the terroir is Atlas Peak Vineyards. The top wine is the Consenso Cabernet Sauvignon, a blend of Cabernet, Merlot, Syrah, and a pinch of Sangiovese. It is a very good example of Napa mountain red, full-bodied with dark berry fruit and an echoing finish. Over time, I would expect the Sangiovese to continue to improve and, at some point, surpass the Consenso. At present, there is a regular and a reserve bottling. Both versions contain Merlot and Syrah, with a dash of Petit Verdot in the regular. It is a very inviting wine, with more complexity, especially in the reserve, than most California Sangiovese. In the reserve, the Sangiovese was co-fermented with the other varieties which may add to the complexity of the finished wine. The estate Chardonnay can be delightful, with bright citrus fruit balanced by a minerally edge. A new project at Atlas Peak Vineyards is the production of a series of mountain Cabernets from Howell Mountain, Mount Veeder, and Spring Mountain, which looks very promising.

## CARNEROS

In dealing with the appellations of Napa Valley, one never quite knows what to do with the Carneros AVA. At first glance, Carneros appears to be a bureaucratic balls-up of the first degree. First, it finds itself in two political divisions: Napa and Sonoma. The Napa side is the largest bit – in terms of vineyards at any rate – and contains most of the best-known wineries. The Carneros AVA is a sub-appellation of both the Napa Valley AVA and the Sonoma Valley AVA, just as Stags Leap District, Howell Mountain, and so on are sub-appellations of Napa Valley. So what you have is one AVA that is a sub-appellation of two completely distinct AVAs.

But in the end, the bureaucrats got it just about right. The Carneros AVA actually makes perfect sense if you ignore the purely political division of Napa and Sonoma. Carneros was established strictly according to microclimatic influences. The Sonoma Mountains, a finger of the coastal range, form the western boundary of Carneros, while the northern boundary lies in the southernmost hills of the Mayacamas Mountains. The Napa River forms the eastern boundary and the Southern Pacific railroad line the southern. The elevation ranges from sea level in the south to over 300 metres (about 1,000 feet) in the western hills of the Sonoma side.

It has been argued that Carneros could be further divided into Alta Carneros and Baja Carneros since there can be a major difference in climate and soils between northern and southern Carneros. There are also climatic differences between western and eastern Carneros. Also, the idea of a railroad track being used as a "natural" marker is simply silly. Why not have the edge of the Bay as the southern boundary?

But at any rate, what you have is something very close to a true appellation. My approach is to follow that lead and consider the district as a whole, including a little Sonoma in the Napa story. We'll try to sort out the wines made in Carneros; what they have in common, what they don't have in common, and what impact the particular terroirs of Carneros have on those wines.

For a physical overview and proper historic perspective on the Carneros district there are two superb viewing sites. The first is the terrace of Domaine Carneros on the Napa side of the AVA. Sipping a lovely glass of bubbly you can look south and west over kilometres of vineyards, San Pablo Bay (an arm of San Francisco Bay) and – on a clear day – the city of San Francisco over there across the Golden Gate. Or, drive a few kilometres to the west and take in the view from the Sonoma side of Carneros. This time with a glass of sparkling wine on the patio of Gloria Ferrer, look south and east, again over waves of vineyards and San Pablo Bay, with the academic towers of the city of Berkeley just behind the hill.

Not only are the wine and the view terrific from both places, but the insight into modern viticultural history is also on target. Both wineries were built to make sparkling wine only, but both now also produce table wines. Both source grapes entirely from Carneros and both are large estates. Domaine Carneros is owned by the French Champagne house of Taittinger and Gloria Ferrer by the Spanish cava giant, Freixenet.

Although wine grapes were planted in Carneros by the mid-nineteenth century, the region's modern viticultural history began in the 1970s and 1980s, centred on grapes used for sparkling wine production – Pinot Noir and Chardonnay – though with some interest in table wine, to be sure. Plantings in Carneros differed in at least one important way from those elsewhere in Napa and Sonoma: vineyards tended to be much larger and mono-varietal. Elsewhere, vineyards had been planted on relatively small hillside plots or on flat land, replacing orchards.

From the time the first Europeans arrived in Carneros – replacing the elk, grizzly bear, and Native Americans – the concentration had been on raising livestock, cattle, sheep, and goats; the name Carneros refers to sheep. This meant that there were large tracts of land available for planting to grapes, rather than scattered plots, which matched well with the move toward mechanization in the vineyards in the 1960s and 1970s. These newly planted vineyards, often more than forty hectares in size, were farmed and harvested uniformly, and rarely divided into separate vineyard blocks as is common today. This approach worked fine for sparkling wine production California-style, but has had a lingering negative impact on the development of Pinot Noir and Chardonnay for table wines. It was only with replanting in the 1990s, as a result of phylloxera, that growers began paying attention to clonal selection and to differences in the lay of the land, the sheer look of the place.

If you could stand somewhere near the summit of Mount Veeder at the western edge of the Mayacamas Mountains a few miles north of Carneros and look roughly south-southeast toward San Francisco Bay, you would note that despite many descriptions to the contrary, Carneros is not a flat landscape. What you see are the broken southern-most reaches of the Mayacamas Mountains as they crumble into the Bay. Some of the steepest vineyards I've ever walked in Napa have been in Carneros.

These hillsides are not especially high, around ninety to 120 metres (300 to 400 feet) above the Bay in the eastern Carneros and about sixty metres (200 feet) higher in the west. But they do present a jumble of sun and wind exposure, as well as soils with a higher gravel content than the clay soils in the narrow flatlands between the hills and in the areas just beyond the hills that border the Bay. You go to those hillsides to find the best Pinot Noir and perhaps Merlot.

Another very common, indeed almost obligatory descriptor for Carneros is "cool". The phrase "cool Carneros" turns up in almost every story about the region. Cool compared to what? Compared to other sub-appellations in Napa Valley, it is cool, although the Oak Knoll district runs it a close second. Cool compared to Santa Maria, an outstanding Pinot Noir region in Santa Barbara? No, not really. Cool compared to parts of the Russian River Valley in Sonoma County? Not at all. In fact, André Tchelistcheff, whose name seems to pop up at every turn in Napa, thought it would be possible to make good Cabernet Sauvignon in

Carneros, given the proper hillside exposure. No one has done it yet, but I suspect someone will at any time.

That aside, the dominant climatic influence in Carneros is maritime. The Pacific Ocean and San Francisco Bay create the fog and wind that characterize the region. Unlike Napa Valley and Sonoma Valley, shielded by mountains from the main thrust of Pacific winds, Carneros is open to the Bay and through that connection to the Pacific, which leads to a typical maritime fog pattern. As air over the interior land mass heats during the day, it rises, pulling in cool air from above the ocean. These chilly winds can be felt during mid-to-later afternoon in Carneros (and somewhat up-valley in Napa, especially in the Stags Leap District) slacking as the temperature falls. Fog moves in during the night and burns off about mid-morning.

This weather pattern is prevalent during the growing season. The afternoon winds help prevent the spread of mildew and mould on the vines, but they can also stress the vines by drawing water from the leaves faster that it can be replaced. Annual rainfall in Carneros is lower than elsewhere in Napa or Sonoma, fifty centimetres (twenty inches) a year or less. Soils are very shallow, from sixty to ninety centimetres (two to three feet) above a hard clay pan which blocks the vine roots from growing deeper into the water table, making irrigation a useful tool for growers in controlling vine vigour and fruit yield.

There have been some recent attempts to dry-farm in Carneros, despite the lack of rainfall. For example, Acacia has a small dry-farmed vineyard block and is looking at expanding it as water tables fall and state and federal agencies become more reluctant to give permits to take water from streams or creeks. In recent years, the California Department of Fish and Game (DFG) has made it a policy to restore fresh water tidal marshes along the Bay, so it is very difficult to gain a permit to collect run-off water in vineyard reservoirs during the winter rainy season. Growers are turning to reclaimed water and simply using less water, usually under four hectolitres per vine per year. In the Central Valley of California, which is much warmer with sandy soils, water use may reach forty hectolitres per vine per year.

The two dominant Carneros soils, the Haire and Diablo series, were formed recently in geological terms, less than two million years ago during the ice ages. They were formed as the water of San Francisco Bay receded. They are both dense with low fertility and high clay content. There is a small percentage of more loamy soils, often high in volcanic content, which were carried down from mountains on the northern edge of Carneros by creeks and rivers. These are more fertile soils.

Although Beaulieu and Louis M Martini were buying grapes from Carneros in the 1930s and through the 1960s, no one bothered to identify them as Carneros grapes and they were dumped into a general red wine or white wine blend. At the time, California wines only needed to have fifty per cent varietal fruit to carry the varietal name on the label. There was certainly a generous portion of Carneros Pinot Noir in a lot of Beaulieu and Martini Cabernets of that period.

As mentioned above, wineries purchased land in Carneros because they could buy large tracts that were easy to farm on the cheap. It was not uncommon to plant forty hectares with a single clonal selection of one variety. In essence, Carneros existed at that time as a factory farm to feed the low-priced generic blends of the large Napa wineries. But slowly, things began to change. Louis M Martini bought eighty hectares of land in Carneros and a few years later began clonal experiments with Pinot Noir and Chardonnay. Several of the clones developed during that period are still in use in California. André Tchelistcheff also convinced the owners of Beaulieu to buy land in the 1960s and a new wave of vineyard development began, led by growers like Rene di Rosa, the Hudson family, and the Sangiacomo family.

Perhaps the best date to mark the beginnings of the modern era in Carneros was the establishment of Carneros Creek Winery in 1972. For the first few years, Francis Mahoney made Zinfandel, Cabernet Sauvignon, and Pinot Noir from grapes grown outside Napa. However, the reason he had opened a winery in Carneros was because he believed the district could become the "burgundy" of California. In 1977, his Carneros Pinot Noir won a number of awards and he was off and running. Mahoney also worked with viticulturists from UC Davis on Pinot Noir clonal selection, aimed at establishing the best clones for Carneros and, along the way, demonstrating the quality of Carneros Pinot Noir. In 1987, he released his widely praised Signature Pinot Noir, a development from his clonal work.

Through the remainder of that decade and the 1980s, viticulture in Carneros was dominated by sparkling wine production. (In terms of volume, that is still true.) Domaine Chandon has extensive holdings as do Mumm Napa, Schramsberg, and of course, Domaine Carneros and Gloria Ferrer. These producers either own vineyards outright or control them through long term contracts. (*See* Appendix IV page 247.)

But at the same time, others were following Mahoney's lead at Carneros Creek and trying to make something like a "burgundy" in California. There was Chardonnay too, of course, but I don't know of a single producer of Carneros Chardonnay who talked about making a "white burgundy". The Chardonnay was there to keep the market happy. No one thought they were breaking new ground. The whole "Burgundy in California" image hasn't helped Carneros. On the contrary, it has probably done more harm than good. Too much praise too soon may have led to a complacency that more or less put Carneros to sleep for a decade or so. (In a curious parallel development, Oregon Pinot producers had the same problem.)

Mike Richmond was one of the Pinot pioneers in Carneros. He was a founder of Acacia Vineyard and the winemaker there for many years. He is now general manager of Bouchaine Vineyards. He recalls that the model was burgundy, even if the taste profile was hardly burgundian. "That was the logical starting point as Burgundy defined the standard for quality," he says. "Fruit was picked at a specific chemistry and wines were made with particular techniques, all influenced by observations of Burgundy." According to Richmond, Carneros wine-growers have become "liberated from the Burgundian model" over time and now have the freedom to find methods that work in their location. "We aren't Burgundy and we have become proud to admit it," he adds.

Asked how the concept of terroir has been played out in Carneros, Richmond says, "Terroir, as the concept of the growing environment in total, including the human interaction with the place, means very much to us. Wine quality is largely determined by terroir. That said, I find it terribly difficult to make consistent and absolute claims about the flavours that relate to a particular terroir. The terroir of knowledge – the common knowledge shared among winemakers within an appellation – may be as significant a contribution to flavour as the soil and climate".

In a sense, Carneros winemakers were trying to make a burgundy that never existed, except in the imagination of American wine consumers. The image of burgundy was a rich, dark wine: a wine perhaps served at the table of the Fairie Queen, perhaps having more to do with Algeria than Burgundy.

Two more pioneers, David Graves and his partner Dick Ward, established Saintsbury in Napa Carneros in 1981. Their early wines were clearly cast in the then-Carneros style of bright cherry varietal character. Now, as Graves noted in a recent interview, the style is much richer. "The wines are darker, more concentrated and tannic." He says the change started in the vineyard. "We have been replanting with better clones, more in the black fruit camp, which are capable of producing grapes with more stuff in them."

Anne Moller-Racke also arrived in Carneros in 1981. She came with her husband Marcus Moller-Racke, whose family had extensive wine holdings in Germany. The family had just bought Buena Vista in Sonoma Carneros and young Marcus had been sent to sort it all out. In 1983, after some time spent learning the operation, the family put Marcus in charge of production and he appointed his wife as manager of the vineyards, which at the time totaled 218 hectares. When the Moller-Rackes divorced in 1991, there were 382 hectares of vines, including the 104-hectare Tule Vista Ranch, which Anne developed with dense spacing and a full palate of clones and rootstocks.

Shortly after the divorce, Marcus returned to Germany and Anne took a break from wine to return to college, studying business and art history, an odd juxtaposition of interests. A few years later, she returned to Buena Vista (still owned by the Racke family, so she found herself working for her ex-husband) as a consultant. Because of phylloxera, she spent a great deal of the 1990s replanting the vineyards she had originally planted in the 1980s. In 1997, she was named vice president of vineyard operations at Buena Vista. Full circle, it seems.

Anne became increasingly intent on developing Tula Vista Ranch as an estate, somewhat in the Burgundian mode, for artisan wine production. So when Allied-Domecq bought Buena Vista in 2001, she wisely retained Tula Vista – which she had renamed The Donum Estate – as a Racke holding and began to develop it as the heart of a Pinot Noir-focused Carneros operation. Anne's mission statement is breathtaking: "I want to produce the ultimate Pinot Noir. I'm not interested in making an international style wine. In the end, wine is made on passion and it must be placed in the context of the vineyard, the terroir. I frankly can't define terroir and I don't know where it comes from," she adds quickly, stepping away from the whiff of corporate arrogance that marks the "mission statement".

Not surprisingly, she believes that the vineyard is more important than the appellation itself. "Carneros, as an appellation, is in transition. In the 1980s it was dominated by sparkling wine," she says, "but that is no longer true." Anne is one of those who believes the difference in Carneros is not between east and west, Napa and Sonoma, but between northern and southern Carneros. "Western Carneros is more affected by wind, therefore the growing conditions are harsher and cooler. Wind has a huge impact, especially on Chardonnay. Southern Carneros is closer to San Francisco Bay and, again, the temperatures are lower. The chief difference in soils is that along the creeks there is more silt and the soils are richer. On the ridges, soils are more gravelly and shallow," she explains. "I want my wines to have a sense of place. To express not only the vintage but show their origin that can be traced throughout the years," she adds.

In tasting Pinot Noir, Moller-Racke says, "I want my Pinots to have intensity and power but also elegance. I don't want my wines to be simple or one dimensional." She adds that the delicacy of Pinot offers more nuances because the varietal character is not so overpowering but more restrained. "It demands more from the wine drinker," she says.

Is Pinot the only game in the Carneros? That's the easy assumption and, for sure, Pinot now dominates the red wines. Chardonnay is a constant, but there are some intriguing dark horse candidates. Michael Havens, owner of Havens Wine Cellars, believes that in the long run, Carneros will be better known for Merlot and Syrah than Pinot Noir. Havens is also a fan of Albariño, Pinot Grigio, and Riesling as possible white varieties for Carneros. The wines he makes from some of those varietals make a strong supporting statement for his position. In the end the strength of Carneros may lie in such diversity, but for the near future, it's all about Pinot Noir.

## The Best of Carneros

### ACACIA
2750 Las Amigas Road, Napa, CA 94559. Tel: 707 226 9991; Fax: 707 226 1685; Email: info@acaciawinery.com; Website: www.acaciawinery.com
Vineyards: 58ha
The winery was founded by Mike Richmond and a group of partners in

1979. The concept was to produce single-vineyard Pinot Noir and Chardonnay. Early wines were of good, sometimes exceptional, quality but the market was not ready for vineyard designated Pinot Noir at the time and in 1986, the winery was sold to the Chalone Wine Group. Richmond stayed on for several years, as did winemaker Larry Brooks. Richmond is now the general manager of Bouchaine winery and Brooks has established his own winery, Campion Wines. In recent bottlings, Acacia has returned to the designated vineyard approach and is making some seriously good Pinot Noir in a richer, more concentrated style than the traditional lighter cherry-berry Carneros style. In late 2004, Constellation Brands bought Chalone, thus acquiring Acacia.

## ARTESA VINEYARDS & WINERY
1345 Henry Road, Napa, CA 94559. Tel: 707 224 1668; Fax: 707 224 1672;
Email: info@artesawinery.com; Website: www.artesawinery.com
Vineyards: 162ha

Artesa is the Napa outpost of the Raventos cava family of Catalonia, producers of Codorníu. It was built in 1990 and called Codorníu Napa. Report has it that the family felt they had to stake a claim in Napa because their fierce rivals, the Ferrer family, producers of Freixenet cava, had built a winery a few kilometres to the west in Carneros Sonoma. The winery was built mostly underground with the expectations that the soil roof would grow a thick crop of wildflowers. That would have been nice, but the wild flowers never caught on, nor did the sparkling wine. In the late 1990s, the sparkling wine was virtually dropped in favour of table wines. Don Van Staaveren from Chateau St Jean was brought in as the winemaker and given a free hand. Early efforts have been good, especially the Chardonnay and Cabernet Sauvignon, which is not grown in Carneros.

## BOUCHAINE
1075 Buchli Station Road, Napa, CA 94559. Tel: 707 252 9065;
Fax: 707 252 0401; Email: info@bouchaine.com; Website: www.bouchaine.com
Vineyards: 42ha

Bouchaine has the longest history of any Carneros winery. The original winery on the site was built in 1899 by the Garetto family and revived by the same family in 1934 following Prohibition. In 1980, the winery (which had been used as a crush facility by Beringer) regained its separate identity. Early Pinot Noir and Chardonnay met with indifference and in 1982, Jerry Luper was hired away from Chateau Montelena as the winemaker. (Luper was part of the winemaking team of Montelena's Chardonnay that swept the boards at the 1976 Paris tasting.) Things improved under Luper, but when he left in 1986, Bouchaine went into a great drift. An occasional good Pinot Noir from estate vineyards show the potential, however, and Mike Richmond, the co-founder of Acacia is now the general manager. There is a renewed focus on estate Pinot Noir and early efforts are more than promising.

## CAMPION WINES

1339 Pearl Street, Suite 101, Napa, CA 94559. Tel: 707 265 6733; Fax: 707 265 7614; Email: lbrooks@campionwines.com; Website: www.campionwines.com
Vineyards: n/a

Larry Brooks made nineteen vintages of wine at Acacia, so he knows Carneros Pinot Noir as well as anyone. When he left Acacia he set up shop as a consultant. In the late 1990s he began making single-vineyard Pinot Noir from three growing areas: Edna Valley in San Luis Obispo County and the Santa Lucia Highlands in Monterey County and Carneros. The Carneros bottling is sourced from several vineyards, including one on the Sonoma line. Brooks focuses on a mix of clonal selection. Wine is made in the traditional style and Brooks declassifies ruthlessly to keep quality high. His Carneros Pinot Noir is in very limited production but is well worth seeking out if you want to taste the latest in classic Carneros Pinot. In partnership with Mike Richmond of Bouchaine, he also makes Amethyst wines, including a Nebbiolo (eighty per cent) and Sangiovese blend made from Carneros fruit, which is one of the best examples of Nebbiolo I've ever had from California.

## CARNEROS CREEK

1285 Dealy Lane, Napa, CA 94559. Tel: 707 253 9464; Fax: 707 253 9465; Email: wineinfo@carneroscreek.com; Website: www.carneroscreek.com
Vineyards: 73ha

Carneros Creek is still at the top of its game, turning out distinctive Pinot Noir, with a new emphasis on single-vineyard production. The Mahoney Estate series is particularly good. Carneros Creek has recently introduced a Carneros Syrah which demonstrates why some producers are getting very interested in that varietal in the Carneros District. The Briarcliff Wine Group, a marketing company, is now part-owner of the brand.

## DOMAINE CARNEROS

1240 Duhig Road, Napa, CA 94581. Tel: 707 257 0101; Fax: 707 257 3020;
Email: website@domainecarneros.com; Website: www.domaine.com
Vineyards: 81 ha

Construction of this rather grand château began in 1987. Designed as a homage to Taittinger, the French Champagne house and one of the founding partners, the structure outraged the locals. It looms above the highway as if it had been transported directly from Champagne, about as grand and imposing as you can get. At the time, a neighbour said that the arched gateway to the entry cost more than his entire winery. Oddly enough, it works. As the years go by, it looks just right, sitting there on a knoll above a sea of vines. And the wines are outstanding, made in an elegant style akin to Taittinger. They are easily near the top of California sparkling wines, especially Le Rêve, a luscious 100 per cent Chardonnay with full, rounded flavours. There is also a delicious Brut Rosé. Eileen Crane began making Pinot Noir in the early 1990s and has slowly increased production. There are several different bottlings, the best being the Famous Gate, available only at the winery and in a few European markets. It's a dark and brooding wine with intense wrap-around flavours.

## THE DONUM ESTATE

24520 Ramal Road, Sonoma, CA 95476. Tel: 707 939 2290; Fax: 707 939 0651; Email:lhandley@thedonumestate.com; Website: www.thedonumestate.com
Vineyards: 60 ha

It was clear from the first vintage (2001) that Donum belongs in the ranks of the best of Carneros. The property is on the first low range of hills north of San Francisco Bay on the Sonoma side of Carneros. There are about sixty hectares of vines, first planted by Anne Moller-Racke in the 1980s. Donum also leases and manages the Ferguson block, a twenty-three-hectare vineyard planted in 1974, mostly to the Martini clones, a classic California Pinot clone. Early Pinot releases are rich and seamless with vibrant fruit mingled with forest floor and earthy aromas. The mouthfeel is silky and lush. (For more details of Donum, *see* page 64.)

## GLORIA FERRER

23555 Highway 121, Sonoma, CA 95476. Tel: 707 996 7256;
Fax: 707 996 0720; Email: info@gloriaferrer.com; Website: www.gloriaferrer.com
Vineyards: 97 ha

Gloria Ferrer, owned by the Ferrer family (Freixenet) inspired by the solid look of a Catalan "*mas*" or farmhouse, fades into the windy hillside of Carneros. Spacious terraces look toward San Francisco Bay. The building and underground *caves* are surrounded by vines, which are put to very good use by the winemaking staff headed by Bob Iantosca. Established in 1988, the top of the line sparkler is the Royal Cuvée, named in honour of a visit to the winery by King Juan Carlos of Spain. It's a blend of Chardonnay and Pinot Noir and is not only very good, but an outstanding value-for-money wine as well. Made in a fruit-forward California style, it offers a good deal of complexity as well. The blanc de blancs is also outstanding. Vineyard manager Mike Crumley has done important work on clonal selection for Pinot Noir and Chardonnay and the winery's table wines from those varietals are worth seeking out for their expression of Carneros style.

## MADONNA ESTATE

5400 Old Sonoma Road, Napa, CA 94559. Tel: 707 255 8864; Fax: 707 257 2778; Email: mail@madonnaestate.com; Website: www.madonnaestate.com
Vineyards: 67ha

Owned by the Bartolucci family, Madonna Estate, formerly known as Mont St John, makes wines from organic vineyards. The family's first vineyard was established in 1922 in Oakville and wine production began in 1933, following the repeal of Prohibition. At one time, it was one of the largest vineyards in the state. In 1970, the Oakville estate was sold and the family bought land in Carneros and planted it to Chardonnay and Pinot Noir. Much of their production is sold to other wineries. Acacia has in the past made a Madonna Vineyard Pinot Noir. The wine quality has been somewhat uneven in the past, but in recent years quality has shot up and also become more consistent. The Madonna Estate Due Ragazze Riserva Pinot Noir, in very limited production, is an outstanding wine, which fits right in at a blind tasting with burgundy.

## SAINTSBURY

1500 Los Carneros Avenue, Napa, CA 94559; Tel: 707 252 0592; Fax: 707 252 0595; Email: info@saintsbury.com; Website: www.saintsbury.com
Vineyards: 22ha

Founded by good friends David Grave and Dick Ward in 1981, Saintsbury earned deserved praise for bright cherry-fruit centred Pinot that caught the public fancy from the start. The wines were always elegant and well-balanced; ready to drink from the start, but also capable of ageing in the five to eight year range. The Saintsbury Garnett, a lighter version and somewhat less intense, became a great restaurant favourite. Saintsbury Chardonnay, both regular and reserve bottlings, is right at the top of Napa Chardonnay. The vineyards were replanted in the early 1990s and the new wines are looking more complex and richer than the wines of the 1980s.

## SCHUG CARNEROS ESTATE WINERY

602 Bonneau Road, Sonoma, CA 95476. Tel: 707 939 9363; Fax: 707 939 9364; Email: schug@schugwinery.com; Website: www.schugwinery.com

Vineyards: 17ha

Walter Schug was trained as a winemaker in Germany. He came to the USA in 1961 and worked for E & J Gallo for several years before becoming winemaker at Joseph Phelps. In 1990, he started his Carneros winery in Sonoma, where he makes Chardonnay and Pinot Noir. The Pinot is all Carneros fruit, made in a traditional style with minimal handling. It's an attractive and silky wine with bright, lingering fruit and good ageing potential. It's the kind of wine that doesn't stand out in a blind tasting, but on the table it has an elegant appeal and a quiet charm.

## TRUCHARD VINEYARDS

3324 Old Sonoma Road, Napa, CA 94559. Tel: 707 253 7153; Website: www.truchardvineyard.com

Vineyards: 109ha

The Truchard family were grape-growers near Lyon in France before emigrating to Texas in 1887, where they planted vines again and built a winery. The Texas enterprise didn't survive Prohibition, but Tony Truchard revived the family tradition when he planted a vineyard in Carneros in 1974 and sold grapes to a number of wineries, including Carneros Creek. Truchard started making his own wine in 1989. He now has 109 hectares planted to ten different varieties, an unusual number of grapes for Carneros. Soils are a mix of clay, shale, sandstone, and volcanic debris. Truchard wines are so consistently good across the board that it is hard to give them any sort of ranking. Certainly – and typical for Carneros – the Chardonnay is excellent, with tasty tropical fruit and a creamy mouthfeel. The Pinot Noir is usually superb, silky and rich with darker fruit tones than many Carneros Pinots. The Syrah is also outstanding. It is grown on hillside vines on volcanic soils and tends toward the Côte-Rôtie model. Truchard also produces the only Zinfandel made entirely from Carneros fruit, a wine featuring soft tannins and luscious fruit – a sort of Pinot drinker's Zinfandel. There is also a delicious Roussanne, a better than average Cabernet Sauvignon in most years, a surprisingly rich Cabernet Franc, a somewhat herbal occasionally interesting Merlot, and most recently, a spicy, zippy Tempranillo.

## CHILES VALLEY

Grapes were grown in Chiles Valley in eastern Napa as early as the 1850s on land owned by Joseph Chiles. His land was part of a Mexican land grant called Rancho Catacula. Today there are just under 405 hectares of vines in the Chiles Valley District AVA, with perhaps another 200 hectares that could be planted out of a total of 2,428 hectares. The AVA, as approved in 1999, follows almost exactly the property line of the Catacula land grant. Vineyards are planted between 240 and 300 metres (800 and 1,000 feet). Above that, the slopes are too steep and topsoil is virtually non-existent.

Chiles Valley runs northwest to southeast, creating an open funnel for prevailing northwesterly winds. The steady air-flow produces substantial cooling during the day and, in combination with the altitude, relatively dry air. During the night, this drier air leads to more rapid cooling than in most of the Napa Valley. In addition, the narrow valley is surrounded by hills up to 670 metres (2,200 feet) high which concentrate the cooler air flowing down the hillsides toward the valley floor where the vineyards are located.

Also, the relative distance from the San Francisco Bay and the Pacific Ocean allows the summer fog to move in much later – often only an hour or two before sunrise – than in the main Napa Valley. By the time the fog does reach the Chiles Valley, the air temperatures have dropped much more dramatically than in the Napa Valley, thereby causing much lower temperatures during the night and a slower heat build-up during the day.

The growing season starts later than in the main Napa Valley due to much colder winter temperatures, often dropping to -7°C (20°F) or slightly lower. It often snows in Chiles Valley at higher elevations above the vineyards. Along with these cooler temperatures, there is a danger of severe frosts in April and May. Even with a late start, the growing season in Chiles Valley is longer than much of Napa because of the cool summers. (Pope Valley, just to the north, has a significantly higher average temperature because it is entirely enclosed by mountains and receives no maritime fog.)

Soils are well-drained loams on the valley floor with alluvial fans above the flood plains. The AVA is entirely within the watershed of the Napa River, though lack of water can be a problem for growers. There is no true ground water in the area, only surface water, which can penetrate as deep as thirty metres (100 feet). In coastal California, most of the rain falls in the winter, so growers keep a watchful eye on the rain gauge and vineyard reservoirs.

The Bordeaux reds and Zinfandel are far and away the best grapes for wine in Chiles Valley. The cool weather pattern leads to grapes with a firm tannin structure, slow to open up, and capable of extended ageing. Volker Eisele, who has grown grapes in Chiles Valley for more than three decades, believes the taste profile of his wines is somewhere between a Bordeaux and a mid-Napa Valley wine. There is some reasonable Chardonnay and a little Riesling grown in Chiles Valley, but it seems a waste of good Cabernet or Zinfandel land.

Overall, even though Chiles Valley could be called a mountain appellation, it differs considerably in temperature and soil conditions from Howell Mountain and Atlas Peak, the other two eastern Napa mountain AVAs. It has more in common with Spring Mountain on the west side of Napa, at least in climate. It seems likely that as available vineyard land elsewhere in Napa becomes more scarce, there will be additional plantings of Bordeaux varieties in the Chiles Valley District.

## The Best of Chiles Valley

BROWN ESTATE
3233 Sage Canyon Road, St Helena, CA 94574. Tel: 707 963 2435;
Email: info@brownestate.com; Website: www.brownestate.com
Vineyards: 16.2ha
The Brown family began planting vineyards in 1985, beginning with about three hectares of Zinfandel. There are now over sixteen hectares of vines, including eleven hectares of Zinfandel, 3.5 hectares of Cabernet

Sauvignon, and 1.8 hectares of obligatory Chardonnay. In the early years, the grapes were sold to other winemakers, but in 1996 the first estate Zinfandel was released. The Zinfandel has been outstanding from the first, with full flavours, yet balanced and harmonious. A limited amount of Cabernet Sauvignon, powerful and dense, was released late in 2004.

## GREEN & RED VINEYARD

3208 Chiles Valley Road, St Helena, CA 94574. Tel: 707 965 2346;
Email: greenandred@napanet.net; Website: www.greenandred.com
Vineyards: 12.5ha

Founded in 1977, Green & Red is named for the red iron soils, streaked with green serpentine rock, a typical soil formation in Chiles Valley. There are three separate vineyards, totalling 12.5 hectares of vines. The first vineyards were planted in 1972, on the site of a vineyard originally planted in the 1890s. There is some Chardonnay, but Green & Red is best known for its estate Zinfandel. The Chiles Mill Vineyard Zinfandel has spicy black pepper tones, while the Chiles Valley, a blend of three valley floor vineyards, is somewhat more luscious and silky. Green & Red also makes a "California" blend Zinfandel from grapes grown outside the AVA.

## VOLKER EISELE FAMILY ESTATE

3080 Lower Chiles Valley Road, St Helena, CA 94574. Tel: 707 965 9485;
Fax: 707 965 9609; Email: info@volkereiselevineyard.com;
Website: www.volkereiselevineyard.com
Vineyards: 24ha

Volker Eisele and his family own twenty-four hectares of vines, planted to east, west, and south facing slopes as well as the valley floor. After buying the property in 1974, he began extensive replanting of the vineyards as well as restoring natural habitat along creeks and streams. The vineyard is planted to more than seventy per cent Cabernet Sauvignon, with smaller amounts of Merlot and Cabernet Franc and a little Sauvignon Blanc and Semillon. The vines are organically farmed and some areas are dry-farmed. The winery is on the site of the Lomita Winery, dating to the 1870s. Only three wines are made: a Cabernet Sauvignon with a small amount of Cabernet Franc added; Terzetto, a blend of Cabernet Sauvignon, Cabernet Franc, and Merlot; and Gemini, a Semillon and Sauvignon Blanc blend. (Terzetto refers to the trio sections of Mozart's operas.) All three wines possess the supple elegance of a classic Bordeaux. The Cabernet Sauvignon will likely age in the twenty year range.

## DIAMOND MOUNTAIN

Jacob Schram put Diamond Mountain on the wine map early on, making wine there in the 1860s, but few followed his lead. The rocky redwood canyons were not as easy to plant as the flatlands in the valley below. Soils were thin and slopes were steep. Jack and Jamie Davies came in 1965 to make sparkling wine at the historic Schram estate, but the modern pioneer for table wine – and Cabernet Sauvignon in particular – was Al Brounstein who founded Diamond Creek Vineyards in 1968.

The Diamond Mountain AVA includes some 2,023 hectares of land, but only about 202 hectares are planted to grapes. It lies west of Calistoga, bordered by Spring Mountain to the south, the Sonoma County line to the east, and the Petrified Forest Highway to the north. Vineyards are planted above 610 metres (2,000 feet), with the AVA's lower boundary set at 120 metres (400 feet).

Day time temperatures often top 38°C (100°F), but can quickly fall more than 4°C (40°F), when the sun sets and cool breezes push up the deep mountain canyons from the Russian River watershed in Sonoma County to the west, often followed by heavy fog. Soils are a mix of volcanic rock and ash, clay laced with gravel, and quartz. The topography is so folded that there is huge variation in soils even within a small area, so many growers have followed Brounstein's lead and tended to keep vineyard lots small.

Production is also small, with most wines sold through a mailing list, at the cellar door or in a few restaurants. Only Sterling Vineyards (which is not physically located on Diamond Mountain) makes enough wine for general distribution. Sterling is the largest grower in the AVA, with about forty-eight hectares planted on its Diamond Mountain Ranch. The vineyard had been a prune orchard and was first planted to grapes by William Hill, a Napa land developer with a fancy for wine grapes, in about 1970. Hill had planted Chardonnay, but those vines were pulled and replanted to Cabernet Sauvignon, Merlot, and Cabernet Franc.

In many ways, Sterling's Diamond Mountain Ranch is typical of the AVA. The vines are planted at an altitude between 457 and 518 metres (1,500 and 1,700 feet) on very steep slopes. Sterling (in common with other Diamond Mountain growers) invested considerable research, not to mention cash, in developing drainage and erosion controls as part of an award-winning environmental plan. As elsewhere in the appellation, soils are thin and volcanic. The vineyard is also dry-farmed. The poor soils and lack of water lead to small clusters of intense and concentrated fruit.

The Cabernet flavour profile of Diamond Mountain differs somewhat from other mountain-grown Napa Cabernets. They can be brutally tannic, and often were in the early 1990s, until winemakers learned to deal with that tannic structure and rounded out the rough edges, putting more emphasis on the fruit. The wines are certainly still dense and concentrated, but the best have layered fruit, good balance, and acidity. They do need at least a few years in bottle to be enjoyed and longer ageing in the fifteen to twenty year range is recommended for most.

Bill Dyer, who made wine at Sterling from Diamond Mountain Vineyards in the 1980s and now has his own small winery on Diamond Mountain, believes the flavour profile for Diamond Mountain in general often features chocolate and anise, with some spice and subdued berry character. In his own vineyard, which is on a northeast slope, the grapes ripen quite late, which seems to allow flavour and aroma development and tannin maturity without excessive sugars.

The AVA is young, so there are few wineries beyond Diamond Creek and Sterling with any sort of track record, but a number of promising new producers are worth a close look.

## The Best of Diamond Mountain

### ANDREW GEOFFREY VINEYARDS
836 Chiles Avenue, St Helena, CA 94574. Tel: 707 968 9770; Fax: 707 968 9711; Email: peter@andrewgeoffrey.com; Website: www.andrewgeoffrey.com
Vineyards: 5ha

A fairly new winery, off to an excellent start with an approachable and balanced Cabernet Sauvignon, showing intense but rounded fruit and good ageing potential.

### CONSTANT WINES
2121 Diamond Mountain Road, Calistoga, CA 94515. Tel: 707 942 0707; Fax: 707 942 0249; Email: info@constantwine.com; Website: www.constantwine.com
Vineyards: 16.5ha

The Constant family restored the nineteenth-century farmhouse and planted a small Cabernet vineyard where owner Fred Constant makes a limited amount of powerful wine and plays bocce ball. I'm not sure how good his bocce ball game is, but the wine is a treat.

## DIAMOND CREEK VINEYARDS
*See* Chapter 9, page 136.

## DIAMOND TERRACE
1391 Diamond Mountain Road, Calistoga, CA 94515. Tel: 707 942 1189;
Fax: 707 942 1372; Email: diamondterrace@earthlink.net;
Website: www.diamondterrace.com
Vineyards: 2ha

Looking for the most distinctive wines, Diamond Terrace's already tiny two-hectare vineyard is divided into three separate blocks with the grapes fermented separately before blending. The finished wine is bold and rich, with complex layers of flavour and a long finish. It has the fruit for early consumption but should age and improve in the bottle for several years.

## DYER WINE
1501 Spring Mountain Road, Calistoga, CA 94515. Tel: 707 942 5502;
Email: info@dyerwine.com; Website: www.dyerwine.com
Vineyards: 1.2ha

Bill and Dawnine Dyer make a few hundred cases of absolutely superb Bordeaux red from a small vineyard which they planted in the 1990s. Bill now consults for several wineries, including Marimar Torres Estate in Sonoma County. Dawnine was the winemaker at Domaine Chandon for twenty-five years, making sparkling wine and table wine. Their first release opened to rave reviews in 1996 and the luscious Cabernet blend has been getting better ever since. Hard to find but worth a search.

## GRAESER WINERY
255 Petrified Forest Road, Calistoga, CA 94515. Tel/Fax: 707 942 4437;
Email: richard@graserwinery.com; Website: www.graserwinery.com
Vineyards: 4ha

Graeser makes limited amounts of Cabernet Sauvignon, Cabernet Franc, and a red blend that are complex, luscious, elegant, and harmonious wines. The wines invariably show bright fruit, centring on raspberry and cherries, with good structure and balance. Enjoyable while young, they will age and improve in bottle for up to fifteen years. Graeser is the only Diamond Mountain winery open for public tasting. Compared to other Diamond Mountain wines, they are reasonably priced.

### REVERIE VINEYARDS

1520 Diamond Mountain Road, Calistoga, CA 94515. Tel: 707 942 6800;
Fax: 707 942 6803; Email: info@reveriewine.com; Website: www.reveriewine.com
Vineyards: 12ha

Although Reverie was founded in 1993 as a specialist in Bordeaux blends, it has also experimented with Barbera, Tempranillo, Grenache, and Roussanne. The wines are all estate-grown and bottled unfiltered, with the Reverie Special Reserve made from the best barrels of Cabernet Sauvignon, Petit Verdot, and Cabernet Franc. The wines are stylish and richly powerful, yet balanced and elegant. The regular bottling of Cabernet tends more toward spicy, aromatic fruit and is meant for earlier drinking. A separate bottling of Cabernet Franc is a super wine, loaded with raspberry and cherry fruit with a dash of anise.

### VON STRASSER WINERY

1510 Diamond Mountain Road, Calistoga, CA 94515. Tel: 707 942 0930; Fax:
707 942 0454; Email: winemaker@vonstrasser.com; Website: www.vonstrasser.com
Vineyards: 4ha

Rudy von Strasser, who came to the area in 1990 and bought property adjoining Diamond Creek Vineyards, led the move to establish the Diamond Mountain appellation. He makes rich and powerful Cabernet, a regular and a reserve, as well as two vineyard-designated Chardonnays and a Zinfandel, all from purchased fruit. The Cabernets are of exceptional quality, deep and rich with long ageing potential. The Zinfandel, jammy and intense, is the only wine made in the appellation. The Chardonnays show tropical fruit and butterscotch, with good balancing acidity.

## HOWELL MOUNTAIN

Howell Mountain, the volcanic cone that towers above St Helena on the east side of Napa, is thick with wine history. The first vineyards planted on Howell Mountain in the 1880s by Charles Krug were sparked by the drive to improve the quality of Napa wines. Experienced growers and winemakers like Krug believed that wine quality could be greatly improved by planting more grapes on hillsides above the valley floor.

Krug thought that Howell Mountain, with its red volcanic soils and vineyard sites above the fog line, would be ideal. Others followed his lead. Many of the new plantings were small vineyards, cleared out of the forest by businessmen from San Francisco who came to Howell Mountain to build summer cabins, an early example of "lifestyle" plantings in Napa. By the 1890s, Howell Mountain Cabernets were regarded as some of the best in California.

One of the best-known wines of the time was made by Frenchmen Jean Adolph Brun and Jean V Chaix, who formed a partnership in 1877 to make wine in California. They had a winery in Oakville called Nouveau Médoc and by the early 1880s built the Brun & Chaix Winery on Howell Mountain. A century later, when the winery had long been moribund, it was bought by Francis and François DeWarvin-Woltner, former owners of Château La Mission Haut-Brion, keeping the French connection going. (The winery, now called Ladera Vineyards, is under new ownership.)

By the end of Prohibition in 1933, there were only a few functioning vineyards remaining on Howell Mountain. But the area began to be noticed again with the wine boom of the 1960s. New vineyards were established and new vines were planted, mostly to Cabernet Sauvignon and Zinfandel with a scattering of Rhône varieties.

Howell Mountain was granted AVA status in 1983. The BATF ruled that in order to be included in the appellation, the vineyards must be at least 426 metres (1,400 feet) in elevation, which was a remarkably sound decision. As it stands, Howell Mountain is a meaningful appellation on its own and as a sub-appellation of the Napa Valley AVA, because it is in the Napa River watershed, if only just barely. Howell Mountain vines tend to bud up to three weeks later than grapes on the valley floor. However, due to an inversion layer which keeps temperatures high at night, they are generally harvested earlier. Soils are shallow and poor and the vines get the full force of the afternoon sun.

The red wines have a distinct character, combining a briary intensity with a hard edge that can seem off-putting if the wine is not handled right or given a chance to develop a little bottle age. At their best, these are wines stripped to the bone; they can seem austere at first glass, but if you stick with them you'll be rewarded with outstanding Cabernet Sauvignon and Zinfandel.

It is somewhat surprising that plantings are so limited on Howell Mountain. There are only about 200 hectares of vines, and probably half of that was planted recently. The steep hillsides are expensive to plant and Napa County's regulations on hillside planting can make it even more difficult. An added obstacle is the town of Angwin, which is the seat of a large college owned by the Seventh Day Adventists church. The Adventists are strongly opposed to alcohol and have fought any winery or vineyard expansion, apparently fearing that tourists, crazed and out-of-control on $100 bottles of Cabernet and armed with corkscrews, will overrun the area, tempting college students to buy Riedel glasses and take to drink, perhaps putting young Adventist women at grave risk.

For whatever reason, although many wineries on the valley floor – including Beringer and Duckhorn – take grapes from Howell Mountain, there are few wineries in the appellation. Burgess Cellars, an outstanding producer, is sometimes included with Howell Mountain wineries, but is in fact just outside the appellation, as is Viader.

## The Best of Howell Mountain

### DUNN VINEYARDS
*See* Chapter 9, page 143.

### LADERA VINEYARDS
150 White Cottage Road South, Angwin, CA 94508. Tel: 707 965 2445;
Fax: 707 965 2446; Email: info@laderavineyards.com;
Website: www.laderavineyards.com
Vineyards: 75ha

This historic estate has been through a number of changes since it was bought by the former owners of Bordeaux's Château La Mission Haut-Brion in the 1980s. In a move that left folks in Napa more than a little puzzled, Francis and François DeWavrin-Woltner planted Chardonnay in the heart of Howell Mountain red wine country. They began selling it *en primeur* under the Château Woltner label at prices higher than anyone at the time was charging for California Chardonnay. It was rather good, actually, made in a flinty austere style, and attracted a kind of mini-cult following. The winery was eventually sold to the Stotesbery family, who have got rid of the Chardonnay, replanting to Cabernet Sauvignon and other Bordeaux reds. The stone winery, which was built in the 1880s, has been refurbished, complete with the *de rigueur* Napa *cave*. The first Cabernets were made from a vineyard the Stotesberys own on the valley floor near Yountville. Ladera, by the way, means "hillside" in Spanish.

## LA JOTA

1102 Las Posadas Road, Angwin, CA 94508. Tel: 707 965 3020; Fax: 707 963 4616; Email: info@lajotavineyardco.com; Website: www.lajotavineyardco.com

Vineyards: 11ha

Home winemaker Bill Smith was looking for property in Napa to plant a few vines when he found the remains of the 1890s La Jota winery on Howell Mountain. He bought the old building and began replanting the vineyards in 1974. He and his family added a few hectares of Cabernet Sauvignon and Zinfandel vines each year. They sold most of the grapes for several years, but in 1982, with the help of neighbour Randy Dunn, they took their first Cabernet Sauvignon to market and followed with a Zinfandel the next year. Over the years La Jota has produced Viognier and Cabernet Franc as well, but it is the Cabernet Sauvignon that gets the attention and deservedly so. The wine is much in the style of Dunn's; perhaps a bit more tightly wound and intense. It ages beautifully and is always in the front ranks of California Cabernets. The winery is now owned by the Mercian Corporation, the Japanese parent company of Markham Vineyards and Glass Mountain Winery. Mercian has invested a good deal of money in *caves* and a general update of the property. To this point, the wine hasn't been spoiled.

## LAIL VINEYARDS

1127 Pope Street, St Helena, CA 94574. Tel: 707 968 9900; Fax: 707 968 9911; Email: info@lailvineyards.com; Website: www.lailvineyards.com

Vineyards: 2.5ha

Established in 1995 by Robin Lail, the daughter of John Daniel Junior, who owned Inglenook for many years (*see* page 18). The flagship wine, J Daniel Cuvée is made from a small Cabernet Sauvignon vineyard called Mole Hill, planted at a 487-metre (1,600-feet) elevation in the early 1990s. The soils are stony and very shallow and the vineyard is on the edge of a steep gorge that runs up from the valley floor, creating an unusual microclimate. The wine, which includes some Merlot, is a harmonious and elegant example of the Howell Mountain style.

## LAMBORN FAMILY VINEYARDS

(The Napa Wine Co) 7830 St Helena Highway, Oakville, CA 94562;
Tel: 925 254 0511; Fax: 925 254 4531; Email: mike@lamborn.com;
Website: www.lamborn.com
Vineyards: 3.5ha

When Bob Lamborn bought twelve hectares on Howell Mountain as a secluded hideaway in the 1970s, he had no idea that he would become the producer of a near cult Zinfandel. He had been looking for a place to get away from the pressures of his life as a private detective when he found the site. When he learned that there had been a vineyard on the site, he planted 3.5 hectares of Zinfandel. His neighbour, Randy Dunn (notice how his name keeps turning up?) helped make the wine. The Zinfandel is briary with intense fruit and firm tannins, capable of some ageing. Lamborn also makes a tiny amount of Cabernet Sauvignon.

## LONG VINEYARDS

PO Box 50, St Helena, CA 94574. Tel: 707 963 2496; Fax: 707 963 2907;
Email: info@longvineyards.co.uk; Website: www.longvineyards.com
Vineyards: 8ha

Zelma Long and her then-husband Robert started this small winery in 1977 when she was the winemaker at Robert Mondavi. Although the couple are now divorced, they still own the winery together. The Chardonnay is remarkable, having firm structure and good fruit, combined with a spicy, minerally edge. The Cabernet is huge and sometimes a bit too chewy. Most years Long Vineyards makes a good Riesling, which is on the sweet side.

## SUMMIT LAKE VINEYARDS

2000 Summit Lake Drive, Angwin, CA 94508. Tel: 707 965 2488;
Fax: 707 965 2281; Email: summitlakevineyards@msn.com;
Website: www.summitlakevineyards.com
Vineyards: 8.5ha

This is one of Napa's hidden jewels for visitors and a real "discovery" wine for those who think they know Napa. The Brakesman family bought the estate in 1971. At about 700 metres (2,300 feet) in elevation, the 8.5-hectare vineyard is planted to Zinfandel, Cabernet Sauvignon, and Petite Syrah (their spelling). The site was first planted in 1917, just before Prohibition. At the same as time the Brakesmans bought part of the historic vineyard, a few hectares were also bought by Robert Lamborn to supply grapes for his Lamborn Family Vineyards, although the wine is made elsewhere. The Brakesman family have added to the old-vine Zinfandel vineyards and consider Summit Lake a Zinfandel winery, although they also make a few hundred cases of Cabernet Sauvignon which is sold only at the winery. Their first winemaker was Jerry Luper, the legendary Napa winemaker who now has his own winery in Portugal. The Zinfandel is typically concentrated, built for age, and filled with delicious black cherry fruit with a chocolate edge.

## MOUNT VEEDER

Winemaking in the Mount Veeder area of Napa dates to the 1860s, but it has always been known more for quality rather than quantity, with vines scattered in small plantings through the thickly wooded Mayacamas Mountains on the border between Napa and Sonoma. The appellation, approved in 1990, now includes about 405 hectares planted from a total of some 6,070 hectares, about the same as in the 1890s.

The Christian Brothers and legendary cellar master Brother Timothy (Anthony Diener) are an important part of Mount Veeder's wine history. The Institute of the Brothers of the Christian Schools, to give the order its full name, was founded in Reims in 1680 to offer free education to the children of the poor. The Brothers made wine and brandy at Martinez, east of San Francisco, to raise money for their schools. In 1931 they bought the nineteenth-century Gier Winery on Mount Veeder and established a novitiate there as well as making wine and brandy. In 1950, they bought Greystone Winery on the valley floor, which is now the western headquarters of the Culinary Institute of America. The Brothers' winery on Mount Veeder was later purchased by Hess Collection winery.

The appellation is named after an 815-metre (2,677-feet) volcanic peak in the heart of the region. It was named for a nineteenth-century Presbyterian pastor who loved to hike in the area. At least ninety per cent of the appellation remains undeveloped and heavily wooded, including oak, madrone, California laurel, and redwood. Mountain lions are often spotted, as well as coyotes, and there have been sightings of the rare Pileated woodpecker.

Most of the vineyards are above the fog line and facing east, with the mountains protecting them from warmer afternoon sun, giving the vines a relatively long and even ripening period. Westerly winds come straight from the Pacific, helping keep temperatures cool. Rainfall can reach 127 centimetres (fifty inches) annually, although the average is closer to eighty-nine centimetres (thirty-five inches). Soils, which are sedimentary, volcanic, and fairly thin, drain rapidly and there is little ground water, meaning grape maturity can be controlled by irrigation. The infertile soils also help keep yields low, often as little as 2.3 tonnes per hectare.

Unlike Napa's other mountain appellations, Chardonnay plays a fairly large role in Mount Veeder vineyards, making up about one-third of the plantings. In fact, some argue that Mount Veeder Chardonnay compares favourably with Carneros, perhaps even overshadowing it. In truth, it is simply a very different wine. Mount Veeder Chardonnay has stone-fruit flavours with a dash of citrus and can be a little harder than Carneros, with a minerally edge. They also age quite well. I have tasted Mount Veeder Chardonnay, notably from Mayacamas Vineyards, with over a decade of bottle age that shows good texture and complex layers of flavour. The other side of the Chardonnay story is sparkling wine, oddly enough. Domaine Chandon has major plantings of Chardonnay in the appellation. It adds length and power to the Chandon base wine.

Cabernet Sauvignon makes up about forty per cent of the vineyards and no other single variety is over ten per cent. The character of Mount Veeder Cabernet is quite distinctive, with a much different flavour profile than other Napa Cabernets. The best have a briary base flavour with dark berry fruit, hints of black pepper, and a dash of sage and lavender, which would be recognized by anyone hiking in California's coastal mountains as the essential aroma of chaparral.

Carole Meredith, who owns Lagier Meredith Vineyard with Steve Lagier, believes that Mount Veeder wines really do taste like the place. Meredith, a UC Davis professor who has done important work in DNA identification of wine grapes, says that she comes in for a bit of teasing from her colleagues about using the "t-word".

Meredith and Lagier make only Syrah, but the "t-word" certainly looms large in any discussion of Mount Veeder wines. They are, in a very different way, as recognizable as Stags Leap District wines and as closely linked to their origin, to their terroir, as the wines from that AVA. Over the past several years, the Mount Veeder appellation has been one of the most exciting in Napa, with more than a dozen new artisan wineries springing up, producing exceptional wines of extraordinary promise.

## The Best of Mount Veeder

### CHATEAU POTELLE
*See* Chapter 9, page 128.

### CRANE FAMILY VINEYARDS
PO Box 2067, Napa, CA 94558. Tel: 707 259 0175; Fax: 707 259 0399;
Email: info@cranefamilyvineyards.com; Website: www.cranefamilyvineyards.com
Vineyards: 3ha
One of the new wave of Mount Veeder wineries, with a Cabernet
Sauvignon and a Merlot taken from a vineyard planted in the mid-1990s
on alluvial loam. Both wines show nicely balanced fruit and good
structure for mid-term ageing. Keep an eye on this one.

### LONG MEADOW RANCH WINERY
1775 Whitehall Lane, St Helena, CA 94574. Tel: 707 953 4555; Fax: 707 963
1956; Email: info@longmeadowranch.com; Website: www.longmeadowranch.com
Vineyards: 10ha
Ted and Laddie Hall began developing Long Meadow Ranch at the 335
metre (1,100 feet) elevation in 1990. Budwood for the Cabernet
Sauvignon came from the famed Bella Oaks Vineyard in Rutherford
and the Jordan Vineyard in Alexander Valley of Sonoma: impeccable
parentage. The Halls planned the ranch as an organic estate, including
vineyards, olive groves, cattle and horse breeding, an organic kitchen
garden, and poultry. The Halls believe that the compost created from the
animals on the estate, plus cover crops, help create the soils to grow
great grapes. Tastings of early releases of Long Meadow Ranch Cabernet
Sauvignon, indicate that they are absolutely right. Long Meadow's
consulting winemaker Kathy Corison has created distinctive and elegant
wines with good fruit and balance. Long Meadow is destined to be one
of Napa's great Cabernets.

### MAYACAMAS VINEYARDS
1155 Lokoya Road, Napa, CA 94558. Tel: 707 224 4030; Fax: 707 224 3979;
Email: mayacamas@napanet.net; Website: www.mayacamas.com
Vineyards: 21ha
Mayacamas has been lavishly praised and abundantly ignored over the
past half century or so. In truth, it was a cult winery before there were
such things. During a hike on Mount Veeder in 1936, Jack and Mary

Taylor discovered an old stone winery which had been abandoned at the beginning of Prohibition. They bought the old building and surrounding land and after World War II began planting Chardonnay and Pinot Noir. The Pinot was later pulled out and replanted with Cabernet Sauvignon. Following Robert Mondavi's lead at Charles Krug, the Taylors started a user-friendly news letter and in 1958 sold stock in the winery. Investors received Chardonnay and an invitation to the annual summer picnic. Meanwhile, the Chardonnay was receiving praise on all sides.

The Taylors sold the winery to Robert Travers in 1968. Travers made intense, highly concentrated Cabernet Sauvignon, which could be overly tannic and tough, but in many vintages did develop beautifully in the bottle. The Mayacamas Cabernets from the early and mid-1970s are among the best Cabernets ever made in California. On the other hand, some vintages may never come around. Mayacamas also has a very good Chardonnay.

## MOUNT VEEDER WINERY

1999 Mount Veeder Road, Napa, CA 94558. Tel: 707 963 7111; Fax: 707 963 7867; Email: winemaker@franciscan.com; Website: www.mtveeder.com
Vineyards: 32ha
The winery was established in 1973 and over the years made some remarkable wines, including a barrel-fermented Chenin Blanc, as well as Cabernet Sauvignon and Zinfandel. The wines were wildly uneven but always fun to try. The winery was purchased in 1989 by Franciscan Vineyards, which is now owned by Canandaigua.

## RANDOM RIDGE

PO Box 691, Glen Ellen, CA 95442. Tel: 707 938 9085; Fax: 707 576 0175; Email: info@randomridge.com; Website: www.randomridge.com
Vineyards: 4ha
Tom Hawley and his family make a limited amount of handcrafted wines on a small ranch that straddles the Napa and Sonoma County line at an elevation of 700 metres (2,300 feet). Hawley likes old-vine, head-pruned, dry-farmed vineyards and the varietals he makes vary from year to year. The four-hectare estate vineyard, on the Napa side of the line, is planted on decomposed volcanic soil on a very rocky site. The Cabernet Sauvignon is absolutely splendid. When Hawley isn't making wine, he surfs and writes poetry.

**SKY VINEYARDS**
1500 Lokoya Road, Napa, CA 95442. Tel: 707 935 1391; Fax: 510 540 8442;
Email: info@skyvineyards.com; Website: www.skyvineyards.com
Vineyards: 5.5ha

Lore Olds makes a legendary super-concentrated Zinfandel from vines planted in a 5.5-hectare vineyard at a 640-metre (2,100-foot) elevation, almost at the Sonoma County line. Olds planted the vineyard in the early 1970s. Organically farmed and non-irrigated, it yields wines of incredible intensity yet, surprisingly, often balanced and age-worthy, with good acid structure and tannins. Winemaking is traditional, using a basket press with one tonne fermenters. Production is low, at about 1,000 cases a year. The wine is held in bottle one year prior to release.

**VINOCE VINEYARDS**
1245 Main Street, Napa CA 94558. Tel: 707 944 8717; Fax: 707 944 0145;
Email: info@vinoce.com; Website: www.vinoce.com
Vineyards: n/a

A start-up winery showing promise with a proprietary blend of Cabernet Franc, Cabernet Sauvignon, and Merlot from Mount Veeder vineyards managed by Brian and Lori Nuss. The first vintage in 2000 showed fragrant black cherry fruit, backed by coffee and chocolate. There is also a Sauvignon Blanc from Rutherford grapes.

## OAK KNOLL

The Oak Knoll sub-appellation, officially Oak Knoll District of Napa Valley, was approved early in 2004, however its history goes back to the roots of Napa winemaking. The first vineyard in the AVA was established in the 1850s by Joseph Osborne, who had a vine nursery and also made wine. He is believed to have first introduced Zinfandel vines into California from New England where it was grown under glass as a table grape. After Osborne's death the Eshcol winery was developed from part of his property.

Although it took more than a decade for backers to establish the AVA, it probably has more claim to appellation status than many others. The area is bounded on the north by the Yountville AVA, on the west by the Mount Veeder AVA, on the east by the Silverado Trail, and on the south by Trancas Street/Redwood Road in the town of Napa, making Oak Knoll a truly urban appellation. There are some 1,416 hectares planted to vines with little room left for more plantings, especially as some of the AVA is within the city limits of Napa and is already planted to houses.

The Oak Knoll soils are based on the Dry Creek alluvial fan draining out of an ancient creek bed running north to south from just south of Oakville to the Napa River. It is the largest alluvial fan in Napa Valley. Because of the varied bedrock types drained by the fan, the base soil is very diverse with a combination of gravel and loam.

Oak Knoll is the second coolest appellation in Napa, after Carneros. There can be as much as 6°C (12°F) difference in temperature between Oak Knoll and Calistoga on a warm summer day. Oak Knoll also gets less rain than up-valley areas. This lack of rain means drier, warmer soils which promote earlier bud break. Coupled with the cooler temperatures during the growing season, due to incursions of fog from the south and east, breaking through from Carneros, this means the growing season is longer, leading to slow development of ripeness, resulting in more intense, concentrated fruit. Oak Knoll is one of the few places in Napa where both Chardonnay and Cabernet Sauvignon grow and properly ripen – as well as Riesling, thanks in part to what is probably the longest growing season in Napa Valley.

Although there were only eighteen wineries in Oak Knoll, at the time when appellation status was granted, there were sixty-four wineries that bought grapes from Oak Knoll, according to Janet Trefethen of Trefethen Vineyards, one of the vintners who pushed for the Oak Knoll appellation. Trefethen is the only winery of any size in the appellation. I would expect as Oak Knoll wines become better known as representing a specific terroir, some of the smaller wineries will become more prominent. Beyond that, the best is yet to come from the Oak Knoll District.

## The Best of Oak Knoll District

### KOVES-NEWLAN VINEYARDS & WINERY
5225 Solano Avenue, Napa, CA 94558. Tel: 707 257 2399; Fax: 707 252 6510; Email: info@kovesnewlanwine.com; Website: www.kovesnewlanwine.com
Vineyards: 16ha

The history of this winery goes back to the late 1960s when Bill Newlan converted a walnut orchard to Cabernet Sauvignon. Over the years, the grapes were sold to Clos du Val, Inglenook, and Robert Mondavi. The winery was established in 1981 as Newlan Winery. Early wines were uneven, although the estate Cabernet was usually very good. In 1999, the Newlan family and the Sato family (also grape-growers) formed a partnership and renamed the winery Koves-Newlan. There is now a new emphasis on the Oak Knoll Estate, with an impressive Cabernet Reserve being made for the first time.

## TREFETHEN VINEYARDS
*See* Chapter 9, page 188.

## OAKVILLE
If you stand in the parking lot of Oakville Grocery on Highway 29, which is a popular spot for day trippers to stock up on picnic goodies, you can see most of the Oakville appellation. From east to west, it runs from around sixty metres (200 feet) up the Vaca range right across the valley to the Mayacamas Mountains in the west. On the north and south, it follows political rather than viticultural lines, bordered by the Rutherford AVA on the north and Yountville on the south.

Most discussions of Cabernet Sauvignon in California begin with the Oakville AVA. This is not to say that the best Cabernet is from the Oakville district. There are indeed some very good Cabernets from Oakville, but the Oakville gospel has been very effectively spread through the efforts of Robert Mondavi. Oakville is also the site of the famed To Kalon vineyard, which gives it a leg up from the beginning.

Oakville is generally thought of as mid-valley but is, in fact, more southern than central. It is far enough south to get some fog drifting up valley from San Francisco Bay. Oakville is, on average, 0.6°C (1°F) cooler than Rutherford just to the north, 1.7°C (3°F) cooler than St Helena and 0.6°C (1°F) cooler than Calistoga at the foot of Mount St Helena at the north end of the valley. Those temperatures are averaged out for the entire appellation. Different microclimates within the appellation create a much more varied temperature pattern.

Soils are formed primarily by alluvial fan deposits off the Mayacamas and Vaca ranges and by flood deposits from the Napa River. The sediments vary from fine clays and silts to cobble-sized fragments with plenty of gravel mixed in. The soils also reflect the difference between the Vaca and Mayacamas ranges. On the west side of the valley, where sedimentary rocks are common in the Mayacamas, the soils are Bale loams and clay loams. On the east side, the soils are mainly volcanic materials from the

Vaca range. The soils are well drained and deep, allowing root penetration of at least thirty metres (100 feet).

Oakville, which was approved as an appellation in 1993, first became important in the 1870s, when the To Kalon vineyard was planted. The most important grape in Oakville at that time was Zinfandel. If you look at grape prices at the time, one standard measure of quality, the Oakville district and St Helena were the chief competitors in Napa on that score. There are roughly some 160 hectares of vines in the AVA and some two dozen wineries. After Prohibition, there was no significant action in Oakville until the 1940s, when replanting of the To Kalon vineyard began. There were new plantings in the 1950s and the district was already back up to speed when Robert Mondavi built his new winery in 1966.

Given Oakville's reputation for Cabernet Sauvignon, it is difficult to define the district in a meaningful way on the basis of terroir. The soils are extremely varied to the point that it is really impossible to relate any particular wine profile to a specific characteristic of the appellation. In Oakville, we are really thrown back on the vineyard site, which would explain the relatively short list of Oakville wineries which represent the typicity of the appellation. Craig Williams, who makes wine from Oakville grapes and is director of winemaking at Joseph Phelps Vineyards, says, "To be honest, I don't know how meaningful the phrase Oakville appellation is. There are tremendous differences in exposure, soil, and elevations. I wouldn't necessarily say that we can draw similarities." In general terms, Oakville Cabernet has more in common with Rutherford Cabernet than growers there would like to admit. It is, perhaps, slightly more supple than Rutherford, a bit more charming and missing, in most cases, some of the depth of Rutherford.

## The Best of Oakville

### GROTH VINEYARDS & WINERY
750 Oakville Cross Road, Oakville, CA 94562; Tel: 707 944 0290; Fax: 707 944 8932; Email: info@grothwines.com; Website: www.grothwines.com
Vineyards: 66ha

Groth was established in the early 1980s, but it was not until 1990 that the winery, on the Oakville Cross Road, was in operation. The winery produces only estate wines: Cabernet Sauvignon and a reserve Cabernet, Merlot, Chardonnay, and Sauvignon Blanc. I am not really a fan of the

Chardonnay, which can be over-the-top with its oak levels, but the sleek and powerful Cabernet Sauvignon can be very good. It has, in the past, been awarded 100 points from both Robert Parker and the *Wine Spectator*, but all the same, I don't hold that against Groth. However, like the Chardonnay, the Cabernet can sometimes show more oak, losing fruit and even varietal typicity. In summary, Groth Cabernet has more to do with winemaking techniques than site.

## ROBERT MONDAVI WINERY
*See* Chapter 9, page 151.

## NICKEL & NICKEL
*See* Chapter 9, page 157.

## OPUS ONE
*See* Chapter 9, page 158.

## PARADIGM
683 Dwyer Road, Oakville, CA 94562. Tel: 707 944 1683; Fax: 707 944 9328; Email: info@paradigmwinery.com; Website: www.paradigmwinery.com
Vineyards: 22ha

Owners Ren and Marilyn Harris began growing grapes in the Napa Valley in the mid-1960s. However, they bought the original Paradigm vineyards in the mid-1970s and within the space of fifteen years had replanted twice, once to change the grape varieties and again because of the threat of phylloxera. Marilyn is a third-generation Napa grower; while Ren's distant ancestor was General Mariano Vallejo, the last Mexican governor of California. The Harrises grow Zinfandel, Cabernet Franc, Cabernet Sauvignon, and Merlot, selling most of the crop to other wineries. The Cabernet Sauvignon is a treat, with the typical Oakville fruit and supple balance.

## SADDLEBACK CELLARS
*See* Chapter 9, page 168.

# RUTHERFORD
The Rutherford AVA in the heart of Napa Valley can lay claim to being one of the best known areas in the world for Cabernet Sauvignon, which is usually blended with other Bordeaux reds. In the roughly fifteen square kilometres (six square miles) there are about 1,538 hectares of vines

planted with more than sixty percent of that Cabernet Sauvignon. It is somewhat surprising that the total isn't higher.

The area is just over four kilometres (three miles) from north to south, beginning at the south edge of Cakebread Cellars and ending in the north at Zinfandel Lane. It stretches some three kilometres (two miles) across the valley from the foothills of the Mayacamas range in the west to the Vaca range in the east. The best vineyards are planted on gravelly alluvial fans which are deep, well-drained, and high in sandy loam and sedimentary marine material. These fans demonstrate the important role the Napa River and its drainage system have played in the development of Napa soils. There is not a great deal of elevation change in Rutherford, because the western and eastern boundaries are set at the 150 metre (500 feet) level. From both east and west, the land dips slowly toward the Napa River, giving fairly uniform soils and weather patterns, in contrast to Napa's mountain zones or even the Carneros District.

Historically, the Rutherford area was of huge importance to Napa wines. In the late1880s, just before Napa's first bout with phylloxera, there were just over two million vines under cultivation in the area. In 1900, Georges de Latour, an immigrant from France, bought a small parcel of land next door to Inglenook and named it Beaulieu. He planted the site with rootstock from France which was resistant to phylloxera and de Latour became an important supplier of rootstock as the phylloxera plague spread.

It was after Prohibition (which he survived by producing sacramental wine) that de Latour made his most important contribution to the California wine industry: he hired a young Russian-born oenologist named André Tchelistcheff, who was working in France at the time, and brought him to California. Tchelistcheff was a brilliant winemaker and innovator. He is credited with introducing cold fermentation and controlled malolactic fermentation and played a key role in spreading the use of small barrels in California. He was also one of the first to put an emphasis on the vineyard site. Tchelistcheff was one of the first modern winemakers to call attention to the possibilities of wine grapes in Carneros and in some of Napa's mountain districts, such as Diamond Mountain. As noted elsewhere in this book, his dedication to the open sharing of information among winemakers could well mark the beginning of the modern era in California wines.

But Tchelistcheff is best know for his work at Beaulieu and in the Rutherford district. He is famously quoted as saying: "It takes Rutherford dust to grow great Cabernet". That remark has been worked over in various ways. Some have even insisted that Rutherford Cabernet has a "dusty" quality. Perhaps, but not likely. It seems clear that what Tchelistcheff was talking about was simply Rutherford dirt. Anyone who has ever walked in a vineyard in Napa at high summer is well acquainted with dust. There has been no rain for months; winds whip down off the Mayacamas range in the afternoon, and dust swirls through the vineyard. That's Rutherford dust. Wind-blown terroir.

Tchelistcheff died in 1994, having set Napa on the track toward elegant, supple Cabernet that, unfortunately, is more honoured by word than deed today. It is always a safe bet to call on the dead to make a point, but it is hard to believe that Tchelistcheff would not be appalled at the over-concentrated, overripe, and totally out-of-balance wines now being made in Napa – and in Rutherford as well, I'm afraid.

At a tasting of Rutherford wines not so long ago, I was bemused to hear one winemaker say that he did not care about acidity. The remark was made during a discussion of the potential of a particular wine to age. He noted that what he was after was a high score from those publications that rate a wine on the 100-point scale, because that score translated into higher prices for the wine. To achieve a high score, he went on, all that was needed was an abundance of rich fruit and a blotto alcohol level. The structure and balance of the wine simply did not enter the picture. In short, he was not interested in the future of his wine, once it had achieved its ninety-seven point mark. He added that it was up to the consumer to decide when to drink the wines he made. Not his job.

I was pleased to hear some dissent to that position. John Williams, owner and winemaker at Frog's Leap was particularly eloquent."I would be ignoring my responsibilities as a winemaker if I didn't think of how the wine would taste as it aged." The plus side of that mini-skirmish (and it wasn't the only one) is that Rutherford takes itself seriously. It is seeking to define itself and the wines, even to the point of admitting in some cases that the wine is being made with at least one eye on the 100-point system. Rutherford AVA is not regarded as a mere marketing ploy. Its winemakers are interested in explaining the AVA, not just promoting it. In a larger sense, they are exploring the notion of the specific terroir of Rutherford.

Rutherford does work fairly well as an appellation, with more uniformity of soils and weather patterns that most Napa AVAs. It could be argued that the ideal situation would be an East Rutherford and West Rutherford, since the alluvial deposits on the east side of the river from the Vaca Mountains do differ somewhat from the Mayacamas-based soils to the west. This sorts itself out in a sense because the best-known vineyard sites tend to be in west Rutherford, where the famed Inglenook vineyards (now owned by Niebaum-Coppola) and vineyards associated with the great Beaulieu Cabernets of the 1940s and 1950s were developed.

As mentioned elsewhere, there was an attempt to establish a "Rutherford Bench" appellation as well as an "Oakville Bench" in the late 1980s when the Rutherford and Oakville AVAs were being discussed (*see* Appendix IV pages 255–6). The proposed AVAs would have been on the west side of the valley, above the valley floor in the low hills of the Mayacamas. There is little justification for calling them benchlands in a strictly geological sense, which defines a benchland as a terrace formed by wave action along a sea coast, or a lake or river shore. Supporters of the proposed benches included land that was perhaps not true bench-land, but simply layers of deep alluvial fans. (True benchland can be seen along the Russian River in Mendocino and Sonoma Counties.) The idea was not supported by anyone on the valley floor, which is hardly a surprise. Nevertheless, there is some justification for the idea that hillside sites should be considered apart from valley floor sites. Soils are generally shallow and less productive, sun exposure is different and after-sunset cooling is more pronounced.

As for varietals, obviously Cabernet Sauvignon is the winner. But other red Bordeaux varieties come into the mix. Sauvignon Blanc is my favourite white wine for Rutherford, as for most of Napa. There is a surprising amount of Chardonnay as well: surprising because there are better places to grow Chardonnay. The white wine grapes are, in general, grown closer to the river. Several of the Rutherford wineries that do offer Chardonnay buy grapes from outside the AVA.

Just what is the flavour profile of a Cabernet-based Rutherford wine? That has been debated for well over a century and recently the answers have been clouded by extreme winemaking techniques. And because of these techniques and specific vineyard practices it is probably, in the end, impossible to settle on a single definition of a Rutherford Cabernet.

But we could start with this working definition: Rutherford Cabernet Sauvignon at its best has a rich, sometimes earthy quality, with spice tones, including mint and traces of chocolate with black cherry and black plum fruit. What you want to do, of course, is drink all the Rutherford Cabernet you can lay your hands on and make your own definition. Start with these.

## The Best of Rutherford

### BEAULIEU VINEYARD

1960 St Helena Highway, Rutherford, CA 94573; Tel: 707 967 5200;
Fax: 707 967 9149; Email: bvinfo@bvwines.com; Website: www.bvwines.com
Vineyards: 445ha

The Georges de Latour Private Reserve Cabernets were once a benchmark of Napa Cabernet. Under Heublein, overall production was increased and key vineyards were sold off. Today, Beaulieu is making a strong comeback. Winemaker Joel Aiken has been steadily restoring some of Beaulieu's old glory and Cabernet – both the regular bottling and the reserve – is well back on track. The new owners, Diageo, seem to have made a solid commitment to the historic vineyard, although there is still too much wine under the Beaulieu label (the Coastal Estate series for one) that should have been sold on the bulk market. Recent bottlings of Chardonnay and Pinot Noir from Carneros have been quite good.

### CAYMUS VINEYARDS

8700 Conn Creek Road, PO Box 268, Rutherford, CA 94573.
Tel: 707 963 4204; Fax: 707 963 5958; Website: www.caymus.com
Vineyards: 29.5ha

In 1987, the *Wine Spectator* headlined its cover story on Caymus Vineyards: "Best Damn Cabernet in California". The story was a little more nuanced, but the same assertion could still be made. Caymus, which is named for a Mexican land grant, is owned by the Wagner family, long time Napa growers. They decided to make their own wine in 1972 and in 1975 made the happy decision of hiring Randy Dunn as winemaker. That was also the first year the family produced the Caymus Special Selection, which is the wine that put them on the map. It is a rich and powerful wine, with intense dark fruit and usually well endowed with oaky tannins. It develops slowly in the bottle and typically does not reach its peak for at least fifteen years. The Napa Valley bottling, made from estate grapes, is more inviting early on and usually less weighty than the Special Selection. At different times, Caymus has made Zinfandel and Pinot Noir but now concentrates on Cabernet only at the Napa winery.

## FROG'S LEAP
*See* Chapter 9, page 148.

## HEWITT VINEYARD
1695 St Helena Highway, Rutherford, CA 94573. Tel: 707 968 3633; Fax: 707 968 3632; Email: info@hewittvineyard.com; Website: www.hewittvineyard.com
Vineyards: 24ha

This historic vineyard, first planted in 1880, is now owned by the Chalone Wine Group. It was first bottled as a single-vineyard wine in 2001. The debut vintage was sensational, with classic Rutherford black cherry fruit and a generous dash of chocolate and dried herbs. It may be getting a bit ahead of things to include Hewitt in the Best of Rutherford, but with the winemaking record of the Chalone Wine Group, and the viticultural record of Hewitt, it belongs there.

## NIEBAUM-COPPOLA ESTATE
1991 St Helena Highway, Rutherford, CA 94573. Tel: 707 968 1100;
Fax: 707 963 9084; Website: www.niebaum-coppola.com
Vineyards: 77ha

Beginning in 1978 with his purchase of the historic Gustave Niebaum home (the heart of historic Inglenook estate), film director Francis Ford Coppola has been restoring the estate, bringing the Inglenook vineyards under his ownership. His goal is not just an historic reconstruction, but to bring the wines back to the peak of quality. He is well on his way to success, but a certain unevenness has kept it from being in any sense an Oscar-winning performance. The top of the line Rubicon is a Bordeaux blend that shows flashes of greatness but can also turn up a bit too tannic and oaky. Recently, Rubicon has seemed to become perhaps overly rich and concentrated at the expense of balance. Having said all that, it is always a serious wine and has enormous potential. In the mid-1990s, Coppola introduced the Niebaum-Coppola Estate Cask wine, a 100 per cent Cabernet, all estate grown. It is a super-extracted wine, showing ripe and intense flavours.

QUINTESSA
*See* Chapter 9, page 165.

## STAGLIN FAMILY VINEYARD
1570 Bella Oaks Lane, Rutherford, CA 94573. Tel: 707 944 0477; Fax: 707 944 0535; Email: info@staglinfamily.com; Website: www.staglinfamily.com
Vineyards: 20.5ha

Staglin makes Chardonnay and Sangiovese, but the Rutherford Cabernet Sauvignon is the main plot line. The Staglins bought a twenty-plus hectare vineyard in Rutherford in the mid-1980s and their Cabernets quickly achieved near cult status. The vineyard had once been owned by Beaulieu, with the grapes used in Beaulieu's famed Private Reserve Cabernets. Staglin Cabernet is built to last, probably showing its best in the ten to fifteen year range. There is, once again, the trademark Rutherford black cherry and plum. In youth, the wine can seem awkward and jammy, but with even five to eight years in bottle, it develops a silky mouthfeel and texture.

## WILLIAM HARRISON VINEYARDS & WINERY
1443 Silverado Trail, St Helena, CA 94574.
Tel: 707 963 8762; Fax: 707 963 8762; Website: www.whwines.com
Vineyards: 4ha

Located on the Silverado Trail, William Harrison makes all estate wines in limited quantities. The wines are aimed at the top end of the market. The top wine is called Rutherford Red, a blend of Cabernets Sauvignon and Franc, with a touch of Merlot. In most vintages the Cabernet Sauvignon is more than sixty per cent of the cuvée. It is a complex wine, showing oaky tannins when young but evolving into a complex and elegant wine after a few years in bottle. The Cabernet Sauvignon is a more forward wine, intense and bold. It can be enjoyed a little earlier than the Rutherford Red. A few hundred cases of Cabernet Franc are made most years.

# SPRING MOUNTAIN
Although Spring Mountain was granted status as an AVA well over a decade ago in 1993, and grapes have been grown there for almost 150 years, it is still difficult to pin down just what constitutes a Spring Mountain wine. You might know from the wine in the glass that it's a Spring Mountain Cabernet, but still not be able to define it.

Perhaps the great variation in soils, elevation, and exposures makes it difficult to find common threads. Having said that, as appellations go, it is more justified than many, since most of the district is in the watershed of York Creek, above 120 metres (400 feet) and as high as 685 metres (2,250 feet) in the Mayacamas Mountains west of St Helena. Soils range from older sedimentary soils in the southern part of the AVA, near Mount Veeder, to newer soils of volcanic origin to the north, toward Diamond Mountain. Su Hua Newton, co-owner of Newton Vineyards remains baffled about any attempt to define Spring Mountain terroir. "You really have to go on a vineyard-by-vineyard basis. You can walk 1.5 metres (five feet) and see several different soils."

In many cases, the sedimentary soils underlie thin layers of volcanic debris. The soil structure does vary a great deal from site to site, and often within an individual vineyard. However, all of Spring Mountain soils are shallow and tend to stress the vines, limiting root structure and yield. The soils are also well drained and there is much difference in sun exposure. Those vineyards planted with a southern exposure tend to produce bigger and "fatter" wines; with leaner wines coming from vineyards with northern exposure.

Spring Mountain has a distinctive weather pattern, especially during the summer growing season. (This point is explored in more detail in the Spring Mountain Vineyards profile, see page 102.) There is also heavier rainfall here than in most parts of Napa. Winter storms off the Pacific, only about forty-eight kilometres (thirty miles) west, are pushed higher by prevailing winds when they hit the Mayacamas range. When they run into colder air above the mountains, the water is dropped on the eastern side of Spring Mountain, a somewhat unusual rain pattern for California where the western slopes of the coastal ranges (and the Sierra Nevada inland) are usually wetter.

There are several key differences between the Spring Mountain AVA and the valley floor, all of which influence the wines to some degree. For example, mornings tend to be warmer on Spring Mountain because the vineyards lie above the fog line – thus the 120-metre (400-feet) contour level. This means that the maximum day temperature is reached about an hour earlier on the mountain. But cooling also begins earlier with late afternoon shading and cool breezes blowing in from the coast. Nights, however, tend to be warmer as the cold air settles to the valley floor.

Red varieties make up over eighty per cent of Spring Mountain grapes, with half of that being Cabernet Sauvignon and one-quarter Merlot, which are without doubt the best varietals for the appellation. Contrary to expectations about the nature of mountain grapes, the Merlot in some cases rates higher than the Cabernet, showing a firm structure combined with luscious fruit. Chris Howell, the winemaker at Cain Vineyard & Winery, offers his personal take on Spring Mountain:

> The inherent diversity in this appellation is an issue that is as ineluctable as it is inescapable. This area has been known historically as "Spring Mountain" more by geography and the road, than by wine flavour. Nonetheless, perhaps because of the forests, the cooler air, and the cooler soils, we are beginning to see some common flavours among the Cabernets. If there were just one aroma descriptor, it might be anise. The fruit would be more blackberry than black cherry. Generally the wines tend to be concentrated in tannin, however the tannins seem to be softer and more refined.

The diversity of geography is compounded by the diversity of the people. They tend to be what one might call rugged individualists – they did, after all, choose to go up into the mountains. It isn't surprising that, as a group, they haven't issued a unified field report.

There is one oddity about the Spring Mountain AVA. Unlike Carneros, which cuts across the Sonoma/Napa County political line, the Spring Mountain AVA stops abruptly at the Sonoma line. It stops, in fact, in the middle of the Pride vineyards crush pad. The Pride family has laid in a row of bricks, marking the division. More importantly, the line divides the Pride Mountain vineyards, a plain silly mistake by distant bureaucrats who do not realize that the map is not the territory.

## The Best of Spring Mountain

CAIN VINEYARD & WINERY
3800 Langtry Road, St Helena, CA 94574. Tel: 707 963 1616;
Fax: 707 963 7952; Email: winery@cainfive.com; Website: www.cainfive.com
Vineyards: 34ha
Built on a windy ridge of Spring Mountain in 1983, Cain concentrates on three superb Bordeaux blends. Cain Five is made in a powerful rich style

and is capable of ageing up to fifteen years, typically with lush notes of creamy oak. Cain Cuvée, a lighter version, is not really a second label as it is quite capable of standing on its own. The recently introduced Cain Concept is a Bordeaux blend made from grapes grown on the Valley floor. The "concept" being to make a wine from grapes grown on benchland and hillsides at a lower elevation as a counterpoint to the Cain Five mountain grapes. Early bottlings have been outstanding. Overall, however it is the Cain Five that deserves to be ranked with the best Napa red wines. The terraced vineyards are planted to all five Bordeaux varieties, plus a small amount of Syrah. In the past, Cain made a classy Sauvignon Blanc from the Musque clone, sourced from Monterey County, however that has now been dropped.

## NEWTON VINEYARDS

2555 Madronna Avenue, St Helena, CA 94574. Tel: 707 963 9000; Fax: 707 963 5408; Email: winery@newtonvineyard.com; Website: www.newtonvineyard.com
Vineyards: 54ha

Following his sale of Sterling Vineyards in 1977, Peter Newton and his wife Su Hua Newton began developing a mountain vineyard on a 263-hectare site on Spring Mountain. They hired Ric Forman, who had been their winemaker at Sterling, to help develop the site. Forman helped to lay out the terraces, and the vineyards were planted to Merlot, Cabernet Sauvignon, Cabernet Franc, and a little Sauvignon Blanc. The Newton Merlot is easily one of the best in California. It has remarkable power balanced with a supple elegance and grace. In a world of bland "me-too" Merlots, Newton's stands out. Su Hua believes that the bland quality seen in too many California Merlots is the fault of winemakers. "A lot of UC Davis-trained winemakers follow a formula, a recipe, and that leads to blandness. You can't do that with Merlot." Most years a small amount of Cabernet Franc is blended into the Merlot. However, Su Hua gives all credit to the stony sparse soils of the vineyards. "It all starts with the dirt," she says. Newton's Cabernets are also quite good.

## PRIDE MOUNTAIN

4026 Spring Mountain Road, St Helena, CA 94574.
Tel: 707 963 4949; Fax: 707 963 4848; Email: contactus@pridewines.com;
Website: www.pridewines.com
Vineyards: 69ha

Established in 1991 by James Pride, who was formerly a dentist, Pride Mountain has flirted with cult status but has overall remained true to Spring Mountain terroir. The wooden-beamed winery is on the site of the Summit Ranch winery, which was built in 1890 but had been abandoned during Prohibition. The ruins are now used as a picnic area by visitors to Pride Mountain. The vineyards are very stony with shallow mountain top soils that have a high gravel content. The Pride family grows Merlot, Cabernet Sauvignon, Cabernet Franc, and a little excellent Viognier, bottling them all as varietals. Pick of the crop is the Cabernet Sauvignon, both regular bottling and reserve. The regular bottling is very agreeable when young, typically with chocolate and blackberry elements dominating. It also ages gracefully and could be held for ten to twelve years. The Reserve Cabernet Sauvignon is a more massive wine, made from selected vineyard blocks, and capable of extended ageing. However, the Merlot also has a lot going for it with bright cherry fruit and a chocolate edge.

## RITCHIE CREEK

4024 Spring Mountain Road, St Helena,CA 94574. Tel: 707 963 4361;
Fax: 707 963 4936; Email: RCV@napanet.com; Website: www.ritchiecreek.com
Vineyards: 3ha

Owner Peter Minor planted his vineyard near the top of Spring Mountain in 1967 at an elevation of 610 metres (2,000 feet). The vineyard is only three hectares and includes Cabernet Sauvignon, a little Merlot, Chardonnay, and Pinot Noir. At one time, Minor had Viognier on the property and was one of the first in California to produce a varietal Viognier. However, he couldn't get the fruit to ripen properly every year and he replaced it with the obscure (in California) Austrian variety Blaufränkisch, perhaps the only such planting in Napa. I've never had the courage to ask him why. The winery was built in 1974 and named after the creek which flows through the property. The Cabernet is typical of Spring Mountain, with brilliant fruit and an underlying element of anise and chocolate. It improves in bottle for up to ten or fifteen years.

## ROBERT KEENAN WINERY

3660 Spring Mountain Road, St Helena, CA 94574. Tel: 707 963 9177; Fax:
707 963 8209; Email: rkw@keenanwinery.com; Website: www.keenanwinery.com
Vineyards: 19.5ha

In 1974 Robert Keenan bought seventy-three hectares of land which were situated at an elevation of 518 metres (1,700 feet) on Spring Mountain. The location was the former site of the Peter Conradi winery in the late nineteenth century and had at that time been planted to both Zinfandel and Syrah. The original Conradi winery closed during Prohibition and the vines had long since disappeared when Keenan bought the property. However there were remains of the old winery, which Keenan rebuilt as well as planting Cabernet Sauvignon, Merlot, and Chardonnay vines. Keenan now makes about 10,000 cases of exceptional wines every year, with the Merlot, which is typically rich and layered with bright cherry fruit, being a favourite with consumers. The Cabernet Sauvignon is also focused on cherries, with dark ripe plum flavours; in most years it has the balance and structure for extended ageing.

## SCHWEIGER VINEYARDS
4015 Spring Mountain Road, St Helena, CA 94574. Tel: 707 963 4882;
Fax: 707 963 7980; Email: svwine@schweigervineyards.com;
Website: www.schweigervineyards.com
Vineyards: 14ha

The winery and vineyards at an elevation of some 610 metres (2,000 feet), on a site that had been planted in the 1870s. The first Schweiger vines, mostly Cabernet Sauvignon, were planted in 1981 on volcanic soils For several years, the grapes were sold to other wineries, including ZD and Newton. Schweiger finally became a bonded winery in 1994. Planted vines now include Merlot, Chardonnay, and a small amount of Petite Sirah. The Cabernet is an immense, rich wine, well suited for ageing. Schweiger makes a tiny amount of powerful and inky Petite Sirah, which is becoming something of a cult favourite.

## SMITH-MADRONE VINEYARDS & WINERY
4022 Spring Mountain Road, St Helena, CA 94574. Tel: 707 963 2283;
Fax: 707 963 2291; Email: info@smithmadrone.com;
Website: www.smithmadrone.com
Vineyards: 81ha

Brothers Stu and Charles Smith developed their high mountain vineyards in the 1970s, planting Cabernet Sauvignon, Chardonnay, Riesling, and Pinot Noir. The Pinot Noir was soon dropped. Over the years, they have developed a sterling reputation for Riesling, made in a just off-dry style (*see* Appendix IV page 254). The Cabernet Sauvignon and Chardonnay are well above average.

## SPRING MOUNTAIN VINEYARD

2805 Spring Mountain Road, St Helena, CA 94574. Tel: 707 967 4188; Fax: 707 963 2753; Email: valli@springmtn.com; Website: www.springmtn.com
Vineyards: 91 ha

The grand nineteenth-century château at Spring Mountain Vineyards was very familiar to television viewers of the 1980s as the setting for *Falcon Crest*, the wine-themed melodrama set in Napa. Despite that fame Tom Robbins, who owned the estate, was forced into bankruptcy and the property was bought by a group called The Good Wine Company in 1992, headed by a somewhat mysterious and publicity-shy international investor named Jacob Safra. Safra hired Tom Ferrell, a respected and talented winemaker and winery executive to put together a winery estate in Napa. Ferrell spent several years constructing the new Spring Mountain estate from parts of the nineteenth century Spring Mountain vineyards, including the historic La Perla Estate and the original Spring Mountain Estate. Ferrell has patched together what could turn out to be a powerhouse winery. Early results are more than promising, especially for Sauvignon Blanc, a stunning Syrah, and Cabernet Sauvignon. Keep an eye on this one.

## TERRA VALENTINE

3787 Spring Mountain Road, St Helena, CA 94574. Tel: 707 967 8340; Fax: 707 967 8342; Email: info@terravalentine.com; Website: www.terravalentine.com
Vineyards: 18 ha

In 1995 Angus Wertle, an imaginative business man from Minnesota who fell in love with wine when he was a student at Stanford University, bought Yverdon winery, which had been built in the 1960s. The winery, which Wertle renamed Terra Valentine, is so far up Spring Mountain it is almost in Sonoma. It is a hand-built monument to the individual baroque style of Yverdon founder Fred Aves, a reclusive inventor, who even made the stained glass in the windows. What he didn't do very well was make wine, a situation that the Wertle family has corrected. The Cabernet Sauvignon shows great promise. It's a supple, balanced wine, which is what Wertle is aiming for. "I'm not interested in blockbusters," he says. I hear you, Angus.

## PHILIP TONGI

3780 Spring Mountain Road, St Helena, CA 94574. Tel: 707 963 3731;
Fax: 707 963 9185

Vineyards: 4ha

Philip Tongi is one of the grand old men of Napa winemakers, having started his Napa career at Mayacamas Vineyards in 1958. Over the years he has made wine at Cuvaison and Chapplett and was a consulting winemaker at Chimney Rock. Tongi began planting his Spring Mountain vineyard in 1981. He released his first Cabernet Sauvignon in 1983. Tongi is best known for his rich and concentrated Cabernet Sauvignon, made from an estate-grown blend of Cabernet Sauvignon, Merlot, Cabernet Franc, and Petit Verdot. It is a wine that takes some time to come around. Tongi regularly holds back some of the production for release when it is ten years old. He also produces a very sweet wine from the rare Black Hamburg grape, called Ca' Tongi, which is inspired by Constantia, the nineteenth-century South African wine.

## ST HELENA

Wine-growing in St Helena goes back almost to the beginning of Napa Valley's wine history, now closing in on almost 160 years. In some ways, the St Helena AVA, which was approved in 1995, doesn't seem to differ all that much from the Rutherford AVA to the south. Until you start tasting the wines, that is. Rutherford Cabernet Sauvignon, especially in the past decade, can get a little over the top, sometimes jammy, but this rarely happens in St Helena. A winemaking decision? Perhaps, but there are other reasons.

Historically, St Helena was the centre of Napa's wine industry from the time that Charles Krug built a winery just north of the present town in 1860. Krug was the man behind the formation of the St Helena Viticultural Club in 1876, the same year in which Jacob and Frederick Beringer established Beringer winery. Krug's organization was the first in Napa to encourage vintners to share information on technical questions, an innovation that has become a Napa (and California) tradition. Perhaps his early efforts encouraged a sharper focus on wine and terroir than elsewhere in Napa.

Geographically, the St Helena appellation lies at the narrowest part of Napa Valley, squeezing down to barely 1.6 kilometres (one mile) in width. The soils are dominated by the familiar pattern of alluvial fans that is seen throughout the Napa Valley; as elsewhere, these soils are well-drained with low fertility. One thing that does set St Helena apart is the sheer diversity of the varietals grown there. Rutherford and Oakville to the south are dominated by Cabernet Sauvignon, but St Helena seems to have the capacity to grow first-class Petite Sirah, Zinfandel, and even a little Pinot Noir, as well as the Bordeaux reds. That could be an historical oddity because of the large number of small vineyards of two hectares or less that sprang up around the town of St Helena in the late ninetenth and early twentieth century. There are now about 150 growers in the appellation, a much larger number than any other Napa AVA. There are also a number of wineries with very limited production and distribution within the AVA.

Despite the diversity, St Helena seems to have the perfect climate as well as the right soils for the Bordeaux grapes, including Sauvignon Blanc. The district isn't as hot as Calistoga, nor is it as cool as Oakville and Rutherford. Across the board, St Helena Cabernets can be hard to distinguish from Oakville or Rutherford Cabernets, but they are pretty easy to spot when tasted against the more powerful mountain Cabernets, the cooler area Cabernets, or any over-the-top examples from anywhere. The best of the St Helena Cabernets show bright and elegant fruit, with a silky mouthfeel and good structure. They are wines that can age well into their twenties. Spottswoode Cabernet is a good example. In short, despite the fact that several varieties thrive in St Helena, Cabernet remains the top card.

## The Best of St Helena

### ARNS WINERY

PO Box 652, St Helena, CA 94574. Tel: 707 963 3429; Fax: 707 963 5780;
Email: arnswine@napanet.com; Website: www.arnswinery.com
Vineyards: 3.5ha
The Arns family grows 3.5 hectares of Cabernet Sauvignon on a vineyard east of St Helena at the foot of Howell Mountain at an elevation of between 122 and 244 metres (400 and 800 feet). The wine is made in a traditional manner, including the use of a basket press. Early vintages have been promising.

## CASA NUESTRA WINERY & VINEYARDS

3451 Silverado Trail, St Helena, CA 94574. Tel: 707 963 5783; Fax: 707 963 3174; Email: info@casanuestra.com; Website: www.casanuestra.com
Vineyards: 8ha

A quirky little winery established by the Kirkham family in the early 1970s on the Silverado Trail. Casa Nuestra specializes in Chenin Blanc, although it also makes a reasonably good Merlot and Cabernet Franc. Grapes are all grown on the small estate vineyard (about eight hectares). Casa Nuestra is one of the few California wineries to take Chenin Blanc seriously. It is made in an off-dry style and is quite delicious. The downside is that about the only place you can buy it is the winery itself.

## CORISON WINERY

See Chapter 9, page 133.

## EL MOLINO

PO Box 306, St Helena, CA 94574. Tel: 707 963 3632; Fax: 707 963 1647; Email: wine@elmolinowinery.com; Website: www.elmolinowinery.com
Vineyards: 27.5ha

The winery was founded in 1871 by W W Lyman and named after the nearby Bale grain mill, now the site of a Napa County Park. The winery operated until 1910. It was revived in 1981 by the Oliver family. El Molino is best known for its Pinot Noir, made from grapes grown on the St Helena estate and grapes from the family vineyard in the Rutherford AVA. This is fairly brawny Pinot Noir, especially if you are thinking Carneros, and can sometimes approach the jammy over-the-top profile. As someone once said, it is a Pinot Noir for Cabernet drinkers. Still, at its best it has a marvellous texture and mouthfeel with a silky, lingering finish. The Chardonnay is made in a rich, oaky style.

## JUDD'S HILL

PO Box 415, St Helena, CA 94574. Tel: 707 963 9093; Fax: 707 963 1147; Email: info@juddshill.com; Website: www.juddshill.com
Vineyards: 5.5ha

Judd, Art, and Bunnie Finkelstein (former owners of Whitehall Lane Winery) originally founded this small winery in 1989 in the hills east of St Helena. They have 5.5 hectares of Bordeaux varieties, mostly Cabernet Sauvignon, and make balanced and stylish wines.

## LARKMEAD VINEYARDS

PO Box 309, St Helena, CA 94574. Tel: 707 942 6605; Fax: 707 942 6019;
Email: larkmead@sbcglobal.net; Website: www.larkmead.com
Vineyards: 48.5ha

There have been vineyards on the Larkmead estate since the late
1800s and a winery since at least 1884. There was an important clonal
experimental station there operated by UC Davis in the 1940s where
many of the clones still in use in Napa were developed. The present
owners, the Solari family, bought the site north of St Helena in 1948.
They grow Cabernet Sauvignon and the other Bordeaux reds, as well as
Sauvignon Blanc, Syrah, and Zinfandel. The wines are made at the Napa
Wine Company. The Cabernet can be extraordinary, with layered flavours
and balance.

## LEWELLING VINEYARDS

1951 Olive Avenue, St Helena, CA 94574. Tel: 707 963 1685; Fax: 707 963
1685; Email: lewvyds@napanet.net; Website: www.lewellingvineyards.com
Vineyards: 11ha

Vineyards were first planted on the estate at the west edge of St Helena in
1864 by pioneer horticulturist John Lewelling. His great-granddaughter,
Janice Lewelling Wight, her husband Russ, and their three sons now have
an eleven-hectare vineyard, part of the original estate and perhaps the
oldest continuously-owned family estate in Napa. Grapes were sold to
Caymus, Markham, Viader, Beaulieu, and other vineyards over the years.
In 1992 the family began making its own Cabernet Sauvignon, which aims
at elegance and harmony which reflects the variety (it is 100 per cent
Cabernet) and the terroir. The wine is bottled unfiltered and unfined.
Production is quite small (under 1,000 cases), but worth seeking out.

## MILAT VINEYARDS

1091 St Helena Highway, St Helena, CA 94574. Tel: 707 963 9758;
Email: info@milat.com; Website: www.milat.com
Vineyards: 9ha

Milat, a family-owned winery founded in 1986, produces only estate-
grown wines including Chenin Blanc, Chardonnay, Merlot, Cabernet
Sauvignon, and Zinfandel. Milat's owners describe their winemaking style
as "minimalist" which is an encouraging beginning. The Chenin is just
off-dry but with high acids, it doesn't taste sweet. It's a great apéritif wine,

or good with Asian fusion cuisine, and is my favourite of Milat's wines. The Chardonnay is one of the few in Napa made in the Chablis style, with the emphasis on the crisp fruit rather than oaky tannins. The Cabernet shows the typical elegant balance of St Helena Cabernets, while the Merlot is perhaps a shade too far on the minty side. Milat is one of the true undiscovered jewels of Napa.

## PARRY CELLARS

3424 Silverado Trail, St Helena, CA 94574. Tel: 707 967 8160; Fax: 707 967 8161; Email: info@parrycellars.com; Website: www.parrycellars.com
Vineyards: 0.5ha

A very limited production winery making a miniscule amount of 100 per cent varietal Cabernet Sauvignon from a vineyard on the Silverado Trail, north of St Helena. I mention Parry only because the wine is so good; graceful and elegant with a luscious mouthfeel.

## SALVESTRIN WINERY

397 Main Street, St, Helena, CA 94574. Tel: 707 963 5105; Fax: 707 963 1382; Email: sales@salvestrinwinery.com; Website: www.salvestrinwinery.com
Vineyards: 10.5ha

The vineyard, originally planted in 1926, grows Cabernet Sauvignon, Merlot, Sangiovese, Petite Syrah, and Zinfandel. Until 1994, the grapes were sold to other wineries, including Freemark Abbey and Raymond. Now Salvestrin makes a small amount of Cabernet Sauvignon and Sangiovese. The gravelly, volcanic soil of the vineyard seems perfectly suited to complex and silky Cabernet Sauvignon.

## SEAVEY VINEYARD

1310 Conn Valley Road, St Helena CA 94574. Tel: 707 963 8339; Fax: 707 963 0232; Email: info@seaveyvineyard.com; Website: www.seaveyvineyard.com
Vineyards: 16ha

In the 1980s, the Seavey family planted a vineyard on a site that dates to the 1870s, producing their first Cabernet Sauvignon and Chardonnay in 1990. The Cabernet Sauvignon has been highly praised for its powerful ripeness and strength. At its best the wine is complex with touches of chocolate and anise.

## SPOTTSWOODE WINERY

*See* Chapter 9, page 181.

## TITUS VINEYARDS

PO Box 608, St Helena, CA 94574. Tel: 707 963 3235; Fax: 707 963 3257;
Email: titusvyd@napanet.com; Website: www.tituswine.com

Vineyards: 20ha

A family-owned estate on the Silverado Trail, making an outstanding Zinfandel from estate grapes. It has a firm structure with good fruit and enough complexity to age well for ten to fifteen years, not always the case with Zin. The vineyard, which is more than forty years old, is dry-farmed, adding to the concentration of the wine without pushing it past the point of balance. The estate Cabernet comes from two vineyards, one on an alluvial fan, which adds an element of well-defined fruit, the other on a stony, infertile, dry creek bed, which gives great concentration to the blend. Titus also makes an old-vine Zinfandel from Mendocino County.

## STAGS LEAP

The Stags Leap AVA is roughly one-hundredth the size of the Napa Valley appellation, which surrounds it. The AVA contains 1,093 hectares with only half of that planted to grapes, primarily Cabernet Sauvignon and related Bordeaux varieties. The district is tucked into a five-kilometres by one-kilometre (3.1-miles by 0.6-miles) area bordering the Silverado Trail and defined by the jagged outcroppings of the Vaca range to the east, the Napa River to the west and south, and Yountville Crossroads to the north. Grape-growing in Stags Leap goes back to the mid-1800s when the Silverado Trail was a quiet horse lane, following the route of a Native American trail toward San Francisco Bay. In 1878, Terrill Grigsby built Occidental Winery, the region's first winery, and the current home of Regusci Winery. Several years later, in 1893, San Francisco entrepreneur Horace Chase built the first winery to bear the Stags Leap name. Today, there are fewer than twenty wineries making wine on a regular basis from the Stags Leap AVA.

The name itself is taken from a massive outcrop of basalt rock, that thrusts some 365 metres (1,200 feet) into the air on the east side of the Silverado Trail. According to legend, the outcrop was named after a huge stag that was chased to the top of the rock by hunters. As the hunters drew near the stag leaped into the valley below, apparently to certain death. But the pursuing hunters were amazed to see the deer bounding down the Silverado Trail, unharmed and free. In some versions of the stories the hunters were Indians, in others they were Spanish and there are even variants which have the stag cornered by a mountain lion or a grizzly bear. Whatever the origin, it's a good story if rather predictable.

The taste profile of a Stags Leap District Cabernet Sauvignon (and Merlot) begins with a supple opening, followed by soft juicy tannins in the centre and a rich perfume of violets and cherries. The best wines are subtle and balanced. There are no sharp elbows poking you in the palate and no harsh unresolved tannins to muddle the long silky finish. Looking at France, Stags Leap wines can be compared to Margaux. On the palate, they have the same velvety quality as Margaux, lacking the dominant structure that can be found in a Paulliac. They have richness without heaviness. Possessing both power and elegance, of all the Napa appellations, Stags Leap wines are perhaps the easiest to distinguish.

It isn't really necessary, of course, to ask why, but it's difficult not to. What makes a Stags Leap wine taste like a Stags Leap wine? Warren Winiarski, the man who helped put Stags Leap on the world wine map doesn't have an answer. "I don't think anybody knows. You could guess forever. It's a combination of all sorts of things that nobody can really identify. Soils? We have volcanic soils, but also upland alluvial soils. Climate? We used to talk a lot about the Stags Leap palisades warming the air as it flowed through, a channel of air coming up from the Bay and holding the afternoon heat to radiate out at night. Stags Leap Cabernet is easier to describe than to say why." He pauses. You can almost see the mental shrug. "I don't think it's possible to say with any degree of certainty what makes a Stags Leap Cabernet a Stags Leap Cabernet."

Winiarski is right, of course. In the end, wine is an elusive creature. It cannot be explained, only enjoyed. But there are a handful of elements in the Stags Leap District which may play a part in the wine profile. There is, most importantly, the soil which is rocky and well drained, derived chiefly from volcanic sources. Many of the better vineyards have a western or southwestern exposure, which opens the vines to more direct sunlight, important for a late-season variety like Cabernet. The Stags Leap District is made up of a series of hills and ridges that create suntraps, holding afternoon heat into the early evening. Tchelistcheff once called the Nathan Fay vineyard in the heart of the Stags Leap District "a little sun basket". This jumbled geography also contributes to a complex pattern of air flow over and around the vineyards.

Then there's the weather pattern. Stags Leap is in the cooler part of Napa, but it isn't as cool as it should be. Pushed up against the Vaca range, Stags Leap District doesn't get the direct winds from San Francisco Bay that sweep through the Carneros region and up the valley. When cooling winds do break through in the late afternoon, as they do for example at Shafer's Hillside Estate vineyard, they are more diluted by warmer air. Also, because of the rocky soils, the immediate microclimate of the vines tends to be warmer due to absorption and radiation of solar energy. As a result of this combination of soils and weather pattern, in most years Cabernet Sauvignon actually ripens earlier than in warmer regions of Napa.

## The Best of Stags Leap

### BALDACCI VINEYARDS

6236 Silverado Trail, Napa CA 94558. Tel: 707 944 9261; Fax: 707 265 7917; Email: cgarrett@baldaccivineyards.com; Website: www.baldaccivineyards.com
Vineyards: 20ha

Baldacci is a newcomer, with its first vintage in 2000, but it is starting strong. There was a vineyard on the site as early as 1916 and the Baldacci family, who are descended from Italian immigrants, replanted in the 1990s to Cabernet Sauvignon and Cabernet Franc. Early bottlings show typical Stags Leap District elegance and flavour profile. Tom Baldacci expects to reach 5,000 to 6,000 cases, all estate-grown. Rolando Herrera has recently been recruited from Stags Leap Wine Cellars next-door as winemaker. Keep an eye on Baldacci.

### CHIMNEY ROCK

5350 Silverado Trail, Napa CA 94558. Tel: 707 257 2036; Fax: 707 257 2036; Email: club@chimneyrock.com; Website: www.chimneyrock.com
Vineyards: 44.5ha

Chimney Rock had a rather unusual beginning. New York executive Sheldon Wilson was looking around Napa for a place to establish a winery in the mid-1980s. He found Chimney Rock, an eighteen-hole golf course for sale on the Silverado Trail. Wilson, an avid golfer, snapped it up and put up a winery. He planted vineyards on nine holes and left the other nine for his morning round. It must surely be the only winery in the world built on a golf course. (Although in southeastern

Napa there is a golf course called Chardonnay.) The emphasis from the beginning was on Cabernet Sauvignon and its cousins, and the wines were always first rate. In the early 1990s, phylloxera forced Wilson to replant. The new plantings are tight spaced with careful clonal selection and the new wines have taken a sharp upward turn. There is a Chardonnay made from Carneros grapes, but the Cabernet Sauvignon and a Meritage blend called Elevage are the main attractions and are often superb.[1] Chimney Rock is a wine to age for ten to fifteen years.

## CLOS DU VAL
*See* Chapter 9, page 130.

## HARTWELL VINEYARDS
5795 Silverado Trail, Napa CA 94558. Tel: 707 255 4269; Fax: 707 255 4289; Email: hartwell@aol.com; Website: www.hartwellvineyards.com
Vineyards: 8ha

Robert Hartwell had been an avid wine collector for years before he bought his own vineyard in 1985. In 1990 he began making a small amount of intense, concentrated, but balanced and harmonious Cabernet. Production is now up to about 2,500 cases, made at the hillside winery which was completed in 1999. The wine clearly shows its Stags Leap origin. Typically, Hartwell Cabernet is elegant and supple, with potential for ageing in the fifteen to twenty year range.

## PINE RIDGE
5901 Silverado Trail, Napa CA 94558. Tel: 707 253 7500; Fax: 707 253 1493; Email: info@pineridgewinery.com; Website: www.pineridgewinery.com
Vineyards: 125.5ha

Founded in 1978 on the Silverado Trail in the heart of the Stags Leap District, Pine Ridge makes wines from several districts in Napa, including Rutherford, but the Stags Leap District tends to out-perform the others, in my opinion. The wine is true to the terroir, with a silky mouthfeel and a firm texture backed up by characteristic Stags Leap District fruit. There is also a luscious Stags Leap District Chardonnay, made in a ripe style.

1. Meritage is a name which is trade marked in the USA and refers to wine blends based on a French model. Reds are made exclusively from Cabernet Sauvignon, Cabernet Franc, Malbec, Merlot, and Petit Verdot. White Meritage blends use Sauvignon Blanc, Semillon, and Muscadelle.

## REGUSCI

5584 Silverado Trail, Napa CA 94558. Tel: 707 254 0403; Fax: 707 254 0417;
Email: info@regusciwinery.com; Website: www.regusciwinery.com
Vineyards: 26ha

Long time growers in the area, the Regusci family took the leap into
winemaking in 1995, restoring the historic Occidental Winery, the first
winery in what is now the Stags Leap District. They produce about 4,000
cases of wine, mostly Cabernet Sauvignon, but also some Merlot and
Zinfandel, all from estate vines. The Cabernet is outstanding, full-bodied
and powerful, but with a delicious underlying core of lovely fruit.

## SHAFER VINEYARDS

*See* Chapter 9, page 176.

## SILVERADO VINEYARDS

6121 Silverado Trail, Napa CA 94558. Tel: 707 257 1770; Fax: 707 257 1538;
Email: info@silveradovineyards.com; Website: www.silveradovineyards.com
Vineyards: 162ha

No Mickey Mouse jokes, please. Silverado Vineyards is owned by the
Disney family, but to their credit, you will not be greeted at the cellar
door by an oversized rodent or wise-cracking duck. What you will find is
outstanding Cabernet Sauvignon and Merlot. I must apologise because I
keep using the word "elegant" to describe Stags Leap District red wines,
but there is simply no getting away from it, and Silverado Vineyards has
a lock on that style. The wines taste good from the beginning and they
keep getting better for years and years, especially the reserve Cabernet.
The Merlot is also superb, supple and harmonious. The winemaking
team, led until recently by Jack Stuart, lets the site speak for itself and it
fairly sings. You can't possibly go wrong here.

## STAG'S LEAP WINE CELLARS

*See* Chapter 9, page 184.

## STAGS' LEAP WINERY

6150 Silverado Trail, Napa, CA 94558. Tel: 707 944 1303; Fax: 707 944 9433;
Email: Kathy.Nelson@BeringerBlass.com; Website: www.stagsleapwinery.com
Vineyards: 36.5ha

This historic vineyard and estate is now owned by Beringer Blass, the
Australian-Californian conglomerate. The winery was originally part of

the Chase family Stags' Leap estate in the mid-nineteenth century. They sold it in 1909 and for many years it functioned as a vacation hotel, although the vineyards continued to produce. During Prohibition, Petite Sirah was planted, known in California as "petty sir". A thick-skinned grape, it was a favourite in the 1920s and 1930s because it could withstand shipment to the east coast for use by home winemakers (*see* Appendix IV page 256–7). In World War II, the estate was used by the USA Navy as a rest area. After the war, it was more or less abandoned, but in 1970, a group of partners headed by a local businessman, Carl Doumani, brought the property and began replanting the vineyard – retaining some of the old-vine Petite Sirah. Over the years, it has been the often berated "petty sir" that has been the strongest entry from Stags' Leap Winery. It is capable of long-term ageing, although there is some question, at least in my mind, on whether Petite Sirah improves in the bottle or simply survives. Beringer Blass is putting a great deal of money and effort into the winery and I would expect improvement in the near future in the Cabernet Sauvignon and Merlot bottlings.

## STELTZNER VINEYARDS
5998 Silverado Trail, Napa CA 94558. Tel: 707 252 7272; Fax: 707 252 2079; Email: wines@steltzner.com; Website: www.steltzner.com
Vineyards: 40.5ha
Richard Steltzner planted his first vineyard in 1966 and was well known and respected as a grower and vineyard manager before he began to make wine in 1977, working in leased space in other wineries. In 1983 he built a small winery, making estate Cabernet from Stags Leap District grapes and a very good Sauvignon Blanc from a vineyard he owns in the Oak Knoll District near Yountville. His Cabernets can sometimes be very tannic, perhaps too tannic although some say they are capable of long ageing. Since the late 1990s, Steltzner has begun to back away from the overwhelming in-your-face style and, for my taste, the wines have become considerably more interesting.

## WILD HORSE VALLEY
Wild Horse Valley is very obscure AVA located mostly in Solano County east of Napa, with a couple of bumps sticking out into Napa. The AVA was granted in 1988. There are a total of 1,335 hectares in the appellation

with only a few hundred hectares, mostly on hillsides in the Vaca range, planted to vines. The AVA is completely outside Napa River drainage. The soils are mostly volcanic on the hillsides, rocky and low in nutrients.

The region lies directly east of the town of Napa and about nine kilometres (six miles) northeast of Carneros. The Tulocay Winery made a dense and generally good Zinfandel from a hillside vineyard in Wild Horse Valley, but those vines have since been pulled and replanted to Cabernet Sauvignon and Merlot, damn it. Heron Lake Winery makes Pinot Noir and Chardonnay.

Wild Horse has, without doubt, the potential to produce very good wines, but to this point, no one has stepped up to do the work. The AVA is sometimes confused with Wild Horse Winery, which is in Paso Robles County on California's Central Coast.

## YOUNTVILLE

Yountville was where it all started. George Yount was a burly mountain man who helped General Mariano Vallejo tame what remained of the savage heart of Napa. He was awarded a forty-six square kilometre (eighteen square mile) Mexican land grand for his efforts and planted the first European vines in Napa in the late 1830s. Today, the town of Yountville is well known as the place where the four-lane highway ends and on busy summer weekends, traffic starts creeping north on Highway 29. (Don't even think of making a left turn unless there is a turning lane.)

As you approach the town of Yountville, there is a large sign advising day trippers that they can visit "forty shops and taste wine" at the next exit, which some cynics suggest is the real "Welcome to Napa" sign. A few yards on down the road there is a much smaller sign advising the true wine buff that the grave of George Yount can also be visited.

It's hard to guess what Yount might have thought of being able to visit forty shops within a few hundred metres of his grave. Being a go-ahead kind of guy, he probably would have thought it was a grand idea and asked where he could invest. After Yount, things were a little slow. There was more activity to the immediate south in what is now the Oak Knoll District, and to the north in Oakville. When the first wave of phylloxera hit Napa in the 1890s, there were under 810 hectares of vines planted in the district. This had dwindled to a few hundred hectares after Prohibition, when one was more likely to see walnut or fruit trees than vines. By 1997, when local wineries applied for AVA status, there were some 1,012 hectares of vines, doubtless an historic high. The AVA was granted in 1999.

Yountville is bordered by the Oakville appellation on the north, Stags Leap on the east, Mount Veeder on the west, and Oak Knoll on the south. Soils are a mixture of volcanic debris from the Vaca Mountains in the east, alluvial silt from the Mayacamas Mountains on the west, and marine sediment left behind when San Francisco Bay receded. This combination of volcanic and marine soils is unusual in Napa.

It's a cool growing area, with morning fog spilling over the Mayacamas as well as pushing north from the Carneros District. Like the other central Napa AVAs, it probably should have been divided into an eastern and western district, chiefly because of soil differences. Also in common with other AVAs that bridge the Napa River, there is a distinct difference in soil depth as you move back away from the river, either to the east or west.

Looking at Yountville's relatively cool climate, it is easy to guess that Chardonnay does well there. However, like the Oak Knoll District to the south, the Bordeaux varieties also come up tops in Yountville: an odd juxtaposition. For example, in the foothills along the Silverado Trail, Dominus Estate makes a supple and elegant red wine that could have stepped straight out of Pomerol.

Given the quality of Yountville grapes, it is a bit surprising that the area is best known for a shopping mall, but that is primarily because the majority of the grapes are sold to wineries outside the appellation. There is not a strong "Yountville" image, compared to some other Napa appellations. In the long run, I believe the quality of the grapes will be regarded as at least equal to the best of the Oakville AVA.

## The Best of Yountville

### DOMINUS ESTATE
2570 Napanook Road, Yountville, CA 94599. Tel: 707 944 8954; Fax: 707 944 0547; Email: info@dominusestate.com; Website: www.dominusestate.com
Vineyards: 50ha

The winery was founded in 1982 by a partnership consisting of Robin Lail and Marcia Smith, the daughters of John Daniel of Inglenook fame, and Christian Moueix, winemaker and director of Château Pétrus. In

1995, Moueix became the sole owner. The fifty-hectare estate was originally planted in the 1880s and came to be known as Napanook. It was the source of grapes for the great Inglenook Cask Cabernets of the 1940s and 1950s. There are three main soil types on the estate: volcanic, heavy clay, and loam. In replanting, a great deal of attention was paid to selecting the right rootstock and varietal to fit the soils. The wines, typically about seventy per cent Cabernet Sauvignon with the rest Cabernet Franc, Merlot, Petit Verdot, and Malbec, have been somewhat controversial in California from the beginning. Many critics found them unbalanced and hard, especially in the early years. By 1990, the wines were on track, although still a little hard and tannic for some tastes. It is a wine that requires considerable bottle age to come around. In 1997, Moueix named Jean-Claude Berrouet from Pétrus as the winemaker and the wines have shown a huge improvement, becoming much more supple, but still with the complexity and structure for extended ageing. In 1996 Dominus introduced Napanook, a second label designed for early drinking and short-term ageing. It is a most agreeable wine and a pleasure to drink.

## GOOSECROSS CELLARS

1119 State Lane, Yountville, CA 94599. Tel: 707 944 1986; Fax: 707 944 9551; Email: wine@goosecross.com; Website: www.goosecross.com
Vineyards: 4.5ha

This family-owned winery just north of Yountville, beside the Napa River, is in transition from white to red, like much of Yountville. For several years, Goosecross made a very good Chardonnay from estate grapes. A few years ago, the Chardonnay was pulled out and replanted to red Bordeaux varieties with the aim of making a Meritage blend. The winery also makes a zesty and delicious Zinfandel, which is the only Yountville Zin. The Goosecross Chardonnay is still quite good; it is made using grapes from outside the AVA.

## WAITING IN THE WINGS

### Calistoga

Bo Barrett, co-owner and winemaker at Chateau Montelena is leading a move to create a Calistoga appellation. Barrett's proposal would create an

AVA of about eighteen square kilometres (seven square miles), including land on the valley floor and up to 365 metres (1,200 feet) in the Vaca Mountains and the Mayacamas Mountains. It would be bounded on the south by the St Helena AVA, on the east by Howell Mountain, on the west by Diamond Mountain, and end in the north at the Napa County border. A Calistoga AVA makes as much sense as many US appellations, although the range of soil types and elevations as proposed makes little sense. The area is best known for Cabernet Sauvignon, with some good Zinfandel as well.

## Pope Valley

This proposed appellation in the northeast corner of Napa is the hottest area in the Napa Valley AVA. It shares the same hot interior valley climate as southeastern Lake County. There are several hundred hectares of vines in Pope Valley, although no wineries worth mentioning are there. St Supéry and Flora Springs are among a handful of wineries that have vineyards there, with Cabernet Sauvignon being the dominant grape. Although Pope Valley is included in the overall Napa Valley AVA, it is outside the Napa River watershed and should never have been added to the basic AVA.

# 9

# The A List

I was looking for a phrase to define what I consider to be the top wineries in Napa. Obviously, I didn't want to go to anything like the Bordeaux classification, for several reasons. Perhaps the best reason is simply that there hasn't been enough time. The first *vinifera* was planted in Napa just over 150 years ago, with post-Prohibition plantings less than a century ago. There's no way I'm going to be foolish enough to put a Napa classification on paper.

Doug Shafer at Shafer Vineyards believes the future of Napa will centre on "great estate wine". I like that: Napa's Great Estates. It struck me as a more fluid, more flexible approach than a rigid classification system. So, like any working journalist, I stole the phrase and went about talking to Napa wine-growers and vintners about Napa's Great Estates. Almost everyone nodded wisely and was pleased to be included. Then I tried the phrase out on Agustin Huneeus at Quintessa.

"Who else are you including," he asked. I gave him a few names. Huneeus smiled that slow smile of his that means "Look out, sucker". He said: "None of those are estate wineries. They all buy in grapes. To be a real estate winery, all the grapes should come from your own vineyards. And none of that label bullshit about controlling the vineyards so you can call it an estate wine. The only way you can control a vineyard is if you own it."

A few days later, I was talking with Janet Trefethen, the co-owner of Trefethen Vineyards. According to Trefethen only about twenty Napa wineries make wine only from the grapes they grow. So if I accept Huneeus' definition of an estate and if Trefethen's numbers are anything like right, and they are certainly close to right, my "Great Estates" approach was in trouble.

It's a question that would hardly come up in France, where I believe the prevailing view would match that of Huneeus. Growers in France would generally sell their grapes to a cooperative or to a négociant. In California, there are more choices. First, you can produce an estate wine from vineyards that you own: the French model. Second, you can produce an estate wine from vineyards that you do not own but that you control. Exactly what "control" means is a little fuzzy and subject to sometimes whimsical interpretation. Are you confused? That is most likely what the bureaucrat who wrote the regulation in the mid-1980s intended. (Until then, estate-bottled meant that the vineyards had to be contiguous with the winery.) Third, you can bottle the wine as "vineyard designated" wine, no matter who controls the viticultural practices, so long as the grapes do indeed come from that single vineyard. Finally, you can take grapes from anywhere you want in the appellation and bottle it as a "Napa Valley" or "Carneros" or for that matter "California" wine, which is the handy appellation covering the entire state. In other words, a blended wine.

The system has an inherent conflict. The winemaker, we assume, wants the best possible grapes to make a wine in a particular style. Maybe the winemaker feels that to achieve his goal steps must be taken to cut the crop level or to use some other viticultural technique that is going to either add to the grower's farming costs or lower the grower's income in the case of a smaller crop. What to do?

Given the natural conflict between growers and vintners, there is a surprisingly high degree of cooperation – certainly more than one would expect with cash on the line. This is especially true in regions like Napa where it's all about quality. Also, contracts are now being written that give the winery the right to dictate certain viticultural procedures, like leaf pulling or dropping green crop. In return, the grower can charge extra for those services. Another approach is to pay the grower by the hectare, rather than by the tonne. This presumably gives the grower a fair return on the harvest, even if he is asked to cut the crop from, say, 5.5 tonnes to 2.7 tonnes per hectare. The growth of vineyard designated wines is another factor that can bring the independent grower and vintner closer together. If your vineyard name is on the label, you want the wine to be good. On the other hand, the vineyard name can take on such a cachet on its own that the grower might feel he doesn't need to heed vintner directions.

At any rate, despite positive gains in working together, there remains a certain tension between grower and winery which would obviously not exist under the French estate model. Which means that my Great Estates concept seemed to be sinking without a trace. What to do? Give it up, that's what. There are true estate wineries in Napa, and a few of them made my final cut, most didn't. But a bright light flashed when I realized that those final cut wineries that were my personal selection of Napa's "alpha wineries" – the top dogs, as it were. Thus, my A List. There are twenty-one wineries, but this number is purely arbitrary. It could have easily been thirty-five, but there must be a cut-off somewhere.

A number of factors went into my A List choices: track record; how long the winery has been making great wine (although in a few cases I ignored that); what impact the winery has had on the overall quality and direction of Napa wines; whether the wine represents the vineyards. But the most important factor was: does the wine taste good? Would I like a second glass? Finally, in what way does it qualify as a classic Napa wine? In the end, this highly personal selection is intended only as a sign pointing the way, not as something cast in stone. It is a rough sketch for a map that, at the moment, does not exist. At any rate, if you are a newcomer to Napa wines, I feel confident in recommending any of these twenty-one. If you are a Napa wine veteran, perhaps one or more of these twenty-one will help refresh your memory.

## BERINGER BLASS ESTATES
2000 Main Street, St Helena, CA 94574. Tel: 707 963 7115; Fax: 707 963 1735; Email: linda.hirashima@beringerblass.com; Website: www.beringer.com
Vineyards: 4,168ha

Beringer looms large in the history of Napa Valley and certainly deserves a prominent place in this or any other book about Napa wines. What makes it an even better story is that Beringer consistently delivers the goods. I've been tasting Napa wines for decades and I think Beringer is better now than at any time in the past thirty years. This, despite being largely under corporate ownership during that time.

To begin at the beginning, Jacob Beringer arrived in Napa in 1869, from Germany, via New York. He had worked in wine cellars in Germany and was also familiar with coopering. He got a job with Charles Krug and, with the help of his brother Frederick, who had stayed behind in

New York, put together enough money to buy a ranch across the road (Highway 29) from Krug's winery in 1875. A cellar was built and a tunnel was dug by Chinese labourers, so that by the end of the 1870s, Jacob was making 100,000 gallons of wine. Frederick joined him in 1884, building the imposing (some might say ostentatious) Rhine House on the property, a structure which is now familiar to countless thousands of wine tourists.

In the late nineteenth century, the Beringer brothers bought property on Spring Mountain and planted more vineyards, as they believed the wines from mountain vineyards were superior to valley floor wines. Beringer still makes vineyard select wines from several mountain sites. The reputation of the wines grew and the family continued to make wine right through Prohibition for sacramental use.

Following World War II, the quality of the wine declined, perhaps because of a shortage of cash, and the winery was eventually sold to the Nestlé corporation of Switzerland in 1970. At that point, most Napa wine people thought, "Well, there goes the neighbourhood". There has not been a happy history of multinational companies and California wine. They were wrong. Nestlé pumped the necessary money into the winery, acquired more vineyards, and hired an outstanding winemaker named Myron Nightingale to run the production side. Beringer's reputation soared throughout the 1980s and early 1990s, riding on the single vineyard mountain wines and the outstanding Reserve Cabernet wines. Nestlé sold the winery to a group of investors, known as Beringer Wine Estates in 1995. In 2000, Beringer was acquired by Foster's, the giant Australian brewers, and merged with Mildara Blass. It is now officially operated as Beringer Blass Estates. Through Beringer Blass, Foster's also owns Chateau St Jean, Windsor Winery, and Chateau Souverain in Sonoma; étude, Stags' Leap Winery, and St Clement in Napa; and Meridian Vineyards on the Central Coast. Beringer Vineyards is by far the largest property, with an annual production of 3.5 million cases and just over 4,000 hectares of vines.

I know what you are thinking: there's no way a winery of that size can make quality wine. You are so wrong. Beringer has done it by putting the right people in the right place and doing the right thing at the right time. For instance, Beringer was way ahead of the curve on the whole food and wine connection. Chef and writer Madeline Kamin was holding seminars and suggesting food and wine pairings at Beringer while other Napa wineries were serving chunks of processed cheese and stale bread to tasting room visitors.

In 1976, Nightingale hired a young winemaker named Ed Sbragia as his assistant. When Nightingale retired in 1984, Sbragia took over and has since pushed the Beringer wine profile ever higher. He is now known as the "wine master". In 1979, Nightingale made another good move, bringing in Robert Steinhauer to manage Beringer vineyards. I believe it is Sbragia and Steinhauer who are responsible for Beringer's high standing. They have an excellent working relationship, which is not always common between winemaker and vineyard manager. Perhaps because Sbragia's father was a grape-grower and home winemaker, it is a little easier for him to make the connection between grapes and wine, which some winemakers never see. Sbragia and Steinhauer have worked especially closely on the Beringer Private Reserve programme and the Vineyard Select wines.

It is in those wines that Beringer shines. The Private Reserve is made from several different vineyards, changing with the vintage. Sbragia says the Cabernet Sauvignon from each vineyard is so distinctive in character that it is almost like working with separate varietals, which gives him a larger canvas to work with. He began making the single-vineyard wines in 1994. Sbragia takes a minimalist approach to these wines, which are aged in new Nevers oak for about two years. "Oak can be as individual as grapes, and different coopers bring out different nuances just as winemakers do. Some barrels are spicier, some have more caramel and vanilla notes," Sbragia says.

In working with the single-vineyard wines, Steinhauer likes to call himself a "viticultural consultant" not a vineyard manager. Until 2003, he was in charge of all Beringer vineyards. Now he works only with Private Reserve vineyards and some Pinot Noir vineyards on the Central Coast. He sees an evolution in the single-vineyard wines as the vines adjust to the winemaking and the winemaking adjusts to the vines. In any given year, Sbragia and Steinhauer might make up to eight single-vineyard wines, including:

Bancroft Ranch, at an elevation of 550 metres (1,800 feet) on Howell Mountain. The soil is volcanic white tuff, very shallow, very infertile. The wine is powerful and concentrated with rich tannins, typical of the area.

Chabot Vineyard is in the St Helena AVA, just east of the Silverado Trail. The area is sometimes called Glass Mountain because of the shiny chunks of obsidian in the soil. Chabot has elements of mint laced through black cherry and blackberry fruit. Chabot was the vineyard that supplied the first Beringer Private Reserve in 1977.

Marston Vineyard is in the Spring Mountain AVA at about the 610-metre (2,000-feet) level. It has an earthy, mineral quality with soft tannins and a high fruit profile.

Quarry Vineyard is in the Rutherford AVA. Soils are volcanic and rocky, very low in nutrients. The wine is typically elegant, with dark fruit aromas and a touch of chocolate.

Rancho del Oso vineyards is near the Bancroft Ranch vineyard at the 550-metre (1,800-feet) level on Howell Mountain. Soils are red volcanic, as against the white volcanic soils of Bancroft. The wine is dense, with blackberry and ripe raspberry elements.

St Helena Home Vineyard is in a sloping alluvial fan. Steinhauer says the fruit characters, black cherries, anise, and spice, are the result of "perfect soils and the perfect climate for Cabernet". It is a key component of the Private Reserve wines.

State Lane Vineyard is in the Yountville AVA, the most southern of the Beringer Cabernet vineyards. Soils are shallow loam over a rocky gravel base. The wine tends to be somewhat fruit forward, with a ripe plum and spice character.

Steinhauer Ranch, the former Tre Colline vineyard is another Howell Mountain beauty. Soils are red volcanic and well drained. The wines are dense with an earthy-minerally edge and firm tannins. The vineyard was renamed in honour of Steinhauer's twenty-fifth year at Beringer.

## Summing up

Obviously, you come to Beringer for Cabernet Sauvignon and especially for the Private Reserve and vineyard bottlings. The Private Reserve is always near or at the top of Napa Valley Cabernet. It is, in many years, a very concentrated wine with a firm tannic structure, but Sbragia manages to maintain a balance and harmony beyond the concentration. The Private Reserve will age in the twenty to twenty-five year range. A Merlot from Bancroft Ranch on Howell Mountain is typically dense and tannic, with good ageing potential. Beringer also makes a Knights Valley

Cabernet from Sonoma grapes that is less intense than the Private Reserve. The Chardonnay can be a bit too oaky for my tastes, although when it is right it has a charming baroque richness. There are also two Pinot Noirs from Carneros and a promising Zinfandel made from Lake County grapes. Beringer makes at least two lines of budget wines, Beringer Founders' Estate and Stone Cellars by Beringer.

## CAKEBREAD CELLARS

8300 St Helena Highway, Rutherford, CA 94573. Tel: 707 963 5222; Fax: 707 967 4012; Email: cellars@cakebread.com; Website: www.cakebread.com

Vineyards: 61ha

I was standing at the top of the world with Bruce Cakebread. Or near enough to it that it didn't matter. We were talking about mountain lions and bears. It's hard to keep them out of vineyards, especially if the vineyard is on Howell Mountain, almost 610 metres (2,000 feet) above sea level and high enough above the Napa Valley floor to cause feelings of awe and exclamations of "Oh, Wow!". It's only the bears that eat grapes. Lions have the feline indifference to anything not flesh or catnip. "I wanted to have a look at the bear," Bruce explains. "He was knocking down every fence we put up, and if he didn't knock it down, he climbed over it. I thought: 'A bear like that, I've got to see'. So I came up here with my two dogs about two in the morning. Found some bear scat. It was still warm when I touched it. Suddenly, I thought, 'What in the hell am I doing here? Let the damn bear have a few grapes', and I hustled back to the truck". There aren't many wine-growing regions of the world where bears are considered a vineyard pest. But that's Napa.

Bruce is the son of Jack Cakebread, who founded the winery in 1973. Jack, who had studied photography under Ansel Adams, was in Napa on assignment, taking pictures for a book, when he stopped at the house of friends for lunch. He had truly fallen in love with the valley and happened to mention to his friends over lunch that if they ever wanted to sell their property, he would buy it. It turned out they did want to sell and Jack bought their ninety-one-hectare property, including an old house and barn, which became the first Cakebread winery. Jack's decision to move to Napa was not one of those "lifestyle" decisions: he was not a rich man looking for a trendy hobby. He owned a garage in Oakland. (How untrendy can you get?) It was just something he felt he had to do.

I've often thought that Jack's personality is reflected in the wines and how they have developed over the past three decades. Part visionary artist and part hard-nosed businessman, he recognized early on the importance of the vineyard. At a time when a lot of Napa growers were still planting Cabernet Sauvignon and Pinot Noir in the same vineyard – and maybe some Chenin Blanc as well – Jack began to seek out vineyards that represented a special character for a particular variety. Besides the Howell Mountain vineyards, the Cakebread family now owns benchland vineyards in Oakville and Rutherford, as well as Carneros in the south and Calistoga in the northern and warmer part of Napa.

The vineyards have been slowly pieced together over the years, with the caution of a businessman careful not to over-extend and the eye of an artist, shaping and adding nuance to the wines. The range of sites gives the winery experience in Napa terroir that most lack and it has been put to good use. Cakebread Cellars has never had the flash of some Napa performers, but over the years, the reputation of its wines has grown solidly to its present position as one of Napa's great estates, with the Sauvignon Blanc and three different bottlings of Cabernet Sauvignon getting special respect.

Bruce, who was the winemaker from 1979 until 2002, when he became president of the company, isn't one to use that standing as a signal to sit back and collect dividends. His new quest is nothing less than to change the way wine is being made in Napa and California. "I've come to realize that sugar maturity and grape maturity are different. In fact, they are barely related," Bruce said one afternoon as we walked through one of Cakebread's vineyards on the Rutherford bench. "I want to achieve grape maturity at lower sugar to hold down the alcohol level."

There are several reasons that alcohol levels have been creeping up in Napa. More powerful and "cleaner" yeast strains are more efficient at converting sugar to alcohol. The new round of disease- and virus-free clones may also be playing a role, producing grapes that are converting sunlight to sugar at a faster rate. However, the most important reason is "hang time". Hang time is wine-grower speak for letting the grapes go unpicked for as long as possible at harvest – thus "hanging" on the vine. Beginning sometime in the late 1980s, hang time became a mantra in California. Wine-growers explained that the longer a grape stays unpicked, the more concentrated the flavours become. Oddly enough, no one asked if concentration was what wine was all about. It was a good example of California-think in action. If a little of something is good, then lots more of it must be really good.

There is some value in the hang time theory. Certainly there was too much reliance in California on "picking by the numbers". Winemakers inevitably walked the vineyard with a refractometer in hand, checking sugar levels in the grapes, rather than tasting. They might taste, but if the numbers didn't support the taste, then the numbers were right. So hang time did make winemakers look at the maturity of the fruit, rather that just check the numbers. But on the downside, grape sugar levels do increase with longer time on the vine, which means that alcohol levels are also up. Twenty years ago, most Napa Cabernet was about twelve or 12.5 per cent alcohol. Today alcohol levels routinely go above fourteen per cent. That doesn't do anything good for the wine. It creates a hot feeling in the mouth and often a jammy unbalanced wine.

What Bruce wants to do is decrease the amount of time the grapes spend on the vine. "I'd like to see our Cabernet Sauvignon spend a shorter time on the vine. Now, it's typically 130 to 140 days from the middle of bloom to harvest. I would like to see that down to 115 to 120 days." Never mind the numbers. What Bruce is talking about is picking grapes that would yield a wine with more suppleness, more elegance than many of the overripe, concentrated monsters that score high with the critics but leave wine drinkers with a dried-out palate, wondering what hit them. "Alcohol is like putting peanut butter on a sandwich," Bruce explains, using a very American metaphor. "A little bit adds a nice texture and flavour, but if you add too much, all you taste is peanut butter." His goal is to show more complexity in wine, not more concentration. "I'm not looking for the big, ripe wines. I want softer tannins and suppleness in a wine that is mature but not overwhelming."

Bruce is very clear that his mission is based in the vineyard. He's looking at water management and control of sunlight to help shape grape maturity and thus wine profile. Another project is a study of soil micro-organisms and their interaction with the vine roots. These micro-organisms convert soil nutrients into food for the vines. As the soils change, the micro-organisms also change, affecting what nutrients go to the vine. Micro-organisms might well be the agents of terroir, controlling directly what elements in a particular site translate into the wine.

During a tasting, Bruce agrees that it is hard to distinguish between Oakville and Rutherford Cabernets from benchland vineyards. However the Oakville Cabernet is perhaps just a touch harder than the Rutherford wine, which in the vintage we were tasting was longer and brighter on the finish. In both appellations the big difference is between the west and east sides of the valley. There is, of course, a clear difference in the Howell Mountain Cabernet, which has much bolder fruit and offers more intense flavours. "What we are looking for is balance, no matter where the grapes come from. We are looking for graceful, elegant wine," explains Bruce.

## Summing up

In most vintages, Cakebread produces four Cabernets. The Napa Valley bottling is a blend of vineyards ranging from Carneros to Calistoga, usually with a good bit of Merlot in the blend. The wine shows black cherry fruit and has a well rounded and elegant structure. The Three Sisters Cabernet is made from three steep hillside vineyards just off the Silverado Trail. The soils in these sites are volcanic and rocky. The wine is typically the most concentrated of Cakebread Cabernets, with a firm structure and a blackberry-cassis range of flavours.

The Benchland Select Cabernet is a classic example of Oakville and Rutherford vineyards. It's typically a powerful but supple wine showing dark fruit, spiced with chocolate and dried herbs. The Vine Hill Ranch Cabernet comes from a single benchland vineyard in the Oakville AVA. It's a layered and complex wine with dark fruit and firm tannins laid over a silky texture and mouthfeel. Overall, Cakebread Cabernets show a balanced and supple profile. They are delicious when young but can handle ageing in the fifteen to twenty year range.

As well as Cabernet Sauvignon, Sauvignon Blanc has always been taken seriously at Cakebread Cellars. The grapes traditionally come from the estate vineyards in Rutherford, but are also sourced from vineyards in St Helena and Calistoga. The wine is produced after the Bordeaux model, with a bit of Semillon and Sauvignon Musque in the blend. The flavour profile is typically centred on citrus, shaded with fig and peach with a minerally edge. About twenty-five per cent of the wine is fermented in stainless steel, which adds a crisp, bright element to the finished wine.

## CHATEAU POTELLE

3875 Mount Veeder Road, Napa, CA 94558. Tel: 707 255 9440; Fax: 707 255 9444; Email: info@chateaupotelle.com; Website: www.chateaupotelle.com

Vineyards: 82ha

In 1980 the French government sent Jean-Noël and Marketta Fourmeaux to California on a mission to find out what was up with California wines. Their families had been in the wine business in France for generations and their mission was to report back on all aspects of winemaking in California, from the vineyard to winemaking philosophy. In short, they were industrial spies. In six months they tasted more than 2,000 wines. Then they decided their future was in California.

They returned to France to file their report, pack up their two young daughters and came back to California to stay in 1983. At first, they made wine in leased space, while they carried on an extensive search for vineyard land. They had decided that they liked the intensity and character of California mountain wines and when they found a property on Mount Veeder, at an elevation of 550 metres (1,800 feet), they knew they had found a home. They named the estate, which is located in a small valley, Chateau Potelle. The first harvest there was 1988. "When we came, most people didn't have a notion of how to grow grapes in the mountains," Marketta says. "Now the consumer is just learning that mountain wines don't taste like valley floor wines. Mountain wines are more focused, with a great density of flavour, a little more austere than valley floor wines. It takes the wines longer to open up."

Potelle's vines, in common with most Mount Veeder vineyards, face roughly east, so they don't get the intense afternoon sun of west-facing vineyards in the Vaca Mountains across the valley. Potelle's vineyards now total eighty-two hectares with nine different soil types, plus east, west, north, and south exposures, which obviously leads to great diversity in ripening and flavour profiles. I have been tasting Potelle wines on a regular basis since the first vintage and I've always found the underlying character to be supple and elegant; they are wines of harmony and balance. According to Marketta, this is achieved largely by the harvest decision. When the grapes are picked may well be the most important decision in the winemaking process. "I want to harvest when the tannins are ripe, but still keep depth and diversity in the wine," she says. "I want to keep the complexity of the grape. I don't want jammy wines."

The vineyards are farmed "naturally" but Potelle avoids the organic label. The couple wants to be able to intervene if necessary to save the crop but most of the farming practices are organic. The grapes are dry-farmed, an important element in reflecting the site. Grapes from each of the nine soil types are fermented separately. All Potelle wines are fermented by wild yeast. In explaining why they do not use commercial yeast, Jean-Noël uses the Potelle VGS Chardonnay as an example. "It grows on six different soil types. Each type of soil brings out different flavours in the grapes. If you innoculate with commercial yeasts you are making these terroirs uniform instead of enhancing their differences. You are basically standardizing your wines instead of enriching them from these differences."

Natural fermentation is also a very slow process in comparison with inoculated fermentation. The 1997 VGS Chardonnay was in fermentation for seventy-nine days, compared with a seven to ten day fermentation for innoculated yeast. "That extra length is critical to the quality and texture of the wine. The length of the fermentation allows all the ingredients and flavours to combine together to make a wine of more complexity, more roundness and richness. The finish of the wine is tremendous. Because of such a complete integration of flavours the wine stays with you forever," says Jean-Noël. Potelle wines are gravity racked and are never pumped. They are bottled unfiltered and in many cases unfined.

Chateau Potelle also makes wines from other areas. There is a vineyard on the Silverado Trail planted to Bordeaux varieties and a vineyard on the Central coast planted to Zinfandel and Syrah. The winery has, from time to time, made Zinfandel from Sierra foothill grapes. But it is the VGS bottlings that have put Potelle on the A List. (VGS officially stands for Very Good Stuff.) VGS wines – Cabernet Sauvignon, Chardonnay, and Zinfandel – are made only from Mount Veeder fruit. All of the VGS bottlings are capable of extended ageing, including the Chardonnay, which remains youthful and intense right past its tenth birthday.

## Summing up

Chateau Potelle Zinfandel has been my favourite for several years. It has typical mountain intensity, but at the same time is a charming wine, with rounded mouthfeel and a lingering finish. The VGS Cabernet has great complexity; it shows ripe fruit in the mid-palate and a long, layered finish with a pinch of smoke. The VGS Chardonnay is a stunning wine. It has good acidity and balance, well-integrated oak, and a rounded complexity on the finish. One of Napa's best.

## CLOS DU VAL

5330 Silverado Trail, Napa, CA 94558. Tel: 707 259 2200; Fax: 707 252 6125; Email:cdv@closduval.com; Website: www.closduval.com
Vineyards: 133.5ha

Bernard Portet and John Goelet founded Clos du Val winery in 1972. Goelet represented a group of investors that also owned winery property in Australia; while Portet grew up at Château Lafitte in Bordeaux where his father was the technical director. Goelet originally hired Portet to manage a château in Bordeaux that he was trying to buy. "When that deal fell through, he sent me to look for a place to build a winery in California," explains Portet. During a visit to California in 1970 Portet was impressed with the power and fruit of Napa Cabernet and Merlot, but believed it could be even better if made with more complexity, in a more balanced style, and with slightly less alcohol. In short, Portet wanted to make a Napa wine that would be more like a Bordeaux. Not that he ever tried to imitate Bordeaux, what he was after and what has been largely achieved at Clos Du Val is a Napa wine with the elegance and finesse of a great Bordeaux.

The story goes that Portet found the site where he believed he could make such a wine (he was a graduate in oenology from the School of Agronomy at Montpellier) during a sweltering hot day in Napa. He was driving down the Silverado Trail in the Stags Leap District when he felt a cool breeze. It was one of those "Eureka!" moments. The Stags Leap District had long been considered too cool to fully ripen Cabernet Sauvignon, although Nathan Fay had first planted Cabernet there in 1961 and a few brighter lights such as Warren Winiarski had realized that the area was good for something besides prune orchards.

The first Clos du Val Cabernet Sauvignon was made in 1972 from purchased Stags Leap grapes at Cuvaison Winery. Steven Spurrier thought the wine good enough to compete in the famous Paris tasting of 1976 (*see* page 26). It didn't win – in fact finishing eighth in a field of ten and behind all the Bordeaux starters – but just being there was enough to get Clos du Val off to a good start.

Three levels of wine are now made at Clos du Val. The Classic series –

Cabernet Sauvignon, Merlot, and Chardonnay – are popular blends of Napa Valley fruit. The limited production estate wines include Carneros Pinot Noir, Stags Leap District Cabernet Sauvignon, and Ariadne, a Stags Leap blend of Sauvignon Blanc and Semillon. The Reserve wines are made only in exceptional years. They include Cabernet Sauvignon and Zinfandel from Stags Leap and Chardonnay from Carneros.

Clos du Val is very near the southern edge of the Stags Leap District, the coolest part of the AVA. The vineyard is planted on gently sloping land, east of the Silverado Trail and well away from the Napa river. Soils are well-drained sandy loam with very little clay. There are several alluvial fans in the vineyards from ancient streams that drained off the Vaca Mountains to the east into the river, giving some sections of the vineyard an exceptionally high gravel content. These conditions naturally put a lot of stress on the vines and no doubt play a part in shaping the understated Clos du Val Cabernet style.

When he started Clos du Val, Portet's winemaking philosophy was radically different from that of most other Napa producers. "First of all, I was from a culture where wine was on the table every day. I couldn't conceive of making wine which was not complementary with food," he says. Another difference between Portet and his Napa colleagues at the time was the lack of connection in Napa between the vineyard and the wine cellar. With very few exceptions, most winemakers seldom saw the grapes until the day the fruit arrived at the crush pad. "I was trained as a winemaker in France, but before I learned about winemaking, I was taught viticulture. Here I found that the grapes were bought by the winery manager. People were amazed that I would go out and walk the vineyards," Portet recalls.

At the time he was establishing the distinctive Clos du Val style, many producers in Napa (and elsewhere in California) were insisting on 100 per cent varietal wines. There was the feeling that, somehow, if it wasn't all Cabernet it was a lesser wine. Portet begged to differ. "I was raised in Bordeaux where it is about getting the best blend possible," he says. "There is not the emphasis on variety that there was in Napa. I was intent on blending to achieve a more complex wine while they were trying to get varietal intensity."

I recall a seminar that Portet gave for the press in around 1980, in which he demonstrated that even apparently insignificant amounts of

Merlot could have an impact on the flavour profile of Cabernet. It is that kind of attention to detail which I believe has been an important factor in keeping Clos du Val very near the top of the list for Napa Cabernet. But Portet and his crew aren't content with the past. John Clews, director of winemaking, admits that he is pretty happy with the wines. "But we are making a few changes," he says. "We are looking at getting a little more Cabernet Franc in our estate Cabernet, along with the Merlot. We love the aromatics we get from Cab Franc grown in Stags Leap. It almost has a Chinon quality. It is such a lovely blending tool to use with Cabernet Sauvignon and Merlot," he explains.

Clos du Val is also one of the wineries taking a closer look at Merlot in the Carneros AVA, where some very interesting examples are showing up, despite the cool climate. The winery already has a considerable presence in Carneros, where it has Chardonnay and Pinot Noir vineyards. The Clos du Val Pinot is a particularly charming expression of that varietal. It is planted on hillside vineyards in very poor and shallow soils (rather an oxymoron when talking about Carneros vineyards) only about five kilometres (three miles), from San Francisco Bay. As Pinot Noir has become more popular in California, some winemakers are pushing for a bolder expression of the varietal: more tannic with more dominant oak tones and a darker colour. Some of these new wave Pinots are being made by winemakers more accustomed to working with Cabernet – and unfortunately, the style seems to be catching on. But Clos du Val is clearly not buying into that approach. Its wines are elegant and drinkable with soft tannins. They are not, however, throwaway wines. They have a sleek underlying power that is quite attractive and are capable of ageing in the eight to ten year range.

Clos du Val Cabernets are true keepers. Wines from the 1970s are still drinking very well. The wines are fairly high in tannin, but the tannins are soft and the acid levels are high, which is one of the keys to ageing. Clos du Val keeps a large library of older vintages although Clews admits that frankly he is careful about who they were offered to. "I've found that very few Americans know what to expect from older wines. They look for fruit from the start, but older wines are more complex. The fruit is there and comes back, but it isn't obvious," he says. Old or young, Clos du Val wines are anything but obvious, a stylistic characteristic that has caused problems for those wine critics who prefer international fruit bomb wines. Clos du Val wines take a little time to get to know, but once you know them they are worth hanging out with.

## Summing up
Clos du Val Reserve Chardonnay is made from Carneros vines, is barrel-fermented and spends ten months in French oak barrels, seventy-five per cent new. Typically, the oak is hardly noticeable, coming through as a faint toasty layer under the creamy centre. It is a truly refreshing wine, capable of improving over five to seven years in the bottle. Carneros Pinot Noir is fermented in open-top stainless-steel tanks and aged twelve months in French oak, about one-third new barrels. It's a luscious wine with supple black-cherry fruit and aromas and a spicy edge. The Reserve Zinfandel is aged twelve months in oak, only twenty-five per cent new barrels. It's a lovely wine, silky and supple with a long finish, made in what is called a "claret" style to distinguish it from the monster Zins favoured by some. The regular bottling of Cabernet Sauvignon is made entirely from Stags Leap District fruit. Typically, about five per cent Cabernet Franc is in the blend. It is aged up to seventeen months in French oak, one-half new barrels. It's a subtle wine with the usual Clos du Val understated fruit on the opening. The finish is velvety and complex with layers of flavour. The Reserve Cabernet typically has slightly more Cabernet Franc in the blend and is aged five to six months longer in barrel with a higher percentage of new oak. It is, for sure, a powerful and rich wine, yet has a balance and elegance that sets it apart from most Napa Cabernet Sauvignon.

## CORISON WINERY
987 St Helena Highway, St Helena, CA 94574. Tel: 707 963 0826;
Fax: 707 963 4906; Email: mail@corison.com; Website: www.corison.com
Vineyards: 4ha

One morning I was sitting in Cathy Corison's small and strictly utilitarian office, tucked into a corner of the mostly finished Corison Winery on Highway 129 outside St Helena. Much of the room was filled by a long table with a few chairs around it. There were three Riedel decanters on the table and a scattering of letters and other papers, but no sense of clutter. There was a computer and fax machine, a telephone, and a few bottles. The tasting "room" was a small table wedged among the barrels just inside the door. Well, it doesn't take much room to taste Corison wines. There are two Cabernets and surprisingly, a delicious Gewürztraminer made from grapes grown in the cool Anderson Valley of coastal Mendocino County some 160 kilometres (100 miles) northwest. ("I love Alsatian wines," Corison explains.) That is, it doesn't take much room in a physical sense. Sensually, tasting Corison wines is a much larger commitment.

Corison's office was a place for working, not impressing and, in that, it echoed the rest of her winery, which was crowded with barrels and a snarl of hoses when I arrived. I had walked in just as a limousine turned up carrying four earnest wine pilgrims. (They had arrived strictly by appointment, no day trippers, please.) The winery itself was designed to look like a barn, to blend into the Napa grape-scape, although barns in Napa are quickly disappearing now. "We broke ground in the spring of 1999," Corison explains. "I was told the winery would be ready for the crush that fall. But it wasn't even close. We didn't have water or electricity. We had to rent a generator and run a hose from a house on the property. It still isn't really finished, but it works." But Corison is not the kind of woman to let little things like no lights or running water bother her. She arrived a few minutes late for our appointment. (I had resisted the temptation to peek at her computer screen.) "Sorry. I had to run to the lab," she said. An intense woman with an air of calm concentration, she wasn't at all flustered by being late. The truth is, I had arrived right on time for our appointment, to the minute. Not done in California wine country.

Corison's 1999 Kronos, made from the fruit of vines I could see when I looked out of her office window that morning, is one of the best Cabernets in Napa. There are four hectares of vines in the Kronos estate. They were just coming into leaf and had that gnarled, twisted look that old vines have when they are almost bare of green. "I bought this place for the dirt," she says – and she isn't talking about the kind of dirt you would take a broom to. The Kronos vines are Cabernet Sauvignon, thirty years old, and planted on a rootstock called St George. It's a rootstock that is seldom used now in Napa or elsewhere in California. Of course, Corison didn't buy her winery estate because it was planted on St George. Like she said, she bought it "for the dirt".

Kronos is on benchland, around sixty metres (a few hundred feet) above the Napa River. In general, these sites on the west side of the valley are stony alluvial soils with plenty of gravel. Treated properly, the vines in this stretch produce some of the most concentrated and intense fruit in Napa or elsewhere in California. The soils are shared by the Rutherford, St Helena, and Oakville AVAs in a narrow strip of land that runs right up the edge of the Mayacamas range. Kronos Cabernet expresses that benchland terroir in textbook fashion. Corison's second Cabernet, a blend of vineyards from the Rutherford and St Helena AVAs, is not as intense and brooding as the Kronos, but there is no doubt of its origins.

Corison, who got hooked on wine while a sophomore in college on her way to a degree in biology, is a Cabernet specialist and a Napa specialist. She has never worked anywhere else. She headed straight for Napa after getting a masters degree in oenology from UC Davis in 1978, starting as an intern at Freemark Abbey. (Corison doesn't make a big deal of it, but at the time, there was only one other woman working in the cellars of Napa Valley.) She spent almost a decade as the winemaker at Chappellet and was more-or-less responsible for putting it on the world's wine map. Although she doesn't like to call herself a consultant, she also made the first Cabernet Sauvignon at Staglin Cellars and was responsible for breakthrough Cabernets at York Creek and Long Meadows.

Corison's approach to winemaking is centred on respect for the vineyard. "I think of myself as a very traditional winemaker," she says. I like to walk the line between power and elegance, approachability and ageing. I want my wines, first of all, to be elegant, then aromatic and well focused. If it is handled right, benchland wine has a wonderful perfume." Corison thinks of wine as a living thing, with various ups and downs. "My wines can fool people because they are approachable when young and the tannins are soft. But they are built to age. Rutherford wines can be very long-lasting made the way I make them."

She is no fan of the high alcohol fruit bombs that seem to be showing up everywhere. "I don't buy into the ultra-ripe style. I think one very important decision is to learn to judge when grapes are ripe. It's something I've learned to do better over the years." There is already plenty of concentration in a properly ripe benchland Cabernet, but Corison does some extended maceration. "It's always a trade-off. With extended maceration you do lose fruit. There's no recipe for it," she says. As for filtration, Corison's philosophy is to filter as little as possible. "If a wine is properly made, it should be stable," she explains.

Corison makes 2,500 to 3,500 cases of wine a year, averageing about 400 cases of Kronos and 3,000 of the Napa Cabernet. "I have chosen over the years to keep it small," she says. "There is always pressure to grow, but there are many reasons to stay small. I'm much closer to the wine. I don't think I can work the wines right unless I stay close to them," she admits. "But in the end, I can't make wine any better than the grapes that come in."

## Summing up

Corison Cabernets have an underlying supple silkiness that is quite distinctive. They are juicy with a touch of olives and spice, lively and bright on the palate, and very drinkable young, but should be held for at least ten years (the Kronos longer) for maximum pleasure.

## DIAMOND CREEK VINEYARDS

1500 Diamond Mountain Road, Calistoga, CA 94515. Tel: 707 942 6926;
Fax: 707 942 6936; Email: info@diamondcreekvineyards.com;
Website: www.diamondcreekvineyards.com
Vineyards: 10ha

Al Brounstein, the founder of Diamond Creek Vineyards and the first person to plant grapes in the Diamond Creek appellation in modern times, is a self-admitted smuggler. In the mid-1960s he knew he wanted to plant vines in Napa. He didn't yet own land, but he was planning ahead. On a trip to France, he took cuttings from two *premier cru* sites in Bordeaux (don't ask, don't tell) and flew into Mexico with them. He then flew them into the US from Tijuana in his own plane. (I hope, for his sake, the statue of limitations has expired for vine smuggling.)

Those cuttings were the beginnings of Brounstein's ten-hectare estate vineyards on Diamond Mountain, which he began planting in 1968. He had bought a twenty-eight-hectare property the year before, going against the advice of many to buy property on the valley floor where it was "easier to farm". Brounstein wanted nothing to do with "easy" – he was after good wine. Napa pioneer Jacob Schram had led the nineteenth-century planting on Diamond Mountain, but no one had planted vines there after Prohibition. When Brounstein asked André Tchelistcheff and Louis Martini where to look for land to grow Cabernet Sauvignon, they sent him to Diamond Mountain. Good move.

When Brounstein bought the property it was heavily wooded and he had no idea how much was plantable. But it turned out that he identified three small sites that could be planted. Red Rock Terrace is a 2.8-hectare north-facing vineyard planted on red volcanic soil; Volcanic Hill is 3.2 hecatres planted on white volcanic ash; and Gravelly Meadow is planted beside Diamond Creek on, as you might guess, gravelly soil. Later on Brounstein planted a very small vineyard which he calls Lake Vineyard, and a few years ago he planted a 0.4-hectare Petit Verdot vineyard on a hillside above Lake Vineyard.

Rather than blending the grapes from the three basic vineyards, Brounstein wisely kept them separate and in 1972 made three different wines. Tasting his young wines, Brounstein realized that he didn't have just one Cabernet, he had three. After hosting some test tastings with the trade and press, he released those three Cabernets, rather than one, a bold move for the time. Brounstein made the decision because of his knowledge of French wines and his appreciation of the concept of terroir.

In the early years, Diamond Creek caught the imagination of wine consumers who wanted big, bold flavours with aggressive tannins. What they didn't realize was they were also getting keepers, wines that would age and develop beautifully in the bottle into graceful and supple Cabernets. Going into the 1990s, Diamond Creek's style evolved. The wines became rather more subtle and harmonious going in. This has won Diamond Creek new fans and for long-term ageing, the wines are likely to be better than the wines from the first twenty years.

At Diamond Creek Brounstein has brought an amateur's zeal to Napa Cabernet. His background was in the pharmaceutical business, so his interest in wine was that of the passionate wine drinker. He was, in a sense, one of the first of the "lifestyle" Napa vintners, a group that has got a bad rap in the 1990s. Brounstein does have some of the quirkiness one sees here and there in that group. He has made the estate into a very pleasant sort of park. The kind of place one would have expected a slightly eccentric eighteenth-century English country gentleman to create. He has engineered two small lakes and about a dozen waterfalls, as well as planting thousands of roses and other flowers. (I looked, in vain, for a faux Roman ruin folly.) In later years he has even turned to painting, creating the labels for the 2002 wines as a thirtieth anniversary token.

But despite the rather charming and endearing frills, Brounstein is the first to admit that it all starts with the dirt and the microclimate of the canyon setting for Diamond Creek. There is a gap in the Mayacamas range that allows cool Pacific breezes that have moved inland up the Russian River Valley in Sonoma to break through in the late afternoon, creating cool nights which keep acid levels up. Soils are chiefly volcanic, with gravel near the creek.

Wines from Red Rock Terrace tend to be the most accessible of Diamond Creek's bottlings, featuring velvety tannins with fruit centred on cherry and blackberry. Gravelly Meadow is a cooler site and is the lowest yielding of the vineyards. The wines have an earthier aspect with riper fruit that can tend toward jammy, but is always intense. Volcanic Hill wines can be austere and withdrawn when young, but they age the longest of any, with deep flavours that are long lasting and elegant. Occasionally, a separate bottling is made from tiny Lake Vineyard, which is the coolest vineyard on the property. In a warm growing season, it yields wines of exceptional quality, supple, balanced, and long lasting. The younger Petit Verdot vines are planted in a heat-trapping canyon above Lake Vineyard. Petite Verdot represents no more than two per cent of any of the bottlings. Harvest usually takes at least a month with as many as twenty passes through each vineyard.

Brounstein is not the winemaker, of course, and doesn't pretend to be. Jerry Luper was a consulting winemaker for many years and during that time he had a team of consulting winemakers. Perhaps this peer approach to the wines is one of the things that has kept Diamond Creek on a steady course over the years. It is not winemaking by committee – there is a winemaker on the spot who is in complete charge of day-to-day operations – but rather winemaking with an eye on the terroir. As Brounstein's wife Boots, who has been one of the winery's guiding spirits from the beginning, puts it, "They make sure we stay on track and stay true to the vines". The Diamond Creek style has evolved, as it should, but the unifying vision has always come from Brounstein. At eighty-plus and slowed somewhat by Parkinson's Disease – he would vehemently deny that he "suffers" from Parkinson's: he doesn't suffer from anything – Brounstein is still clearly "the guy in charge".

His vision of a terroir-based winery, with a nod to Bordeaux, has extended to his pricing policies as well. Diamond Creek was the first California winery to break the $100 per bottle price in 1987. At the time, there was something close to outrage in the trade press that anyone would have the effrontery to price a California Cabernet at the same level as First Growth Bordeaux. Now, of course, the field of $100-plus California wines is rather too crowded. However, Diamond Creek remains one of the few that can justify that price.

## Summing up

Diamond Creek wines are one of the best buys in Napa for long-term ageing, twenty years and beyond. Vintages from the early 1980s were reaching maturity in 2000. Vintages from the 1990s will be drinkable earlier, but I would anticipate that a wine from, say, the great vintage of 1995, should reach peak form by 2015 or a few years later. Given only moderate ageing time, perhaps five to eight years, Diamond Creek wines take on an elegance and suppleness that is astonishing. Also, even after a decade or more in bottle, the separate vineyards do retain their individuality, expressing the site.

### DUCKHORN VINEYARDS

1000 Lodi Lane, St Helena, CA 94574. Tel: 707 963 7108; Fax: 707 963 7595; Email: welcome@duckhorn.com; Website: www.duckhorn.com
Vineyards: 71ha

When Dan and Margaret Duckhorn founded Duckhorn Vineyards in 1976 it was the thirty-eighth post-Prohibition winery in Napa. You could say the Duckhorns have grown along with the Valley, but their growth has been focused. The first wines were a Merlot and a Cabernet Sauvignon, but the winery now has four Merlots, five Cabernet Sauvignons, a Sauvignon Blanc, and a declassified wine called Decoy, as well as a Napa Valley proprietary red wine called Paraduxx. (One is tempted to make jokes about the Duckhorns going quackers, but best not.)

All told, Duckhorn owns about seventy-one hectares of Napa vineyards up and down the Valley, which supply more than half of the winery's grape needs. Duckhorn makes a blended Merlot and a blended Cabernet Sauvignon which both have the basic Napa Valley appellation. One step up from those are the Estate Grown Merlot and Estate Grown Cabernet. There are three single-vineyard Cabernets: Patzimaro Vineyard, Monitor Ledge Vineyard, and Stout Vineyard. Duckhorn also makes a Howell Mountain Merlot, which is representative of the appellation, and a single-vineyard Merlot, the justly famous Three Palms Vineyard.

All of this makes Duckhorn a very California-style operation, with wines blended across both a basic appellation (Napa Valley) and a sub-appellation (Howell Mountain), as well as vineyard-designated wines. Completing the picture, Duckhorn recently expanded north, with a Pinot Noir-only winery which is based in the Anderson Valley of Mendocino County. Both Dan and Margaret have a passion for Pinot Noir and believed they had to go outside Napa to make the kind of Pinot they wanted. The resulting wine is rather more dark and brooding than most Napa Carneros versions.

Beginning in the late 1980s, Duckhorn has followed a deliberate shopping policy of buying Napa vineyards, looking for distinctive properties to meet specific wine needs, looking at particular soil and microclimate. The vineyards are located on alluvial fans marking stream beds and on slopes at the base of Howell Mountain and Spring Mountain. Only one vineyard, the home vineyard or Marlee's Vineyard, is on the river. With its deep sandy loam soils, laid down by thousands of years of flooding, it is an ideal location for Sauvignon Blanc and Semillon. It is a bit of an oddity that Duckhorn's flagship wine, Three Palms Vineyard Merlot, comes from a vineyard they do not own. Other wineries, including Sterling Vineyards, also get grapes from Three Palms. Despite getting onto the single-vineyard trend early, according to Dan there is still a great deal of blending going on between vineyards, even for the estate wines. Duckhorn deals with about thirty-five growers for the basic Napa Valley blends and has its own farming company in place. "We ferment separate blocks and monitor them, down to as small as 0.2 hectares. What we are looking for is diversity of site which is the key to blending," says Dan.

With more than twenty-five years of experience in Napa – and that's not just surviving, but with a fairly high level of success – Dan has seen the region's wines change in ways that bother some producers. "The focus is now on concentration. It's all about concentration," he explains. "Viticultural techniques including hang time, how the wine is fermented, and treatment in the winery, are all aimed at greater concentrating. It's what the market is telling us to do," he admits, not looking too happy about it. It is brave and perhaps a little rash of Dan to admit that Duckhorn wines have changed in response to shifting market demands. But on the other hand, he is running a business. And there isn't much point in following your winemaking muse if she leads you to the bankruptcy court.

One could say the wines have evolved. There has not been an abrupt change that you can point to. The development in the wines could only be detected in a vertical tasting going back to the early 1990s. Perhaps, I suggest half-seriously, we need to include the market as a factor in the Napa definition of terroir? However you look at the proliferation of overripe, super-concentrated wines coming from Napa and elsewhere (and I, for one, tend to view it with alarm), it is changing the face of Napa wine, as Duckhorn acknowledges. "Everyone wants to be the next Screaming Eagle," he says, referring to the Napa cult wine, known for its great concentration and intensity – and its very high price. Duckhorn wines may be more concentrated now than they were a decade ago, but they are not over the top, maintaining balance and harmony within a more powerful structure. Another change Dan has noticed is that no one asks about ageing any more. "When we started, every time I did a tasting or a winemaker dinner, someone would want to know how long the wines would age. Now, no one seems to care. It's all about fruit."

Whatever has happened to the red wines, the Duckhorn Sauvignon Blanc has continued in a very agreeable Graves style. "We've been under a lot of pressure to move toward the grassy New Zealand style," says Dan. "We are swimming upstream with our style, but we will stick with it." Much of the fruit for the Sauvignon Blanc, which generally contains about twenty-five per cent Semillon, comes from the home vineyard, but grapes may be sourced from other parts of Napa, focusing on warmer sites with well-drained alluvial soils.

Duckhorn's decision to build a new winery, costing $14 million, for his Paraduxx brand, which has been made since 1994, was a bold move. The wine is an unusual blend of Zinfandel and Cabernet Sauvignon, with a little Merlot in some vintages. Typically, the blend tends to be roughly two-thirds Zinfandel and one-third Cabernet. The question of why do a Zinfandel/Cabernet Sauvignon blend does come to mind. Dan believes the fact that the blend is highly unusual, at least in modern times, is the great strength of Paraduxx. There are no parameters except to produce a good wine every year. The blend also gives Duckhorn a wine that in some respects stands outside the competitive cult Cabernet crowd – and it plays into an old Napa Zinfandel tradition. The name? An alternative spelling, if you will, of a pair of ducks. The label changes every year, with a different painting of two ducks.

## Summing up

Merlot is the prize winner at Duckhorn without a doubt. Though the Cabernet can be very good and is worth looking out for, and the Sauvignon Blanc is one of the valley's best. Paraduxx is something of a dark horse and I suspect as it moves out on its own it is simply going to get better and better down the line. But it's the Three Palms Merlot you want to put your money on. Typically, the Three Palms offers balanced tannins with ripe cherry and chocolate fruit, a splash of raspberry, and an earthy background. In many vintages it barely meets the legal definition of a varietal wine, which is seventy-five per cent because there is often a good bit of Cabernet Sauvignon as well as Cabernet Franc and Petit Verdot in the blend. It is a keeper, and should age in the fifteen to twenty year range, although it is generally accessible when younger. Three Palms is aged in new French oak for about twenty months.

The Howell Mountain Merlot takes a somewhat different approach. In most years, it is a more powerful, full-bodied wine with more obvious tannins and darker fruit with a spicy chocolate edge. In most years there is a significant amount of Cabernet Sauvignon in the blend. It is not as approachable as the Three Palms, but should age in the same range. It spends about twenty months in all new French oak. The Estate Grown Merlot is a pretty wine, with integrated tannins and a silky mouthfeel, reflecting good Merlot varietal character. Most years there is a good Cabernet Sauvignon, in the range of about fifteen per cent, in the blend. You can drink it young but it will be more complex and rewarding five to eight years from vintage. It also is aged in new French oak for eighteen to nineteen months.

Of the Cabernet Sauvignon portfolio, Dan has recently been making two vineyard-designated wines. The Patzimaro Vineyard is in the St Helena appellation at the base of Spring Mountain. Because of cool night winds off the mountain, following fairly warm days, the acidity levels stay high, leading to wines that show a supple balance and pleasing elegance. The Monitor Ledge Vineyard Cabernet Sauvignon is in the alluvial fan of Selby Creek, more or less on the valley floor off the Silverado Trail in the warmer northeastern part of the valley, near Calistoga. Soils are gravelly and very lean which leads to intense fruit and wine with a tight structure. The Duckhorn Estate Grown Cabernet Sauvignon is a wine for early drinking, with ripe fruit and soft tannins. In any given year, as many as thirty lots of wine go into the blend.

Decoy, Duckhorn's second label, is a terrific everyday good value wine. The varietals change with each vintage, but are based on Cabernet Sauvignon, Merlot, Cabernet Franc, and Petit Verdot, blended from declassified wine from young vines, experimental lots or other wines that don't make the cut into the higher priced programme.

## DUNN VINEYARDS
805 White Cottage Road, Angwin, CA 94508.
Tel: 707 955 3642; Fax: 707 955 3805
Vineyards: 8ha

Randy Dunn was the winemaker at Caymus Vineyards from 1975 until 1985. During that decade he made some of Napa's greatest Cabernets, including a series of legendary Caymus Special Selection. "I learned one very important thing while at Caymus," says Dunn. "Keep it simple. When I started they were making about 7,000 cases of wine. When I left they were up to about 100,000 cases. I decided when I left, I didn't want to get big." Dunn has been true to his decision. His production level at Dunn Vineyards has been at about 4,000 cases for many years. "I figure I could double that without losing quality, but I'd rather have the time for living," he says.

Sitting on an aluminum beer keg outside the door of his wine tunnel – Dunn refuses to call it a *cave* – at his winery and residence high atop Howell Mountain, Dunn states: "It takes a lot of beer to make good wine." There's a California truism. It is a cool, windy day on the mountain. To the west, across the lowlands of Napa Valley, you can see fog hanging in the redwood canyons of the Mayacamas range that separates Napa from Sonoma. To the east, but for a slight early summer haze, you could see the hilly edges of California's Great Central Valley. From this vantage point, you can also see part of Dunn's eight hectares of vines, as well as a mixed hardwood and conifer forest, a small pond, and a field where Dunn and his son are laying irrigation pipes and preparing a vineyard to plant Petite Sirah.

The winery isn't really hard to find. That is, if Dunn decides to fax you a map. To say he doesn't encourage visitors is a vast understatement. He has been known to hide in the old barn when unexpected visitors arrive. There are no signs anywhere, either on the main road or the shared driveway that give any clue to the aspiring visitor that he or she is anywhere near Dunn Vineyards. As you turn up the one-lane drive, there is a huge Valley oak on the left, with a tire swing, an American icon of the 1950s posing for a Norman Rockwell painting; a little further on there is a bocce ball court, perfectly laid out and well used.

Dunn's house is next left and beyond that is the winery itself. To those accustomed to the ego-boosting structures of Napa Valley, it would be hard to believe this was the home of one of the best half-dozen Cabernets in Napa. There is little evidence of a winery beyond six stainless-steel tanks housed under a series of steel arches topped with plastic sheeting. Then you see the heavy redwood doors of the wine tunnel, where Dunn Vineyards Cabernet is quietly ageing in barrel. Near that are the remains of an old structure, made of stone and redwood, that was built in the late 1800s as a stage coach stop, although no one knows where the stage started or where it was going. Perhaps over the mountain from St Helena to the community of Berryessa, now drowned under a reservoir. This structure, called the White Cottage, was Dunn's first bonded winery and home until he had the tunnel dug and built the house just up the hill, where he lives with his family. When you can find Dunn, he will usually be in the vineyard or in the cellar, or sometimes sprawled under a tractor, making repairs. He's mid-sized with a bristly white moustache, typically wears a white cowboy hat and, yes, does ride horses. But he also flies a twin-engine turbo-prop plane, sails, has a house on the Sea of Cortez in Mexico, and has lately taken up tennis.

When people talk about Napa lifestyle these days, they usually refer to multi-millionaires who have made way too much money in the computer business, or real estate or some other non-wine related enterprise, who are attracted to Napa for the obvious reasons, and sometimes even make good wine. Dunn is in Napa because he loves the place and he loves good wine. His pickup truck has a bumper sticker reading: "I am a tree-hugger and dirt-worshipper". Dunn is all about wine.

The particular day I visited, he had just closed a deal on twenty hectares of timbered land a few miles away near the modest town of Angwin. The sale came with a state-approved plan to clear cut the timber and a vineyard consultant's estimate that some nine or ten hectares were plantable for a vineyard. Dunn doesn't intend to cut a single tree or plant a single vine. Once all the paperwork is finished, he will establish the parcel in a land trust that cannot be developed. The cynical would say that the deal provides a good tax break for Dunn, which is true. But the fact is, Dunn really is a tree-hugger. When I asked how he came to his mountain top, I was expecting him to launch into a lecture on soil types and microclimates. Instead he explains: "It was such a pretty spot. And I thought it would grow nice grapes". How's that for deconstructing the hi-tech California approach to winemaking? In a somewhat more conventional mode, Dunn points out that mountain grapes yield a more intense and long lasting wine that grapes from the valley floor. "That is," he added, "if they are made right". As for the soils, Howell Mountain is mostly red volcanic soils, well drained, and low on nutrients. His 5.2 hectares of vines are split between several small sites, all on his property, planted at about the 610-metre (2,000-foot) level.

Dunn makes two wines, almost entirely Cabernet-based except for a small amount of Petite Verdot. His Napa Valley bottling was originally made from bulk wine and is now made from wine that doesn't make the cut into the higher-priced Howell Mountain bottling. His winemaking approach is highly traditional, more easily described by what he doesn't do that what he does. He doesn't sort the grapes in the winery because, as he puts it, "they are sorted in the field. I don't pick bad grapes". There is no cold soak and no long maceration. When the young wine is dry, it is taken off the skins. This is of course, contrary to the long maceration model so common in Napa, and elsewhere, designed to "soften" the tannins. "What they call 'tannin management', whatever that means," Dunn mutters. He does adjust for acidity because he doesn't like flabby wines, what he calls "new generation" wines. "There are people who claim they can tell if you hit a wine with acid, that's bullshit. You can't tell unless it's done wrong," Dunn maintains. But Dunn doesn't do much wrong. The proof is in the bottle.

## Summing up

Dunn's Howell Mountain Cabernets are deeply concentrated, ripe but not overripe, with the briary toughness of mountain wines, balanced by massive fruit, all wrapped around a supple backbone that promises long ageing. For all that, they are most certainly drinkable when young and it can be a struggle keeping the corkscrew away from them. If you do manage to hide a few bottles away, they will be drinking very well at any time in the next twenty-five years. The Napa Valley bottling is typically somewhat softer.

## FORMAN CELLARS

1501 Big Rock Road, St Helena, CA 94574. Tel: 707 963 3900;
Fax: 707 963 5384
Vineyards: 27ha

Forman Cellars appears to have been carved out of solid rock about 180 metres (600 feet) up Howell Mountain. There are piles of rock beside the vineyard, walls made of rock, a tasting room of rock – visitors are not especially encouraged – and a barn made of rock. All the rocks were blasted out of the hillside with dynamite, according to Ric Forman, one of a handful of winemakers who changed Napa wines in the 1970s. There are more famous winemakers, but in any serious discussion of Napa wines, Forman's name is sure to come up.

Forman came out of UC Davis with great recommendations from his professors. He worked for a year at legendary Stony Hill and spent a year with the upstart Robert Mondavi. He was the first winemaker at Sterling in 1969. The owners of Sterling had hired him in 1968, but then sent him to Bordeaux and Burgundy to give him a wider knowledge of wine than he had gained at UC Davis. It was a master stroke. "I came out of Davis a complete techie," says Forman. "That visit to France opened my eyes."

Forman Cellars is the winery he started in 1978, the year he left Sterling. In his vineyard dark red trunks of madrone trees and gnarly branches of California Coast oak grow right to the edge of the vines. "When I found this place, it was all overgrown with shrubs and trees," says Forman. "There had been a vineyard here before Prohibition and some of the old vines were still alive." Those vines were Zinfandel, planted on five by five spacing, which told Forman that under the rocky surface there must be gravel to enable the vine roots to go deep in search of water, as the early Napa mountain vineyards were never irrigated. Sure enough, the old vineyard had been planted on a deep alluvial fan of gravel. Forman speculates that it may have been an ancient river, flowing from springs on Howell Mountain down to the valley floor. Forman decided to go his own way after putting in two years with Sterling when it was owned by Coca-Cola (it's now part of the Diageo empire). He has done some consulting but has mostly concentrated on his own estate vineyard, which is at the eastern limit of the St Helena appellation. He also owns a vineyard in Rutherford AVA which makes an extraordinary Chardonnay.

There is nothing particularly unusual in Forman's approach to winemaking. He's still techie enough to shun wild yeast fermentation. He agrees that modern yeasts may be too efficient at doing their job, converting sugar to alcohol, but doesn't like the stuck fermentations and "off flavours" from wild yeasts. He also filters the wine, rejecting the popular unfiltered trend, believing that filtered wines age better. (Ageing is very much on Forman's mind when he makes wine. Anyone who has tasted some of the early vintages of Sterling would be aware of that.) Fining is with egg whites.

It's what happens before the grapes get to the winery that really shapes the profile of Forman's wine. Forman has only a small staff and personally goes through the vineyard ten or eleven times a year. He may be shoot thinning one time, dropping green crop another time, or repositioning the vine shoots another time. There's always something going on where wine grapes grow, and all that time among the vines certainly pays off in the wine.

The estate vineyard is planted to Cabernet Sauvignon, Cabernet Franc, Petit Verdot, and Merlot: all go into Forman's basic blend. Like most other quality-oriented growers, he aims at a yield of just under seven tonnes per hectare, although he cautions that low yield alone is not always the sign of quality grapes. "If the vineyard is diseased or otherwise improperly farmed, low yield is not an indicator of high quality wine." Forman looks for balance and elegance in his wines, somewhere midway between the more assertive even tough mountain wines and the lush valley floor wines. Why do Forman wines taste good when young, but also age gracefully, developing an intense bottle bouquet and rich round-ness after several years? He seems bemused by the question. "It's the soil. Wine comes from the soil. If wine loses that sense of place, we have lost it all," he answers.

## Summing up

Forman Chardonnays are one of Napa's secret pleasures. Like his red wine, the Chardonnay is built to last, with a crisp acidity unmarred by malolactic fermentation. Again, like the red wine, it is delicious when young, somewhat Chablis-like, but ages into a more complex and dense wine after five to ten years in the bottle. Forman's red wine will, in most cases, continue to improve in the bottle for about twenty years. Going in, the younger wines are intensely perfumed, with bright cherry fruit, a touch of chocolate, and soft tannins with an underlying herbal and underbrush quality that is reminiscent of the best Bordeaux. There is also a second label called La Grande Château Roche, quite a fitting name for a wine coming from Forman's rocky terroir.

## FROG'S LEAP

8815 Conn Creek Road, Rutherford, CA 94573. Tel: 707 963 4704;
Fax: 707 963 0242; Email: ribbit@frogsleap.com; Website: www.frogsleap.com
Vineyards: 32ha

Like a lot of other people, I was first attracted to Frog's Leap winery by the name and the official winery slogan: "Time's Fun When You're Having Flies". It didn't take long to learn that Frog's Leap co-founder John Williams not only has a sense of humour, he makes damn fine wine. There is a good reason for the name. When Williams arrived in Napa in the late-1970s from New York, he worked at Stag's Leap Wine Cellars. (Later he worked at Spring Mountain.) In 1981, with his partner Larry Turley, he "borrowed" grapes from Stag's Leap and made 700 cases of Zinfandel and 700 cases of Sauvignon Blanc at an historic Napa property called the Red Barn. In the late 1880s, the Red Barn was a commercial frog farm, supplying the restaurants of San Francisco. The Red Barn had also been a winery, dating back to 1884.

Just to show how far the sloganeering frog jumped, Sauvignon Blanc and Zinfandel are still the best of Frog's Leap, according to some critics. Sauvignon Blanc makes up about half of total production. (Williams and Turley split the partnership in 1994 and Turley started his own winery, Turley Wine Cellars, *see* Chapter 10, page 220.) Williams farms several vineyards, besides the estate vines, in the Rutherford AVA, including four on the fabled – some say mythical – Rutherford bench area west of Highway 29. There is also a Frog's Leap-farmed vineyard in what Williams calls the "eastern bench" which is warmer and has heavier soils with some clay content that Williams believes is ideal for Merlot.

Williams is a strong advocate of organic farming, which he believes leads to healthy vines and, in the end, to wine that simply tastes better. "I am fond of using the example of my health as a metaphor for healthy wine-growing," he says. "I believe that growing a healthy vine is much like taking care of your personal health." He argues, and his wines seem to support him, that the use of herbicides and commercial fertilizers kills the microbial complex of life in the soil. He is also retraining his vineyards to dry-farming, cutting out irrigation altogether. He points out that Napa Valley gets eighty-one to ninety-one centimetres (thirty-two to thirty-six inches) of rain annually, which he claims completely satisfies the water needs of the vines. By not irrigating, Williams believes the vines' roots are forced to go deeper into the soil, pulling up nutrients that are locked away far below the surface. Modern drip irrigation does tend to create a small and sometimes saturated zone of moisture near the surface and vine roots huddle around that zone, much as if they were grown in a large pot. Williams argues that the specific terroir of the site cannot really be known if the vines are irrigated. He also thinks it's just the right thing to do. "The world is running out of water. You can farm grapes without water. It was done for thousands of years."

Williams sees the vineyard and the wine in a holistic fashion that goes way beyond the bottom line. "We know that just being physically fit does not in itself guarantee overall health. You can work out day and night but if you're homeless, jobless, and your air and water are polluted, your prospects for health are dismal. Thus with the vine," he explains. "Do your farm workers have housing and health care? Are you using too much diesel fuel in your tractors? Are you contaminating the ground water? In short – if the environment of farming around the vine is not healthy, it will be difficult to maintain a healthy productive vineyard. This is the concept of sustainable farming. Reduce, reuse, recycle, renew, retain, and revere – mantras at Frog's Leap." Williams has also begun to incorporate elements of biodynamic farming into his approach to the vineyard.[1] He uses the analogy of a pot with three legs:

1. Biodynamic agriculture developed out of the teachings of Rudolf Steiner, an Austrian philosopher in the 1920s. Although many of his theories seem completely whacko, to put in mildly, other aspects such as cover crops, composting, and developing special organically-based sprays have produced positive results in France and California. Jim Fetzer's Ceago Vineyards in Lake County and Benziger Vineyards in Sonoma County as well as Frog's Leap, Phelps, and Quintessa in Napa, have reported great success with biodynamics.

*If personal health or organic growing is one leg and environmental health or sustainable farming is the second – what is the third? In our lives we know that to be truly healthy and happy we must eventually consider our spiritual health. Believe it or not this is also true of plants and indeed all living organisms. Grape vines exist in a natural living stream that reflects from deep in their soil to the cosmos above. Biodynamic farming is one of the ways we are studying at Frog's Leap to learn more about the natural spiritual world of the living systems around us. Drawing on elements of homeopathy, using the natural cycles of the moon and the planetary alignments, and immersing ourselves in deeper undestanding of the farm as a living system can all lead to healthier vineyards. A pot that stands firmly on three legs.*

Willaims calls his approach "traditional farming". Many California wine-growers at least talk the organic game, but biodynamics is still thought to be a little bit too far "out there". Critics ask how the phases of the moon can possibility affect a grape vine in the Rutherford AVA? They seem, on the surface, to have a point. I wonder, though, if you look deep enough at the concept of terroir, at what really shapes the flavour profile of a grape (or a tomato or radish for that matter), if at least the philosophy – if not all of the practices of biodynamics – might not have a role to play. That question certainly comes up when tasting Frog's Leap wines. What would they taste like if John Williams had never heard of biodynamics? There's no way of knowing. All we can really do is look at the wine in the glass and consider how it got there.

## Summing up

The Frog's Leap Sauvignon Blanc is a pure marvel, a fruit feast with style. Absolutely no wood is used in making this wine, nor does it go through malolactic fermentation. Utterly delicious as an apéritif and even better with food, it is close to being my favorite Napa Sauvignon Blanc. Maybe it is. The Chardonnay, made mostly from Carneros fruit, does have just a smack of oak; typically it is balanced and lively, with good varietal fruit. Among the reds, the top of the line Rutherford Red Wine is a blend of Cabernet Sauvignon and Cabernet Franc, usually about four to one. It is a massive wine, rich and impressive. The Cabernet has bright cherry fruit, usually spicy with a hint of mint. At its best it can be complex with layers of flavour. The Zinfandel is patterned on the classic California field blends, with Petit Sirah, Carignan, and Napa Gamay in most vintages. (The field blends were the result of Italian immigrants planting a mix of varieties helter-skelter through the vineyard.) It's a real treat. I hate to keep heaping on praise, but the Merlot is another winner, balanced and elegant with just enough tannic structure to keep it honest.

## ROBERT MONDAVI WINERY

7801 St Helena Highway, Oakville, CA 94562. Tel: 707 226 1395;
Fax: 707 251 4386; Email: info@robertmondaviwinery.com;
Website: www.robertmondaviwinery.com
Vineyards: 566.5ha

Robert Mondavi the winery runs a risk of being the victim of the success of Robert Mondavi, the man. (There is also an uneasy relationship with Robert Mondavi, the corporation.) In an odd way, Mondavi wines have been obscured by the publicity surrounding the winery founder. Many consumers (and some members of the wine trade as well) are so intent on the career of Robert, that the wines get overlooked. Or, even worse, they are made to jump through hoops that the competition is allowed to walk around. There is the somewhat snobbish attitude by some that because Robert has been such a public figure the wines somehow can't stand on their own. There's the unspoken question: if the wines are all that good, why does Robert have to work so hard to sell them?

Mondavi wines are also a moving target, something that some wine critics and others in the trade just don't get. Robert Mondavi wines have never fitted into a comfortable pigeon hole. From the beginning, Robert has restlessly experimented and taken his wines in a new direction. It's the nature of the man himself. If he had been a contented wine marketer in his early fifties, cheerfully selling the same wines that the family had been making for years at Charles Krug, he would never have broken with his brother to start his own winery. Always an innovative marketer, he became an innovative winemaker, or rather inspired his staff and later his son Tim Mondavi to be experimental and innovative.

I was present at a press event (there have always been too many of those) at the winery in around 1990, where Robert commented that maybe because he was getting older, he was finding his taste for wine changing. He wanted to drink gentler wines, more elegant wines. That represented a huge step back from Robert of the 1980s who seemed more interested in powerful, concentrated wines with lavish oak. He made and abandoned international fruit bomb, ninety-nine-point killer wines before the critics learned to love them. When he left them behind in the early 1990s, he also left the critics behind. However, at times, Napa wines of the Robert Mondavi Winery seem to have lost direction in a sea of corporate bottlings designed to increase cash flow rather that speak of quality.

There are encouraging signs that this drift is under control. A new cellar facility that was finished in time for the 2000 harvest is perhaps the best example of the direction Mondavi is going with the top tier of Napa wines, the reserve, appellation, and vineyard-designated reds. Planning for what the Mondavis call the To Kalon Fermentaton Cellar began in the mid-1990s. What the Mondavi team has done is take winemaking a few steps back. The cellar is gravity flow, straight out of the nineteeth century, which means no pumps are used in the movement of the wine. The grapes are delivered directly into 190-hectolitre French oak tanks. There are fifty-six of these fermenting tanks, which are made by French coopers, then disassembled and shipped to Napa for reassembly. Following fermentation, the wine flows down to the next level of the building and goes into small new oak barrels for finishing.

The wooden tanks are not intended to impart any oak character to the wine, rather the intention is to allow a slow micro-oxidation during fermentation and maceration which softens the tannins, adding structure and a supple depth of flavour and mouthfeel to the wine, and most likely adding ageing potential. A side-by-side tasting of the Reserve Cabernet, with one sample that was fermented in the oak tanks and another that was fermented in stainless steel, showed a remarkable difference. The stainless-steel sample seemed harsh and awkward compared to the oak-tank one, yet the grapes were picked from the same vineyard in alternate rows. The oak-tank wine was deeper and richer with a long silky finish. The stainless-steel wine seemed too brisk, too abrupt in comparison.

The costly construction of the To Kalon Cellar, with winemaking technology that was state of the art 200 years ago, was driven by a determination to find a way to capture the terroir of the To Kalon vineyard in the bottle. It is easy enough to make a perfectly acceptable masked and anonymous wine for the world market. It's quite another thing to try to put the essence of one of Napa's most historic vineyards in the wine. Is Mondavi on the right track with the back to the future approach? It's early on but the results are encouraging. Genevieve Janssens, director of winemaking at Robert Mondavi, has no doubt that the oak-tank wines will age longer and develop more complexity in the bottle, even though they are accessible sooner than the stainless-steel wines. "The programme is clearly working," she says. "It's giving us what we expected; complexity, elegance, and a better expression of the terroir."

To Kalon is a benchland vineyard located in the heart of the Oakville AVA. Mondavi, with 223 hectares planted, owns a good part of the original nineteenth-century site. The vineyard runs from the low outcrops of the Mayacamas range almost to Highway 29. It has good sun exposure with infertile, well-drained, gravelly clay loam becoming deeper and more alluvial on the valley floor. Cabernet Sauvignon is the dominant vine in To Kalon, followed by Sauvignon Blanc, Merlot, Cabernet Franc, Malbec, Petit Verdot, Semillon, and a little Sangiovese, Zinfandel, and Syrah.

It is only one of a number of outstanding Mondavi sites, but the Robert Mondavi Winery was slow to move into vineyard-designated wines. Tim Mondavi, one of the first in California to call himself a wine-grower, indicates that it was, at least in part, a marketing decision. Initially, it was necessary to establish Napa Valley, then the sub-appellations, and finally the vineyards. "We didn't want to take away from the overall Napa appellation," he says. We were discussing Mondavi's single-vineyard Pinot Noirs from Carneros, the PNX vineyards, and the Huichica (wee-CHEEK-ka) Hills vineyard (*see* Appendix IV page 250). Tim believes that making Pinot Noir taught him a lot about making Cabernet Sauvignon. "California winemaking lost so much during Prohibition," he says. "Most of the wineries had been closed or were in terrible conditions. The first order of the day to winemakers in the 1930s was simply to clean it up; to make sound, clean wines. The vineyards were somewhat overlooked."

That is an understatement. Vineyards were planted helter-skelter. Grapes were brought into the winery as they ripened and all treated exactly the same. The variety didn't matter: Pinot Noir, Zinfandel, Cabernet, all the same. Throw them in the crusher, put them through the same hot fermentation, put them through every imaginable filtration and bottle. You'd like some Pinot Noir? Of course, we can supply that, sir. No problem. Well, Tim didn't put it exactly like that. He actually put it a little stronger: "Winemaking techniques were brutal. Everything was treated the same." Things got a little better in the 1960s and 1970s but according to Tim, it wasn't until he really got serious about Pinot Noir that he realized the same gentle – and minimal – handling that worked for Pinot Noir might also be a good thing for Cabernet Sauvignon. I'm not sure when Tim got serious about Pinot Noir, but by the early 1990s, there was a noticeable improvement in Mondavi Pinot, which is about the same time Mondavi Cabernet started evolving into a more elegant, supple style.

One of the unexpected delights of the Mondavi line-up is the Fumé (Sauvignon) Blanc. When Robert built the winery in 1965 and the doors opened in 1966, he found himself with rather an abundance of Sauvignon Blanc. At the time, Sauvignon Blanc in California was often made in a slightly sweet style and was even more often tired and oxidized, having that in common with many California white wines of the 1960s. Aware of the excellence of dry Sauvignon Blanc from France, Robert hit on a marketing ploy. The story goes that he especially liked Pouilly-Fumé and decided it was a name that would fly in the USA. As with so many other of Robert's marketing ideas, he was right. It helped that the wine in the bottle was quite good and widely praised by wine critics. The wine remains one of the best Sauvignon Blancs in California, although it seems to have lost a bit of its spicy bite of late. And that tacky frosted bottle has really got to go.

The heart of Mondavi's Fumé is a dry-farmed section of To Kalon known as I-Block. It was planted to Sauvignon Blanc on phylloxera-resistant St George rootstock in 1945 and is believed to be the oldest Sauvignon Blanc planting in North America. Most of the grapes from I-Block go into the reserve Fumé, but a small amount is held out and bottled as a vineyard-designated wine. It is an extraordinary wine with a deep minerally finish, a creamy centre, and layers of flavour.

Janssens loves the wine and believes the Mondavi Sauvignon Blanc is in top form. How would she relate the flavour profile of the I-Block wine to the site? "The mineral quality is from the site; the creaminess is winemaking," she explains. At the time we were standing in I-Block, surrounded by the old thick vines, many of them so battered by time and disease that they had been tied to stakes to keep them from being knocked over by a strong wind. It was another of those Mondavi public relations moments. We were tasting the wine from the vines while standing among those same vines. I have to admit, it worked.

But what hasn't worked – and I believe has confused both the trade and consumers – is the perception that Mondavi has lost corporate focus. Its roots, after all, are in Napa. But the Mondavi Corporation has unleashed a flood of various Mondavi bottlings in the past decade. There is the Mondavi Coastal Range, the Mondavi Private Selections, all of the imports, and, of course, Mondavi Woodbridge which was the first breakaway from Mondavi Napa in 1979. With the exception of the Woodbridge wines, which represent very good value for money, these new wines are often mediocre or worse and all dilute the Mondavi name in the eyes of the trade, if not the consumer. However, as a buyer for a large California wine and spirits retail chain puts it: "If restaurant and retail wine buyers don't stock Mondavi, it doesn't matter what the consumer thinks. The wine isn't there to buy." These are not original insights, by any means. In fact, in a surprisingly frank interview given to a local newspaper on the occasion of his ninetieth birthday, Robert himself blamed his sons Tim and Michael for straying from the original family vision.

The newer wines, made under the direction of Janssens, who came over from Opus One in 1997 where she had been director of production, have a clarity and a focus that speaks well of the future. But the first decade of the new century will be critical for Mondavi. Janssens, who has already established excellent credentials at Opus One and with her own small production winery, Portfolio (see page 213) will have her hands full avoiding the corporate reefs – which have become increasingly dangerous. In late 2004, Robert Mondavi Corporation was purchased by Constellation Brands, a division of Canandiagua Wines of New York. The management at Constellation has announced that it is keen to maintain Mondavi as one of the "stars" of Napa, but at time of writing, it isn't clear what affect the new owners will have on the wines of Mondavi.

However Janssens seems very capable of weathering such storms. She took the main thrust of the attack when James Laube, an influential critic at the *Wine Spectator*, launched an assault on Mondavi wines, claiming that they had become leaner and less interesting, losing the richness and ripeness that Laube appreciated. Mondavi answered that the style had, in fact, become more European and more harmonious. According to Mondavi insiders, Janssens assembled and tasted the wines that Laube had attacked. No backing down for her, a fifth-generation French winemaker. She said the wines were fine and she was not about to change the style.

## Summing up

There are five Napa Cabernets. The basic Napa Valley is a blend, in varying proportions, of Oakville, Rutherford, and Stags Leap AVAs. There is generally about twenty per cent To Kalon fruit in the blend and often a fairly high percentage of Merlot as well as smaller amounts of Cabernet Franc and Malbec. It is aged in small barrels and is the most fruit forward of the Cabernets, with an ageing potential of six to nine years. The Oakville contains usually about sixty to sixty-five per cent To Kalon fruit with a larger percentage of Cabernet Franc than the Napa Valley bottling. It is more muscular and more intense than the Napa Valley wine and shows some of the complexity associated with Oakville Cabernet and with To Kalon in particular. I would recommend ageing between eight and ten years. The Stags Leap District Cabernet has a much higher percentage of Cabernet Sauvignon fruit, usually over ninety per cent. It has the typical silky mouthfeel and powerful centre of Stags Leap Cabernet. It should age well for twelve to fifteen years.

The To Kalon Cabernet shows the intense, layered fruit typical of that vineyard, with thirty-five years being the average age of the Cabernet vines in To Kalon. It is more extracted and concentrated than the rest of the Cabernet range and should develop in the bottle for fifteen years or more. Finally, the Reserve Cabernet comes from several different Napa AVAs, with typically about half the grapes from To Kalon. The flavour profile is deep and rich, layered with black cherry fruit and notes of chocolate and truffles. In most vintages it will easily age for fifteen to twenty years.

At the time of writing, Mondavi makes three Pinots, all from the Carneros AVA. Far and away the best is the PNX, which is made from thirty-year-old vines and is both highly concentrated and opulent, with subtle flavours and a silky texture behind rich almost jammy black cherry fruit. The Huichica single-vineyard Pinot is made from younger vines. The fruit is bright and intense, with the wine showing great promise as the vines mature. The Carneros Pinot is an admirable rendition of Carneros terroir – bright cherry fruit with a hint of raspberry and a touch of spice.

## NICKEL & NICKEL

8164 St Helena Highway, Oakville, CA 94562. Tel: 707 967 9600;
Email: hweiss@nickelandnickel.com; Website: www.nickelandnickel.com
Vineyards: n/a

From Highway 29 the Nickel & Nickel winery has the comfortable look of a successful farm. The two-storey Victorian house has obviously been restored. Behind it, a modern structure that appears to be an up-to-date dairy barn stands to one side of an old-fashioned wooden barn. Looks fine at first glance, then you realize that they didn't build barns like that in Napa. It's actually a barn build in the 1770s in New England which was taken apart, shipped west, reassembled, and restored in the heart of the Oakville appellation. But, you know what, it works. After getting to know the Nickel & Nickel operation, it's no surprise.

The winery was created by the partners who own Far Niente. Only two wines are made there, a Cabernet Sauvignon and a Chardonnay. Both are vineyard blends and the owners wanted to try their hand at single-vineyard wines. Years before, when Far Niente had created Dolce, it was decided that it also should have its own winery, rather than being made at Far Niente. The same logic applied for the single-vineyard wines. The first vintage at the new winery was 2002, although Nickel & Nickel wines were made at the nearby Napa Wine Co from the first vintage in 1997.

By 2003, twenty-two different wines were made and manager Dirk Hampson, who guided the birth of Nickel & Nickel, thinks that number could increase, rather than shrink. Some of the vineyards are owned by Nickel & Nickel, some are under contract. They range from the very cool Jamieson Canyon area south of the city of Napa to Dragonfly, a warm site in the St Helena appellation. There are also vineyards on Diamond Mountain, Howell Mountain, and many points in-between.

What is going on at Nickel & Nickel simply would not have happened only twenty years ago in Napa, perhaps not even ten years ago. Nickel & Nickel is exploring Napa terroir as no one else is doing. Also, to this point, all the wines have not only been single-vineyard but single varieties, an exercise not just in mapping terroir, but in matching varietal to terroir. It's a project that could last a couple of lifetimes, for sure. Hampson is very aware of the importance of the work. "Making a single-vineyard wine is quite different, of course, than blending," he says, during a tasting of seven single-vineyard Cabernets.

As Hampson points out, a single-vineyard wine is about provenance and personality and it could take years to get to know it well. Working with the winemaking team, Hampson's philosophy is to accept what the vineyard offers. "We will try to minimize the defects. Our goal is not to take the wine and make it taste the way we want, but to display the vineyard. I think of a vineyard as being like a friend. With a good friend, you accept the faults. We want the vineyard to define itself, to express its personality through the winemaking."

It's very early days still for Nickel & Nickel, so is it too soon to offer a definition of terroir, in general terms? Hampson takes a stab at it: "Terroir is the personality of the vineyard, as displayed over time as interpreted by humans." I like that. I'm not ready to carve it in stone, but I do like spelling out that time is a factor. Terroir wasn't born yesterday.

## Summing up

Nickel & Nickel wines. They are a moving target, changing with every vintage. I've tasted several Cabernets from the 2000 and 2001 vintage and really found nothing not to like. The wines were quite different, of course, as could be expected. Moreover, the winemaking style did not seem to get in the way of the vineyard expression. The wines all showed an internal harmony and balance, nothing over the top, nothing to bruise the palate. I was especially impressed by a Cabernet from the Coombsville area, an unusual spot for Cabernet in Napa because of the cool climate. The Cab from the Tench vineyard in the Oakville AVA was also impressive in a completely different way, featuring silky mouth-filling fruit. Nickel & Nickel also makes single-vineyard Zinfandel and other varieties, including some Sonoma wines. This is truly an awesome undertaking in defining Napa terroir.

## OPUS ONE

7800 St Helena Highway, Oakville, CA 94562.
Tel: 707 944 9442; Fax: 707 948 2497;
Email: info@opusonewinery.com; Website: www.opusonewinery.com
Vineyards: 42ha

Opus One, viewed from Highway 29 looking east, has the appearance of a Mayan temple that has sunk into a bog. In the courtyard, the image shifts to neo-Greek, with rows of columns creating exterior walkways for no particular reason. The reception area springs forward into the last century, giving the impression of a mid-level insurance company, perhaps in Kansas City, attempting to look chic. Pretentious? Well I guess.

When Robert Mondavi and Baron Philippe de Rothschild announced their joint venture in 1980 it was regarded as a major breakthrough for California wines, comparable in its way to the Steven Spurrier Paris tasting (*see* page 26). This was, so the wine pundits said, proof that California wines could play in the same league with the French. The first vintage was actually the 1979, which was released, along with the 1980 in 1984. The early vintages were all made at the Robert Mondavi Winery and the grapes were also taken from Mondavi vineyards. Mondavi sold a fourteen-hectare section of the To Kalon vineyard to the partnership in 1981. In 1983, the Franco-California partners bought a twenty-hectare parcel across the street, the eventual site of the winery. In 1984, an adjoining nineteen-hectare parcel was added. The land runs from Highway 29 east to the Napa River. The soils are fairly deep clay loam, with pockets of gravel left behind from the wandering Napa River thousands of years ago. The vineyards, including the To Kalon section, are planted to the five Bordeaux red varieties, dominated by more than eighty per cent Cabernet Sauvignon.

Director of operations for Opus until 1997 was Genevieve Janssens, now the director at Robert Mondavi (*see* page 151). Janssens was involved in plans for the construction of Opus and hired the cellar staff. The French were reportedly outraged when Tim Mondavi lured her away to Robert Mondavi. Ground was broken for Opus One winery in the summer of 1989 and construction was finished in 1991 in time for the harvest. One of the most impressive features of the winery is an underground barrel storage area that circles the core of the winery. The partners knew that the site often flooded during heavy winter rains. That can be handled with proper drainage. What they didn't know until well into the construction was that the winery was located above underground hot springs. Not what you want popping up through the floor of the barrel cellar. (There are geothermal hot springs scattered throughout Napa Valley and in Sonoma Valley as well.)

The present public relations establishment says that those springs may be mythical, claiming there is no written record of them. Writing in his 1998 book *Harvests of Joy* Robert seems quite sure that those springs were a threat. "To make a long story short, we drained and sealed the site to protect against water and heat. Then we built a wine cellar that would be waterproofed, insulated, and evenly cooled by an elaborate system of pipes. Miles and miles of pipe, embedded in the floor and ceiling of the cellar." Robert estimates that dealing with the "mythical" hot springs cost $8 million. (When the Nickel & Nickel winery was built nearby, about ten years later, the exact same precautions were taken in the cellar to guard against the possibility of geothermal hot springs breaking through.) In Napa, it's said that there was an unlimited budget for the construction of Opus and that it was exceeded. Beyond that, the winery is well designed. The grapes are delivered to the sorting table in sixteen-kilogram plastic boxes with a destemmer-crusher located directly above the fermenting tanks, so the grapes and juice are moved by gravity flow, not pumps.

Opus One is a great puzzle. The wine can be very good but, it seems to me, that it can be just average. Just average is not good enough when the price is over $100 a bottle. My theory is that Opus is the perfect example of winemaking by committee. Winemaking by committee can be dangerous enough when all concerned are in the same time zone; when on different continents with a different winemaking heritage, it can verge on disaster. Not that Opus One wines have ever been a disaster. It's simply that they should have been great wines, or at least very good wines. The 1995, for example, is a brilliant wine. Why doesn't it have more company? Or, to be honest, perhaps my expectations for Opus were simply too high. A recent vertical tasting going back to 1987, turned up some extremely good wines. Opus can be awkward in its youth but given five to eight years of bottle age, the wines do seem to come together in a generally impressive fashion.

Beyond that, things just may be looking up at Opus. In the past, Opus was made by Tim Mondavi and a winemaker from Rothschild. When Patrick Léon, the last Rothschild representative retired, Michael Silacci, a California winemaker who had worked at Stags' Leap Winery in Napa and other top estates, was finally given full control of winemaking. Tim Mondavi is now a consultant as is Philippe Dhalluin from Rothschild. Silacci has made a number of changes that should put Opus on track to become the wine it should have been all along.

For openers, he is in the vineyard on a regular basis, something that was not always done in the past. Not only is he there, he has put in place a training programme for vineyard workers to help them understand what they are doing and why they are doing it. When a vineyard worker detected an area of mildew growing on vines shortly after Silacci took over, that worker found a bottle of Opus One in his car when he left work that day.

Silacci doesn't just look at the numbers. He has a hands-on approach that is refreshing in these hi-tech days. Another example: Silacci felt that way too much water was being used on the vines. "I decided to see if we could get to zero irrigation. Maybe it won't be possible, but I'd like to try," he says. He is using all the techie instruments to measure moisture in the vines, but he also looks at the vines as well. "If the numbers tell me moisture is low, but the leaves are still turning toward the sun and looking good, I don't give them any water. But if the numbers say the vine doesn't need water, but the leaves are curling away from the sun, I'll water them," he says. A small thing, maybe, but it's an indication that Silacci is present and making decisions that cannot be taken when winemaking is done by committee.

Besides the benefits of a strong on-the-scene winemaker, Opus is just beginning to make full use of its estate vineyards, which have largely been replanted, changing density and row direction. As these new plantings mature, I suspect Opus One will begin to achieve its potential. Yet, in the end, Opus One must take its place on the Napa A List, regardless of my opinion – and I should add in all fairness that I seem to be almost alone in my attitude toward the wines. At the end of the day, what makes Opus a great wine is the influence it has had on the rest of Napa. Opus not only broke price barriers, it also helped break Napa away from the 100 per cent varietal mode while at the same time boosting Napa's reputation as the Cabernet capital of California. And, as mentioned, with Silacci in charge, the wines are improving with every vintage. Whether this will continue is very much up in the air at time of writing. Late in 2004, Constellaltion Brands acquired the Robert Mondavi Corporation and thus half-ownership in Opus One. It isn't clear what impact this will have on the future of Opus.

## Summing up

The varietal composition of Opus One has bounced around considerably since the 1979 vintage, which included eighty per cent Cabernet

Sauvignon, sixteen per cent Cabernet Franc, and four per cent Merlot. The 1987, a great year for Opus One, contained ninety-five per cent Cabernet Sauvignon in the final blend. In 1995, another very good year, there was eighty-five per cent Cabernet Sauvignon. In the 2001, an incredibly good vintage and the first year that Silacci was in control, there was eighty-seven per cent Cabernet. The barrel-ageing programme has been much more consistent, ranging from a low of fifteen months to a high of nineteen months, followed in most vintages by a minimum of twelve months bottle-ageing before release, often longer. At its best, Opus One is an opulent wine, showing dark chocolate (at least when young), black cherry, and hints of black pepper with a creamy centre and a long finish with the dark opening fruit looping back to add layers of luscious flavour at the end. The ageing potential, especially with the newer releases, is up to two-plus decades.

## JOSEPH PHELPS VINEYARDS
200 Taplin Road, St Helena, CA 94574. Tel: 707 963 2745;
Fax: 707 963 4831; Email: jpvwines@aol.com; Website: www.jpvwines.com
Vineyards: 161ha

Joseph Phelps' winery doesn't always get the credit it deserves. But Napa insiders know that Phelps has been a leader since its founding in 1972. Phelps was the first to produce a Bordeaux blend red wine under a proprietary label, with its Insignia, released in 1978. The previous year, Phelps released a Syrah, which helped spark the interest in Rhône varietals in California.

In a sense, Phelps discovered Syrah. There was much confusion in California concerning Syrah, Durif, and Petite Sirah. That confusion probably dates back to the introduction of the grape in California in the 1870s. In 1959, the Christian Brothers planted a small plot of Syrah in Napa, although they may have believed they were planting Petite Sirah. At any rate, Phelps gained control of the vineyard, realized that it was indeed Syrah and made wine from the vineyard in 1974. Phelps later increased its Syrah plantings and went on to make a whole line of Rhône varietals under the Vin du Mistral label.

Phelps became interested in the wine business when his construction company built both the Rutherford Hill and original Chateau Souverain wineries. He liked Napa and he liked wine, so he decided to build his own winery. In 1972 he bought a 271-hectare parcel in Spring Valley just off the Silverado Trail east of St Helena. Phelps planted a sixty-five-hectare vineyard there to a variety of grapes, but including Riesling, Gewurztraminer, and Sauvignon Blanc.

His first winemaker was Walter Schug, a German-trained oenologist, who now has his own winery in Carneros Sonoma. Given Schug's training it isn't surprising that the first wine out of the Phelps stable was a Riesling. The emphasis was on white wines for several years, although it soon became evident that Cabernet Sauvignon was the future for Napa and for Phelps. Craig Williams joined Phelps in 1976 and worked closely with Schug in developing the Cabernet programme. He was especially associated with Insignia, which in its early years was dominated by Merlot, but has since evolved toward Cabernet Sauvignon. He recalls that at the time, other winemakers in Napa were working almost entirely with 100 per cent varietal wines, only blending to "stretch out" a wine. When Schug left Phelps in 1983, he and Williams had established a pattern that was to continue, adding vineyard-designated Cabernets as well as the Napa Valley blend.

Williams is first to admit that quality was uneven during the 1980s. "We went through a challenging period during the late eighties and early nineties where we were having trouble with consistency in some of our grape sources," he says. But beginning in 1989, the redevelopment of estate-owned vineyards in Carneros, Stags Leap, and the Rutherford bench gave Williams and Phelps vineyard manager Bulmaro Montes the raw materials they needed to launch a new era in the quality of JPV wines. "Our wines taste a certain way because of where the grapes are grown," Williams explains. "I'm just trying to add an element of style."

Because Williams does look to the vineyard, I ask him to talk about the Backus Vineyard Cabernet, which has been a bright spot in the Phelps line-up since the early 1980s. The 8.5-hectare vineyard is on the Silverado Trail in the Oakville AVA. It is on a thirty per cent slope, with an elevation starting at about sixty metres (200 feet) raising to about 167 metres (550 feet). Backus was planted in 1975 on St George rootstock, so it escaped the phylloxera wave of the 1980s. "There aren't many old vine Cabernet vineyards around," Williams says. He explains that the soils are gravelly loam with a high iron content and volcanic in origin, but says it was difficult to link the site directly to the wine flavour profile. "I don't really know," he admits. "We are still young at this. We get a tremendous extract level, a lot of colour and tannins, and a kind of bitter chocolate mocha flavour, as well as some minerality. Talk to me again in ten or twenty years." His answer sums up the whole question of terroir in Napa: there is still a lot to learn. "That is going to be the challenge for the next group of winemakers. They will have to step up and try to define the AVAs, the sub-regions and the vineyards, to describe the constant attributes we find in the wine without winemaker interference. It really is difficult to separate what the vineyard gives from what the winemaker does," he says.

Since Phelps has two blended wines, Insignia and the Napa Valley Cabernet as well as the vineyard-designated Backus, Williams has a chance every vintage for a first-hand look at those vineyard attributes. "I would say that there is a little bit of a rustic nature in the Backus. You can see the site coming through. That is both good and bad. We have had to declassify Backus in some vintages, while Insignia is greater than the sum of its parts," Williams says. Over the years, Joe Phelps has given him a pretty free hand, not only in wine production but in vineyard acquisition and development. Phelps now has vineyards in Carneros as well as in the Freestone region near the Sonoma coast. Phelps plans to build a second winery there for Pinot Noir production.

Phelps has also been one of the few Napa vineyards to move into biodynamic farming, which puts even more focus on the vineyard (*see* footnote on page 149). Large parts of the Freestone and the Backus vineyards have been farmed using exclusively biodynamic methods. The feeling is that grape quality will be improved as well as the environment. With its commitment to the vineyards, Phelps is on the right track for Napa's future. Williams is right in saying it is too early to draw up a tidy definition of Napa terroir as applied to a particular region or even vineyard. But they are making a start at Phelps.

## Summing up

Phelps makes a refreshing Sauvignon Blanc in a frankly bold California style, all bright citrus fruit and lively flavours. The Ovation Chardonnay from Carneros fruit can be spectacular, with balanced rich flavours, deep and satisfying. It's the Cabernet and Cabernet blends however that people line up for. The Napa Valley blend is an excellent wine, typically with a layered finish and good structure for mid-term ageing. The Insignia is one of Napa's best and belongs in anyone's "First Growth" ranks. It's an elegant and supple wine with layers of flavour and a rich harmony. It is drinkable when young but ages beautifully. Anyone who has an Insignia from the late 1970s in their cellar has a tiny time capsule of just how good Napa red blends can be. Backus remains my favourite, with its flashes of tremendous power, dark and mysterious. And don't overlook the excellent Vin du Mistral range. Phelps delivers consistent quality year in and year out at a fair price.

## QUINTESSA

1601 Silverado Trail, Rutherford, CA 94573. Tel: 707 967 1601;

Fax: 707 286 2727; Email: info@quintessa.com; Website: www.quintessa.com

Vineyards: 61ha

Quintessa is a good example of why it is impossible to generalize about terroir in Napa. If you look at its location on a map, you would be inclined to think that planting a vineyard dedicated to red Bordeaux varieties just there between the Silverado Trail and the Napa River was a very bad idea. One has read (and believes) that it is foolish to plant Cabernet Sauvignon in Napa anywhere near the river. Soils are too deep and too rich. The water table is too high. There's too much clay. Whatever. There are plenty of reasons not to plant Cabernet Sauvignon near the Napa River.

But then, you go and look at Quintessa and you realize that they got it right. Quintessa, a vineyard of about sixty-one hectares is planted around a man-made lake on a broken range of hills that seem to have split off from the Vaca range in a lemming-like effort to reach the river several million years ago. There are east, west, north, and south exposures in this jumble of soils and microclimates in the eastern end of the Rutherford appellation.

The site had never been planted to wine grapes, or anything else for that matter, when it was bought by Agustin and Valeria Huneeus in 1990. Agustin, a native of Chile who was a top executive of Concha y Toro when that winery began major growth in the 1960s and was later in charge of world brands at Seagram in New York, is an unlikely champion of terroir-based wines. That is, he is if you only look at his résumé. Perhaps because he came up the global corporate ladder (or maybe the elevator in his case, he made it look so smooth) he realized that unless wine represented a particular place, it was just another commodity subject to the whim of the market, like potatoes or rice or coffee.

Agustin is called "Cucho" by family and friends, which means in Chilean street slang something like "wise old cat" – only with just a hint of danger, as in "watch yourself", embedded in the meaning. I first met him in the early 1980s. He had left Seagram and was looking for a property in California, an estate that he could direct without answering to a corporate board. At that time, only a few people in California were talking about "artisan" wines and virtually no one was using the "T for terroir" word. And those who were thinking outside the UC Davis box were certainly not marketing types, which was Agustin's strength.

Valeria is an intriguing mix of hard-headed scientist – she has a degree in oenology and viticulture from the University of Chile and a PhD in biology from Columbia University in New York – and earth goddess. She has a relationship to the Quintessa vineyards which could be described, without irony as spiritual.

After a few false starts, Agustin was tapped to run Franciscan Vineyards in 1985. Franciscan was founded in 1972 and by 1979 had gone through several owners when it was bought by Eckes International, a Germany company that produced spirits and fruit juice. Franciscan was then and remains now a winery that somehow never seems to reach its potential, despite top vineyards in the Rutherford and Oakville appellations. In a few years, Agustin became a full partner and managed to make the winery respectable, both in the market and in wine quality. However, always restless and curious, like a "wise old cat", he found the site he believed would yield a great terroir-driven wine. Valeria agreed and in 1990, they bought the estate that is now Quintessa.

Years later, Agustin recalled, "Several other vintners had been trying to buy it. Joe Phelps, Mondavi, everyone was after it but somehow the owners never let it go. When we made an offer I never thought it would go into escrow. I didn't have any financing in place at all. When my offer was accepted, I had sixty days to find the money." Needless to say, the money was found. And while the wise old cat helped put together a deal selling Franciscan to Canandaigua Wine Company (now Constellation Brands), the New York spirits and beer importer and a producer of popularly priced wines that was making a move into the premium wine business, Valeria was planting the vineyard.

Quintessa was the first vineyard of any size planted from scratch following the return of phylloxera to Napa in the 1980s. Huneeus understood that the return of the dreadful root louse would not have been as devastating if vine rootstock had been more diverse. In the monoculture of the AxR-1 rootstock, the phylloxera population boomed, spreading rapidly. The Quintessa vineyard is now planted with seven different rootstocks, not only to thwart phylloxera but to attempt to match rootstock to soil conditions. There are also thirteen different clones of Cabernet Sauvignon, Merlot, and Cabernet Franc. Valeria estimates that they got about thirty per cent of it right in the way of rootstock and clonal selection matched to site, meaning that by her standards up to two-thirds of the vineyard should be replanted.

She is pleased with the results of biodynamic farming at Quintessa. The entire estate is farmed organically and has been from the beginning, but Valeria has been gradually converting to the biodynamic method for several years (*see* footnote on page 149). By the harvest of 2003 about twenty hectares, almost one third of the vines, were farmed biodynamically. Valeria began with some vineyard blocks that in her opinion were not performing well. "These were blocks of vines that never were included in the final Quintessa blend. But after four years, one of the blocks was in the final cut," she says. In another case, she took two side-by-side blocks, both of which were consistently in the final blend. She started farming one block biodynamically and within two years the fruit was superior to that in the control block. "It is labour intensive. It's much more expensive to farm biodynamically," she adds. It does not, of course, yield to any sort of scientific test, but Valeria believes that the organic and biodynamic approach, which results in a rich soil and plant life in the vineyard, leads to wines of greater complexity and concentration.

The Quintessa winery itself was finished in 2000. Movement of grapes, must, and wine are all by gravity with the wine ending up in barrels in an underground *cave* which has been dug deep into the hillside. The approach to the winery is off the Silverado Trail with a driveway leading to a stone wall which follows the contour of the hill behind it. It's impressive, if a bit overwhelming. I should imagine that as the stone mellows with exposure to wind and rain it will be a little less startling.

## Summing up

Quintessa is a blend of Cabernet Sauvignon, Merlot, and Cabernet Franc. It is a seamless, harmonious wine, elegant and supple. There are no sharp elbows or rough bits sticking out. Someone described is as like tasting velvet. It is a wine that welcomes almost any style of food. And for the people who ask, it is a wine that should age and develop in the bottle for up to twenty years, depending on the vintage, though that is speculation at this point. It will be fascinating to watch Quintessa evolve as the vineyard matures. It is already a very good wine. I suspect that within a few years it will become one of the world's great estates.

## SADDLEBACK CELLARS

7802 Money Road, Oakville, CA 94562.
Tel: 707 944 1305; Fax: 707 944 1325;
Email: hillery@saddlebackcellars.com; Website: www.saddlebackcellars.com
Vineyards: 9ha

Nils Venge was the first Napa winemaker to score 100 points from Robert Parker. Despite that setback, Venge makes one of the world's best Cabernet Sauvignons at his small Saddleback Cellars winery just off the Oakville Cross Road, in the heart of Napa. The 100-point score was for the 1985 Groth Vineyard Reserve Cabernet Sauvignon, which was, indeed a very good wine. Venge was a minority partner and winemaker at Groth.

Saddleback Cellars is next door to Groth. It's a modest concrete block building at the end of a narrow lane. There's a small sign attached to the door, identifying it as Saddleback Cellars and a few old barrels stacked near a picnic table outside. The picnic table serves as the winery tasting room in good weather. Otherwise, guests (who need an appointment) can taste at a table squeezed between stacked cases of wine and rows of wine barrels. There is the obligatory winery dog to greet visitors and, more often that not, Venge himself, a towering Dane, who is often called "The Viking of Napa Valley". Venge wines are still getting high points, although I don't believe he has bagged any 100-pointers at Saddleback, but then he doesn't need to. His wines can speak for themselves.

Venge makes several varietals, including Pinot Blanc, Pinot Grigio, the occasional Sauvignon Blanc, Chardonnay, Merlot, Zinfandel, and Syrah – I must have forgotten something – while holding total production at Saddleback to around 8,500 cases. Why so many wines? He says he likes the challenge. One has the impression that Venge is not happy sitting still. (The name Saddleback Cellars is said to have come from Saddleback Mountain in Orange County in southern California, where Venge was born and raised. But it seems to me more likely it is the result of the time Venge spends in the saddle. His father was an accomplished horseman and Venge has clearly followed in his hoof-steps.) That aside, however many "challenge" wines he might make, Venge is the master of Cabernet Sauvignon and has been from the beginning.

Venge trained at UC Davis in viticulture and oenology, receiving his degree in 1967. The plan was that, armed with this knowledge, he would be able to eventually take over the family wine and spirits importing company in Los Angeles. Instead, he went to Vietnam and when he got back in 1970, he decided that he wanted to grow grapes and make wine, not just sell it. Perhaps his ability to translate Cabernet Sauvignon grapes into such compelling wine came about because of several years he spent in vineyard management with Charles Krug and Sterling. In 1973, he was hired as the general manager and first winemaker at Villa Mount Eden. His first Cabernet, the 1974 vintage was a sensation and he made several more there in the late 1970s that are legendary in Napa. In his spare time, he planted his nine-hectare estate vineyard and started thinking of making his own wine one day. In 1982, Venge became the winemaker and general manager at Groth and released the first Saddleback Cellars Cabernet.

Venge's Cabernets are not subtle. They pack plenty of power, enough to get the favourable attention of the Parkers of the wine world, for sure. But there is something behind that power; a supple and almost elegant harmony that echoes through the palate. Venge ages his Cabernet in new barrels for about thirty months, at least six months longer than many in Napa and a full ten to twelve months longer than some. Also, like his neighbour across the Oakville Cross Road, Silver Oak Cellars, he likes American oak, using roughly forty per cent, which gives his Cabernet, when young, a flash of dill. Despite the extended barrel-ageing, Venge's Cabernets are far from being oak monsters.

Venge shrugs off any attempt to map out how he makes the wines. Although apparently quite sure of what he is doing, he does seem to lack the "ego" gene that is so apparent in many superstar California winemakers. He shuns trends, refusing to use wild yeast and has no use for extended maceration, taking the wine off the skins when it is dry and allowing it to go through malolactic fermentation in the barrel. He is not adverse to giving grapes some time on the vine, the familiar hang time approach, but not to the point that it leads to overripe, over-concentrated wines. He does like what he calls "varietal purity" or 100 per cent varietal wines, although he blends up to six per cent Viognier into the Syrah. But the Cabernets are all Cab all the way.

One hears more and more talk in Napa about "going for the points". That is, making a wine that will score in the high nineties on the 100-point system. If anyone would buy into that approach, it could be Venge, who is the original 100-point guy, but he laughs away the suggestion. "I've heard of people doing that, but I'm not interested," he says. In any survey of Napa's great estates, Venge almost rates a special category. It seems that anywhere he goes is a great estate.

At present, he is the consulting winemaker at several Napa wineries – and any one of them could rank as someone's great estate. Just down the road, Venge consults with Plump Jack, a winery financed by the Getty fortune and owned by the rapidly rising politician Gavin Newsom, who was elected mayor of San Francisco in 2003. Newsom immediately thrust himself into the national picture by authorizing the performance of same-sex weddings in San Francisco's city hall. This was the first official sanction of such marriages in the USA – although San Francisco had long sanctioned same-sex legal contracts that gave gay partners the same legal rights as any other married couple. When asked if he has taken any similarly bold steps in the wine business, Newsom notes that he was the first to use screwcap closures on a Napa Valley Cabernet. He received good press for that decision, too, when he brought out a Plump Jack Cabernet in screwcap in the late 1990s priced at $150. Perhaps his best decision though was hiring Venge to consult on Plump Jack's first offering, a 1995 Cabernet that received exceptional press.

Venge is also the winemaker of record for Keenan Vineyards, a Spring Mountain winery known for its outstanding Cabernets and for Vivani Vineyards, one of the best start-up wineries in Napa in the late 1990s. Beyond that, Venge and his son Kirk, also a UC Davis graduate, are developing the Venge Winery in the St Helena appellation at the foot of Howell Mountain. In 1999, they planted about twenty-eight hectares of vines on the property, and began the process of rebuilding an historic winery on the site which was originally established in 1891. The two operations will be kept separate.

A common thread in all of Venge's work is the emphasis he places on the vines. While tasting over several vintages of Saddleback Cabernet, I try to get Venge to reveal where he keeps the "magic wand" that some critics say he waves over Cabernet. "It's not the winemaker that makes the wine. It's the vineyard, all in the vineyard," he insists. Quite likely, but if that is the case – and being an advocate of terroir-based wines I have little choice but to believe him – then Venge has a knack of choosing the right vineyard when it comes to making Cabernet Sauvignon. Which raises the question of his present estate vineyard. It's the usual make-up of river-based alluvial soils, gravelly and well-drained, less than a mile from the river. Venge's Cabernets certainly have, in common with many other valley floor Cabernets, a friendly palate approach but they also have a deeper structure that promises even more pleasure down the road.

Typically Venge makes no pretence of any magic touch in the vineyard. He knows the area well, having made wine at Groth for many years, that is an advantage. The vines are also dry-farmed. Because the vines have to find their own water, there is a certain amount of self-regulation: roughly, the vines give you what they want, not what can be coaxed from them by the wine-grower's craft. For example, the vines are head-trained and cane-pruned, using only a three-wire support system, rather than one of several trellis-systems touted by current vineyard wizards that allow more sunshine, more concentration, and possible overripe fruit.

## Summing up

Venge's Cabernets are the main attraction, but he makes other wines that measure up quite well. The Chardonnay and Pinot Blanc, both made from estate grapes, are both well above average. The Saddleback Old Vine Zinfandel is made in the rustic – what some might call old-fashioned – style of big California Zin. I find it a super wine, just fun to drink and then drink some more. The grapes come from a traditional grower near Calistoga, in the northern reaches of Napa. Like most old vine Zin made in this style, the ageing potential seems virtually unlimited: it will likely lose its rich undercurrent of spice after ten to twelve years, however. There is also a very good estate-grown Merlot. It is typically a dense chocolatey wine with dark fruit, a whisper of dried herbs, and a medium tannic structure. In most years it has the structure to age for ten to fifteen years. Always curious, Venge has been experimenting with a Syrah and a Sangiovese as well, which are worth looking out for.

Venge makes two Cabernets, the regular bottling and the Family Reserve. The latter is made from selected rows in the estate vineyard and is actually picked, made, and bottled by the extended Venge family. It spends a little longer in oak and is typically dominated by rich, dark fruit with an edge of chocolate and tobacco. The regular bottling is usually made from at least ninety per cent estate Cabernet. The flavour profile leans toward dark berry and black cherry fruit with firm fleshy tones and moderate tannins. It is very drinkable young, but would repay at least ten years of ageing and many years even longer

## SCHRAMSBERG VINEYARDS

1400 Schramsberg Road, Calistoga, CA 94515. Tel: 707 942 6668; Fax: 707 942 5943; Email: info1@schramsberg.com; Website: www.schramsberg.com
Vineyards: 24ha

Schramsberg is not perhaps the bucolic spot that Robert Louis Stevenson found when he trudged up a redwood canyon to visit canny old Jacob Schram, the German immigrant who planted vineyards on the steep slopes of Diamond Mountain, a few miles south of Calistoga, in 1863. But the road is still far too narrow and twisting for bus-bound day trippers and Schram's Victorian house is still nestled snugly into the trees. Visitors need an appointment, just as they did in Schram's day, but there are certainly more of them. Even though the one-lane drive leading to the winery is hard to spot from Highway 29, it seems there is always a line waiting for the tour and tasting. This isn't surprising, given the quality of Schramsberg sparkling wine and its international reputation.

Jack and Jamie Davies became interested in producing a méthode champenoise wine in the early 1960s, when they were shareholders in the Martin Ray Winery near San José, south of San Francisco. Ray was likely the first sparkling wine producer to use the traditional production method as well as the traditional grapes of Champagne – Chardonnay and Pinot Noir – in California. In Napa, Hans Kornell and Beaulieu were making methodé champenoise wines at the time, but not with the traditional grapes. Korbel also made methodé champenoise in Sonoma, using Chenin Blanc, Riesling, and other non-traditional grapes.

In fact, méthode champenoise wines called "Champagne" had been made in California since the mid-nineteenth century. (It wasn't until after World War II that the Charmat process and the transfer process came into widespread use in California.) Paul Masson produced a "medicinal Champagne" right through the years of Prohibition. This could have been what inspired Martin Ray, since he bought the Paul Masson winery from the man himself in 1936. (To step outside Napa for a moment, Ray was well ahead of his time as a vintner. He fought against allowing varietal labelling when the wine contained only fifty-one per cent of the variety. He was a strong supporter of appellation of origin and urged winemakers to pay more attention to what went on in the vineyard. He was widely regarded as a crank and nut.) At any rate, the Davies were so impressed by Martin Ray's sparkling wine that they wanted to have a go at it themselves. In 1965 they found Jacob Schram's old estate and winery in Napa, which had closed at the onset of Prohibition. There had been a couple of unsuccessful attempts to reopen after Repeal, but in Jack Davies words, "it was a real mess when we found it". The Davies restored Schram's original house, expanded the underground caves which had been hand dug in the nineteenth century and built a right-up-to-the-minute modern winery that fits without missing a beat into the redwood-thick hillside.

The Davies turned up in Napa at a good time. There was a keen sense of cooperation at the level of production, even though there was competition in the market. For example, the Davies were looking for grapes and wine to try to get production underway within weeks of moving into the old winery. They were promised 4.5 tonnes of Riesling, which they didn't want. However, Robert Mondavi said he would trade them 4.5 tonnes of Chardonnay from Charles Krug. This was only a few months before he broke with his brother Peter and the family (see page 24). When the Davies called Peter to complete the trade following the breakup, Peter said he knew nothing about it, but would honour the agreement anyway.

During the next few years, the Davies pulled out the remnants of the old mountain vineyard and planted Pinot Noir and Chardonnay. That was a mistake. They were still thinking old Napa, old California. They wanted Chardonnay and Pinot Noir and they had a warm mountain vineyard above the fog level, so they planted what they wanted, rather than what the vineyard wanted. But they did learn from their mistake. That vineyard is now planted to Cabernet Sauvignon and other red Bordeaux varieties. Those grapes were sold to other wineries for several years, but in 2004, Schramsberg released J Davies Cabernet Sauvignon from the 2001 vintage. Several other California sparkling wine producers have taken to table wine, but Schramsberg is the only one to abandon the Pinot Noir/Chardonnay mode and for good reason. That's what their estate vineyard demands.

Instead Schramsberg has made an interesting transition for grape sources for the sparkling wines. It no longer uses any grapes from Napa except Carneros. Typically, it sources from over sixty vineyards in some of the coolest areas of the North Coast, including Anderson Valley in Mendocino County. This, of course, gives the winemaking staff enormous diversity in building the base wine. Schramsberg is the only sparkling wine producer in California to barrel-ferment a significant amount of wine, about twenty-five per cent, which also adds to the sparkling wine palate. There is no intention of adding any oak element through barrel-fermentation, it is done simply to enhance the mouthfeel of the wine. There is virtually constant experimentation going on in the winemaking process as well, with separate lots of wine made reflecting clonal selections, malolactic or not, and other winemaking techniques.

But the common thread that knits Schramsberg together doesn't have anything to do with vineyard site, clonal selection or wine barrels. Schramsberg has stood out from the beginning for extraordinary dedication to quality. The replanting of the home vineyard to Cabernet is an example. At the time the Davies were making their start, the common wisdom in California regarding sparkling wine was that it didn't make much difference where the grapes were grown. It was thought that the production process would eliminate any site specific character in the wine anyway, so why bother. But even though the Davies had no formal training in oenology or viticulture – Jack was a successful business executive and Jamie's background was art history – they did know that to create quality, it was necessary to pay attention to the details. Like what grapes went into good sparkling wine and where was the best place to grow those grapes. So it's a combination: the right grapes in the right places, always looking for ways to make better wine in the cellar, and a dedication to quality. That combination put

Schramsberg on the right track in the beginning and has, by and large, kept them on it ever since.

The Davies also always knew how to work the market as well (*see* Appendix IV page 248). One of their great fans in the early days was a fellow named Dick Nixon, who for a time was president of the USA. I never talked to the Davies' about their politics, but whatever they were, they knew how to get a bottle of their wine on the presidential dining table. Nixon liked what he found in the bottle and when he paid a state visit to China in 1972 (the much discussed visit to Beijing that "opened" China to the west) he asked a White House aide to call the Davies and ask if they could deliver thirteen cases of wine to Travis Air Force Base, which is about fifty miles east of Napa and the jumping-off point for USA Air Force flights to Asia. Jack himself drove the wine to Travis – it was a 1969 Blanc de Blancs – not knowing what the event was, but imagining some sort of White House dinner. To this day Jamie maintains that they were completely surprised to turn on the television one morning and see commentator Barbara Walters raising a bottle of their wine for the cameras in Beijing during a dinner Nixon gave for Chinese leaders.

It is only fair to point out that Schramsberg bubbly is bipartisan. President Carter, a Democrat, served it to President Portillo of Mexico at the White House and to Soviet President Leonid Brezhnev at a state dinner in Vienna. It remained very popular in the Reagan years although the first Bush apparently only served it once. President Clinton called on Schramsberg often, as did the second President Bush, who served the Schramsberg Crémant to Queen Elizabeth and Prince Philip at a Winfield House dinner in 1999. After an early run on the Blanc de Blancs, following Nixon's lead, the Crémant has been the heavy favourite, with only a few bottles of Blanc de Noirs scattered down the presidential years. The record shows no Brut or Reserve wines on the menu. Schramsberg is, as far as I can determine, the only California winery which has created a list of events for visitor inspection, detailing when their wine was served at White House and other official functions.

When Jack died in 1998, many assumed that Jamie would sell the winery or at least turn active management over to her sons. It is true that youngest son Hugh is running day to day operations, but as for selling the estate, "It never entered my mind," says Jamie. She still sets in on tasting for the final blends and can be found most days in her office at the winery.

## Summing up

There are seven vintage-dated Schramsberg bubblies and one which is non-vintage. Mirabelle, the non-vintage brut is one of the best buys anywhere for an everyday sparkling wine. Since Mirabelle is made from the *cuvées* that didn't make the cut, the standards are high. Mirabelle comprises about twenty-five per cent of Schramsberg's production of 50,000 cases. Unusually for a budget bubbly, Mirabelle has about twenty-five per cent reserve wines in the blend.

The Blanc de Blancs, Blanc de Noirs, and Brut Rosé are all outstanding wines, with the Blanc de Blancs an exceptional value-for-quality wine and Schramsberg's top volume wine. The rosé spends roughly thirty months on the yeast and gets its colour from two to three per cent Pinot Noir base wine added to the Chardonnay/Pinot blend before the first bottling and again with the finishing *dosage*. The Blanc de Blancs and the Blanc de Noirs both get about three years on the lees. The Blanc de Noirs normally has about fifteen to twenty per cent Chardonnay in the blend. All have a residual sugar of just over one per cent.

The Crémant Demi-sec is the odd man out in the Schramsberg line-up. The varietal mix is Flora – a cross between Semillon and Gewurztraminer developed at UC Davis (one is tempted to ask why) – Chardonnay, Gewurztraminer, and Pinot Noir. It normally runs to about four per cent residual sugar and is a nice glass of wine for those who like such things.

The heart of Schramsberg is the Brut Reserve and J Schram, without doubt the best sparkling wines made in the USA. The Brut Reserve is aged for six years before release. It's a very rich, creamy wine, with a baked apple and meringue centre that is marvellous. It also matures beautifully if you like a little age on your bubbly. The J Schram is a Chardonnay-driven wine with a toasted nut and sourdough bread profile. It is aged for five years before release. Of the two top bubblies, this one is perhaps more Californian than the Reserve. You can't really go wrong with either.

## SHAFER VINEYARDS

6154 Silverado Trail, Napa, CA 94558. Tel: 707 944 2877; Fax: 707 944 9454; Email: shafer@shafervineyards.com; Website: www.shafervineyards.com
Vineyards: 75ha

It was 1972 and John Shafer was a publishing executive in Chicago. He realized that he didn't want to spend another year in the buttoned down corporate world. "A few years shy of my fiftieth birthday I did something foolish," Shafer says. "I came to Napa Valley looking for a chance to be in business for myself ... for a life change ... for a new place to call home." Like many others coming to Napa, Shafer was an immigrant. Immigrants had been coming to Napa for more than a century when he arrived. They had come from Germany, Italy, and more recently from Mexico. He just happened to be from Chicago.

"I was a city boy, a product of the Chicago suburbs," Shafer wrote in a memoir in 2002, his thirtieth year in the wine business. "My father, a life-long teetotaler, set off to work every day in a hat, suit, and tie, riding the commuter train downtown. My adult life was spent in the cement and asphalt 3-D maze of Chicago in the world of corporate textbook publishing, helping to market and promote products such as the once-ubiquitous 'Dick and Jane' reading books." I don't believe any of the "Dick and Jane" books dealt with Dick and Jane going off to plant wine grapes, but that's what Shafer did. Dick and Jane's loss turned out to be the wine consumer's gain.

Shafer eventually found the place he was looking for in 1972 in what is now the Stags Leap AVA. He recalls: "At first glance, it was not a glorious property to behold. It came with a rundown house and several out buildings. The twenty-hectare vineyard sported a hodgepodge of white and red varietals, all head-pruned ... Beyond these surface details though, this site seemed to have exactly what I was looking for – hillsides of thin, volcanic soils that offered quick drainage. South and west exposures combined with its location in the southern end of the valley offered a nice incorporation of midday heat, much of it radiating directly off the towering palisades, and then of cool late-day breezes from the San Francisco Bay."

What Shafer describes is typical of Stags Leap vineyard sites. Vines were first planted on the property in the 1880s. There is a good chance most of those grapes went into brandy production. A few years later (after the original wave of phylloxera swept through Napa) the vineyard was replanted by an Italian immigrant named Batista Scansi. He put in Zinfandel, Carignan, Sauvignon Vert, and Golden Chasselas. Those grapes probably went to home winemakers during Prohibition in the 1920s, although there is a long and honourable history of moonshine brandy stills in the hills and canyons of Napa.

As Shafer began replanting, he continued to harvest grapes from the existing vineyards. The property came with a contract from the Napa Valley Co-op which in those days acted more or less as an agent for E & J Gallo, so Shafer's old-vine hillside Zinfandel was vinified in St Helena and shipped off to Modesto to appear in Gallo's Hearty Burgundy with the rest of Gallo's Napa purchases. In 1977, Shafer harvested his first crop of Cabernet from two-year-old vines. He sold most of the crop but kept back enough to make seventy-five litres of wine in his basement. In what was perhaps an omen of greatness to come, he bottled his homemade Cab in empty bottles of Mondavi Red Table Wine. In 1978 he made his first commercial vintage. That inaugural wine evolved into today's Shafer Hillside Select, easily one of the best dozen wines in Napa and one of the world's great Cabernets. Today, more than twenty-five years on, it is an astonishing wine, holding its age quite well. It was the first evidence of what the vineyard could offer.

To hear Shafer tell the tale, the '78 was a disaster in the making. "I was fairly new in the valley and wasn't able to get pickers when I needed them," he explained. "In those days, we thought we had to pick at twenty-two or 22.5 brix. I thought the fruit had stayed on the vines far too long when I finally got the grapes picked." Shafer picked fifteen tonnes, which were crushed at Markham winery, fermented at Round Hill, and put in a mix of French and American oak barrels. "I borrowed a truck from Joe Phelps to haul the barrels – there were about forty – back to the basement here." Disasters continued. Just as the wine was starting to go through malolactic, an intense cold stretch hit in January. "I finally wrapped the barrels in electric blankets and brought in space heaters, hoping to create the right conditions for malolactic." His electricity bill must have been rather high but even at that, he said the wine didn't finish malolactic until May. Perhaps that's why it is so good today.

Refusing to be discouraged, the Shafer winery was bonded on Valentine's Day in 1979. "We picked Valentine's Day so that we would remember the date," Shafer explains. The 1978 was released in 1981 to rave notices. After that remarkable beginning, the Shafers admit they lost their way for a few years. Shafer says, "The biggest blunder was following the lemmings over the cliff in the 'food-wine era'."

Shafer's son Doug joined the winery in 1983 after gaining an oenology degree from UC Davis. The present winemaker, Elias

Fernandez, came on board the following year. Both agree that as young winemakers, anxious to make a success of the fledgling family winery, they may have been paying too much attention to the numbers and not "listening to the wine". They hired Tony Soter (then the winemaker at Spottswoode and now the owner of étude) to consult and try to get them back on track. "Tony had the remarkable idea for the time that wine should taste good," Doug says. After two years, Soter told the Shafers that he had "taught them everything he knew" and "he cut us loose", as Doug puts it.

Apparently the Shafers and Fernandez were apt pupils. A couple of the vintages of the late 1980s aside, Shafer wines have been on a winning track for some time. "We learned to make the wine the grapes told us to make, rather than imposing on them the wine we wanted to make," says Fernandez. Of course, what the grapes said they in turn learned from the site, the terroir.

The vineyard blocks are laid out on a series of small knolls below the massive rocky thrust of Stags Leap. The exposure is southwesterly; the soils are shallow, composed of gravelly volcanic debris laid over a base of volcanic shale. The climate pattern consists of warm days and cool nights with a late afternoon wind off San Francisco Bay sneaking over from Carneros to begin the cooling process. At harvest, each block is fermented separately, some blocks going into the Hillside Select, others into the Napa Valley Cabernet. One block in particular, Sunspot, has traditionally been the heart of the Hillside Select.

"Several years ago, during harvest, I looked up at Sunspot just as the sun was coming up behind the vineyards and it struck me what a special place this is. How that block, year in and year out, has delivered such outstanding wine," says Doug. "Sometimes I think not enough credit is given to that kind of consistency," he adds. "I think we really started getting serious about it, or learning how to deal with the vineyard, in about 1987," continues Doug. A programme of sustainable agriculture was put in place, including the use of cover crops and natural predators to deal with vineyard pests. "We started paying more attention to barrels, to toast levels, to how we filtered the wine. We recognized that we had made many mistakes in the beginning." Fernandez adds, " We learned that you can't depend on numbers. You have to go to the vineyard, not just look at numbers."

We were sitting around a massive table at the winery as we tasted wine and the Shafers and Fernandez talked. I mostly listened, putting in a simple question now and then. I could look out into the vineyard and up the hillside. It suddenly struck me that I was hearing something rather unusual – wine-growers talking about all the things they had done wrong, admitting that they had to ask for help, admitting that in the beginning they didn't understand what the vineyard was giving to them. It was astounding to hear this in a business so dominated, so driven by image. It was as if William Faulkner had said, "Yeh, I wrote a lot of crap in the beginning, but I finally began to get a feel for the English language." Here were three people making one of the world's great wines – two of them with oenology degrees from UC Davis – saying that they really didn't start to get it right until they listened to the vineyard. The question comes up, just what did they learn? What did the terroir teach them or rather give the wine?

"It gives a texture, a supple mouthfeel," says Shafer. "A juicy quality," Doug adds. How does the terroir of their vineyard fit into the Stags Leap District profile? Shafer, who was a driving force behind the creation of the Stags Leap AVA, says, "I think the common thread of Stags Leap District Cabernet is the softer, supple tannins we get. There are then house styles that develop. You can emphasize the tannins or other qualities by the winemaking technique, but the supple tannins are there. We can be both big and elegant. We have it both ways," he says. "We walk the line between extraction and elegance," Doug explains, "and when we get both in one bottle, it's really cool." Way cool, I'd say.

## Summing up

It is rare to find a single winery making more than one or two top wines. Shafer has half a dozen bottlings, including the Hillside Select, that are worth a close look. The Red Shoulder Ranch Carneros Chardonnay comes from a vineyard planted in 1990 to five different clones of Chardonnay, chosen for low yield and distinctive flavours. The wine is barrel-fermented using wild yeast and does not undergo malolactic fermentation. The usual barrel time is fourteen months, half in new oak, including two-thirds French and one-third American. Typically the wine has a luscious mouthfeel, spiced by green apple and a splash of mango. The Relentless is made from Syrah and Petite Sirah, all from a single ridge top vineyard in the Stags Leap District. The wine, named in honour of winemaker Fernandez, is typically about eighty per cent Syrah and twenty per cent Petite Sirah, although the percentage changes from vintage to vintage. It normally spends about twenty-eight months in French oak, about eighty-five per cent of which is new. It's a powerful, yet elegant and supple wine, with ripe berry fruit spread over a base of dried herbs with a dash of black pepper. A very intense wine, but never brash.

Most California producers have been less than successful with Sangiovese. The Shafer Firebreak is an exception. Most vintages have a dash of Cabernet Sauvignon. The wine, named after a forest fire several years ago, is from the Shafer estate. It's a luscious wine with wraparound flavours and a long, echoing finish. The Shafer Napa Valley Merlot is bended from vineyards in Stags Leap, Oak Knoll, Yountville, Oakville, St Helena, and Carneros. Most vintages include a small percentage of Cabernet Franc and Cabernet Sauvignon. It is typically a lush wine with a silky mouthfeel and is often the most fruit-forward of Shafer's wines.

The Napa Valley Cabernet Sauvignon is blended from selected vineyards in Stags Leap and the Oak Knoll District and aged for twenty months in barrels, half new and half American. Again, it is typically fruit forward, balanced with supple tannins. The Hillside Select is a stunning wine, made entirely from estate grapes and aged for thirty-two months in new French barrels. Typically, the Hillside Select shows a rich concentration while marinating a juicy, fruity centre, balanced by hints of chocolate and tobacco. I would recommend ageing at least twelve to fifteen years from the vintage date.

## SPOTTSWOODE WINERY

1902 Madrona Avenue, St Helena, CA 94574.

Tel: 707 963 0134; Fax: 707 963 2886;

Email: spottswoode@spottswoode.com; Website: www.spottswoode.com

Vineyards: 16ha

Spottswoode is one of the handful of truly classic Napa estates. Today, it is almost surrounded by the town of St Helena, but the original sixteen-hectare vineyard site is still in vine, at the foot of Spring Mountain in the St Helena AVA. The wine is made in one of Napa's lovely old stone wineries. It was built in 1882 as the Esmeralda Winery and became the Montebello Wine Company at the end of Prohibition. The present name comes from the Spotts family who owned the estate from 1910 until 1972. It's a leafy, inviting place, as is the nearby Victorian home and gardens of owner Mary Novak. She and her late husband, Jack, bought the neglected estate in 1972 at a time when the charming old Victorians were being torn down and replaced by sprawling California ranch-style houses. Over the years, the house has been reclaimed as a lively family centre – the Novaks have five children; three work in the business.

The same kind of attention has been lavished on the vineyards, which are planted to 12.5 hectares of Cabernet Sauvignon, 1.6 hectares of Cabernet Franc, one hectare of Sauvignon Blanc, and 0.2 hectares of Petit Verdot. The Novaks had planted Merlot early on, but Mary says it did nothing for the wine, while the Cabernet Franc adds considerably to the flavour profile. Winemaker Rosemary Cakebread believes the Petit Verdot will add "another colour to the palate". You can see most of the vineyard from the back terrace, sloping up toward the Mayacamas range to the west, with Spring Mountain looming on the right. The vines have been farmed organically since 1985, Spottswoode making the change from chemical growing to organic long before it became a trendy move.

It had not been the Novaks' intention to make wine when they first settled in Napa, moving north from San Diego County. But, following the advice of business associates who praised the remarkable quality of the grapes, they made the first Spottswoode wine in 1982, under the direction of consulting winemaker Tony Soter. The vineyard itself is mostly on the Sulfur Creek alluvial fan. Soils are sandy clay loam that permits good drainage while allowing sufficient water retention. The vineyard microclimate is dominated by cool night air moving inland from the Pacific through the gap in the Mayacamas range south of Spring Mountain. There is an amazing diversity of soils. The combined fourteen hectares of Cabernet Sauvignon and Cabernet Franc typically produces about twenty-four separate lots of wine annually. The wine is made in a modern facility, designed to look like it belongs next to the old stone cellar, which is used as barrel storage.

Again, in classic estate style, Spottswoode makes only two wines, a Cabernet Sauvignon – and no nonsense about meaningless reserve designations – and one of California's best Sauvignon Blancs, made in the Graves style. Let's open with a glass of the Sauvignon. There is very little oak influence. The wine is barrel-fermented but goes into stainless steel as soon as there is a hint of oak, usually within two to three months. There is, typically, fifteen to eighteen per cent Semillon in the blend, which contains grapes from four different vineyards. There are the estate grapes, and also grapes from two vineyards near Calistoga in the warm northern reaches of the valley and a vineyard in Carneros. The Semillon comes from one of the Calistoga vineyards and the Carneros vineyard is planted to the Musque clone of Sauvignon Blanc. The vineyards were originally sourced by Tony Soter. They are mostly dry-farmed and head-pruned.

Spottswoode has not been tempted down the grassy path of New Zealand-style Sauvignon Blanc. "I think even if we wanted to make a New Zealand style, the grapes wouldn't let us," says Cakebread. "We aim for a classically styled wine, a pure expression of fruit." Nor have Cakebread and Beth Novak Miliken, who runs the winery for her mother, taken the tempting road towards international fruit bomb wines or the super-concentrated wines aimed at scores in the high nineties. "Sure, we've talked about it," says Novak Miliken. "But in the end, you have to be true to your personal standards and what the site has to offer." Cakebread adds: "I could never make a wine like that – nor could the vineyard give it to us even if I wanted to. You know, winemakers now play a game of seeing who can wait longest to pick. All the talk is about hang time and concentration. I don't even want to know when anyone else picks."

Tasting through a vertical of Spottswoode wines going back into the mid-1980s, I couldn't help but wonder who it was that first dictated that concentration was what wine was all about. Like many other Napa wineries, Spottswoode has had to replant since the return of phylloxera in the late 1980s. Again, like others, the Novaks took the opportunity to change rootstock and clones. I ask Cakebread if these changes might have an impact on the profile of Spotswoode wine? "In the long run, the new clones and rootstocks won't have a big impact. The site is still giving us what it did before," she says. Asked her favourite Spottswoode vintage, Cakebread doesn't hesitate: "The 1999. If I could make a wine like that every year, I would be happy". I have to agree. The 1999 is the result of a long, cool growing season, with the harvest lasting well into October. It's an elegant wine, lush and focused, and capable of extended ageing.

## Summing up

What does the site offer? The first word that springs to mind is elegance and a supple range of fruit, always luscious, never in your face. There is also an underlying dark spice tone that is consistent throughout the wines and a silky mouthfeel, especially in the wines under ten years old. Beyond that, the wines take on a classic cigar box flavour profile. Without meaning to invite comparisons, I would say that Spottswoode Cabernets would be hard to pick out if there were put into a blind tasting of classified growth Bordeaux. The Cabernet Sauvignon is made from estate grapes, organically grown. Typically, the tonnage is around seven tonnes per hectare. After fermentation, the Cabernet is aged for around twenty months, depending on the vintage, in French oak, of which about two-thirds is new barrels, and held about one year in bottle before release. A small percentage of Cabernet Franc, typically around five per cent is used in the blend. The Spottswoode wines will age for at least two decades, in some cases longer. Anyone thinking of establishing a cellar of California Cabernet would do well to look at Spottswoode as a good place to start.

## STAG'S LEAP WINE CELLARS

5766 Silverado Trail, Napa, CA 94558. Tel: 707 944 2020; Fax: 707 257 7501; Email: winecellars@cask23.com; Website: www.cask23.com
Vineyards: 113ha

There is still something of the professor about Warren Winiarski who, with his wife Barbara, owns Stag's Leap Wine Cellars. Even though he hasn't taught since the 1960s, except by example, when Winiarski takes on a subject that is dear to him, terroir for example, his voice and his body language send out the signal: this is important. Pay attention. You will be tested on this. There is also the underlying passion that great teachers have in common, no matter what the subject.

There is also present the intellectual honesty and curiousity that I remember from my days in graduate school. I once had an English professor who walked in one morning and started reciting *Beowulf* to the class, by memory, in the original Anglo-Saxon English. I understood maybe one word out of three, but it was one of the most moving readings of poetry I have ever experienced. Winiarski has opened the same vistas into terroir for me as that long-ago English professor opened into *Beowulf*. Early on one very hot summer day I went into the Fay and SLV vineyards with Winiarski for a seminar in terroir. "I first tasted wine from this site in 1969. It was a homemade 1968 Caberent made by Nathan Fay and I knew I wanted to plant a vineyard as close to this as possible," he said. "The question is, of course, was that wine an expression of terroir or simply an expression of outstanding Cabernet Sauvignon? I'll never know for sure."

In 1970 Winiarski bought and planted what is now called the SLV vineyard. It is right next to Fay vineyard. At the time, it was planted to plum trees and a few vines: Petite Sirah and Alicante Bouschet. It was this vineyard that produced the grapes for the 1973 Stag's Leap Cabernet Sauvignon which won the 1976 Paris tasting against the best of France (see page 26). That tasting came only twelve years after Winiarski gave up his job teaching a survey course in liberal arts (which might now be called humanities) at the University of Chicago and headed to California with his wife. He had learned to appreciate wine while studying in Italy. He knew, of course, that the winds of change were blowing in Napa and simply followed the American urge to pack up the women and children and head west.

Winiarski came down in the centre of the storm, landing a job at Robert Mondavi in the year the winery opened. For the next few years, he tasted Napa wines by day and at night read textbooks and manuals on winemaking. At that time, most of the Napa Caberents were vineyard blends. There was seldom any thought given to letting a single vineyard speak by itself. By 1970, Winiarski felt the time was right. With a group of partners, he bought the eighteen-hectare property. Two years later, he built the winery on a knoll overlooking the vineyard and the hunt was on. (The site of Winiarski's Stag's Leap Wine Cellars is only a few miles from the historic ruins of Occidental Cellars, built in 1878 by Terrill Grigsby, one of the dashing mountain men who were behind the revolt in 1846 that led to the short-lived Bear Flag Republic. There are the remains of an old stone winery on the Winiarski property that is believed to have been built a few years later by one of Grigsby's sons, a few yards from Chase Creek and the Fay vineyard.)

In 1986, Winiarski was able to buy the Fay vineyard and combine the two estates. Fay had planted his vineyard in 1961 on a site sloping up from Chase Creek toward the rocky Stags Leap palisades. Fay was the first to plant Cabernet Sauvignon in what is now the Stags Leap District and is believed to have planted the first Cabernet vines south of Oakville in the twentieth century. Until Fay proved them wrong, the UC Davis experts considered the area too cool to properly mature Cabernet Sauvignon.

The Fay vineyard, as now planted, consists of twenty-four hectares of Cabernet Sauvignon, two hectares of Merlot, and 0.4 hectares of Petit Verdot. The soils are gravelly bale clay loam and volcanic debris with very rocky sub-soils. That's what it says when you read the fact sheet supplied to the wine trade, the wine media, and consumers interested enough to ask. But Winiarski has a different take. "You see the grey colour of the soil in the lower part of the vineyard?" he asks, referring to the flat area near Chase Creek. "Look. You see how small the pebbles are. These are soils that washed down from the mountain. They are the lightest soils so the water carried them here in a series of alluvial fans." Winiarski points out several slightly raised strips of soil, reaching out like fingers (or the ribs of a Japanese fan) from the mountain toward the creek. Those fingers are concentrations of alluvial soils and are one reason Fay vineyard is split into more than a dozen different blocks.

As the vineyard climbs toward the mountain, the soil starts to change colour, taking on reddish cast at first, then a deeper red, like a weathered brick, as the vines begin climbing the hillside toward the rocky cliffs above. "The red soil is volcanic. It's residual soil too heavy to be washed down," Winiarski explains. "Below, there is the lighter soil, the water element. Above is the heavier soil, the fire element, and they meet somewhere in the middle. The difference in the wines is remarkable. Cabernet from the 'water' soil is supple with a fleshy quality. From the 'fire' soil, it is more concentrated, more spirited. We have identified each block based on its relation to fire and water. It is the middle ground, where the two elements meet, that provides the harmony, that brings the fire and water together – and that is what we blend towards. That is our terroir," he says.

The SLV site, Winiarski's original vineyard, lies at a slightly lower elevation than Fay. Even though it is separated from Fay only by the width of a dirt road, it yields a completely different wine and is bottled separately. In an André Simon lecture titled "The Significance of Terroir," delivered to the Wine & Food Society in the early 1980s, Winiarski said:

> The subject of terroir increases our enjoyment of wine by adding another
> dimension to appreciate: that of locality or origin. We generally believe

*we "know" about things when we know where they come from, as well as how they come to be … We believe that because the grape variety is the same everywhere, the place where the variety is grown offers important information, since it is the unique origin of what we are experiencing and enjoying.*

In Winiarski's view, terroir itself is mute. It has no voice of its own and it can only find expression through human intervention and human choice. Those choices involve many things, beginning with the choice of variety, and involving dozens of viticultural and winemaking decisions. He likes to talk about the vineyard "singing". "To make a tune, all the elements must be in harmony. If you like the song, you can sing it or listen to it again and again without tiring of it. Otherwise, it becomes just noise."

Trading metaphors, the vineyard could be a musical instrument, say a piano. The world is filled with pianists who can play the right notes in a Chopin nocturne, but there are precious few who can get inside the music and create an experience that transcends the scribbles on the page. It is possible to make a "correct" wine that does not really express the terroir, simply a degree in advanced oenology. Perhaps to make it work it has to be knowledge plus intellect plus passion. A poor arrangement or an incompetent conductor can ruin even the best piece of music. Winiarski contends that the international emphasis on big, overripe, and over-extracted wines that became the vogue in the mid-1990s also wipes out terroir.

## Summing up

It's true that Stag's Leap Wine Cellars is all about red wine, no doubt of that. But the Chardonnay is worth a mention as well. The Napa Valley, a blend from several different vineyards, is a pleasing apéritif wine, balanced and oak-shy which is a plus, but the Arcadia Vineyard Chardonnay is one of those few Napa Chardonnays that rate some serious attention. Stylistically, the Arcadia is a homage to Chablis, Winiarski admits. The vineyard, which the Winiarski family bought in 1996, was originally planted in 1973 by a group of partners that included Miljenko Grgich (Grgich Hills) and was the source of that winery's great Chardonnays of the 1970s and 1980s. It was originally called Olive Hills Vineyard but Winiarski renamed it Arcadia. It is in the Coombsville area, south of Napa but just north of Carneros. Far Niente, another outstanding Napa Chardonnay, is from the same region.

Winiarski makes two estate Cabernets every year: the Fay Vineyard and the SLV. You could start with elegance to describe the wines, then go on to speak of opulence, richness, depth, and complexity of flavour. The Fay vineyard bottlings offer a silky mouthfeel and can be a pure delight. They have the balance and structure for long ageing, and intriguing dried fruit and spice in the mouth. It was a Cabernet from the SLV vineyard that won the Paris tasting (*see* page 26). The vineyard, first planted in 1970, was showing signs of disease and age by the 1990s so Winiarski started a block-by-block replanting programme. Typically, SLV wines show darker fruit than the Fay Vineyard with a rich herbal edge centred on rosemary and sandalwood. In exceptional years Winiarski also makes a third Cabernet, the Cask 23, which is a blend of grapes from the Fay and SLV vineyards. The Cask 23 is the ultimate expression of terroir, a subtle interplay of the best elements of the two estate vineyards. It's a rich, enchanting wine to drink, which stands beside the best in the world.

## TREFETHEN VINEYARDS

1160 Oak Knoll Avenue, Napa, CA 94558. Tel: 707 255 7700; Fax: 707 255 0793; Email: winery@trefethen.com; Website: www.trefethen.com
Vineyards: 242ha

Driving north from the town of Napa on Highway 29, you begin to wonder where the vineyards are. There is mile after mile of shopping malls, factory outlet stores, and motels. This could be Omaha, Des Moines or almost any American city that is sprawling in an unsightly fashion beyond its core. Then all at once, the concrete ends and the vineyards begin. You have entered the Oak Knoll District, one of Napa's newer AVAs and the home of Trefethen Vineyards, a historic site just north of the city of Napa.

In 1886, when Napa was only a few buildings clustered around working docks on the Napa River, the Eshcol Winery was built by James and George Goodman. The three-story wooden winery was designed by architect Hamden McIntyre, who also designed Far Niente and Greystone. In 1888, an Eshcol Cabernet Sauvignon took first prize at the San Francisco Viticulture Fair, so the young winery got off to a good start. Wine was made at Eshcol until Prohibition and the vineyards straggled on until the 1960s when the property was bought by the Trefethen family. They began replanting the old vineyards and the long process of restoring the original gravity flow winery, which has been named a National Historic Landmark.

The 222-hectare valley floor vineyard is the largest contiguous vineyard under single ownership in Napa. John and Janet Trefethen also own a twenty-hectare hillside vineyard just at the northern edge of the Oak Knoll District. The Trefethens' first wine was from the 1974 vintage and, in some ways, their experience in restoring and replanting the old vineyard parallels the entire experience of the Napa Valley over the last quarter of the century. When they began planting in the late 1960s, they were advised to plant on AxR-1, virtually regarded at the time as the "universal" rootstock. Well, you know that story and with the onslaught of phylloxera in the 1980s, it doesn't have a happy ending.

Janet says that by 1990, it was time to make a decision. "Do we invest the $87,500 per hectare to replant 222 hectares or do we pull out?" The Trefethens elected to stay the course and began a gradual programme of replanting. At the same time they started extensive field testing of clones and rootstock, wanting to be sure they got it right the second time around. The valley floor vineyard is now planted to Chardonnay, Cabernet Sauvignon, Merlot, Riesling, Cabernet Franc, and a little Pinot Noir. The hillside vineyard is in Cabernet Sauvignon and Merlot.

Soils on the valley floor are loam with sand, clay, and silt and patches of gravel from an old creek bed. The Cabernet is planted in the gravelly soils. The climate is cool, almost as cool as Carneros and quite a bit cooler than Rutherford and the northern part of the valley. On the hillside, soils are sandstone, shale, and loam on an alluvial fan. It's a little warmer than the valley floor and gets slightly more rain in an average year.

The Oak Knoll District (Trefethen is far and away the largest winery in the AVA) has a longer growing season than any other Napa appellation, because of earlier bud break and flowering due to warmer and drier springs and a slightly later harvest than up valley vineyards. It is one of the few parts of Napa that good quality Chardonnay and Cabernet Sauvignon can both be made. Even more surprising is the excellent (almost) dry Riesling from Trefethen.

Trefethen doesn't always grab the headlines. Although it does make a cult-priced wine, the Halo Cabernet Sauvignon, from its hillside estate, it has never broken into those gaudy ranks. Perhaps because the aim at Trefethen has always been to make balanced wines with subtle flavours designed to entice and seduce, not take you by assault. The Trefethens like to say their wines are made in the vineyard. Well, a lot of people in Napa say that, but in the case of Trefethen, it rings true. There is no winemaking style or ideology imposed on the wines. For the most part, what the vineyard gives is what you taste in the glass.

Trefethen first caught the public eye with its Chardonnay, which until the mid-1990s was made in a minimalist style – fermentation in stainless steel, no malolactic fermentation, brisk acidity, and long-lived. As the post-1990 Chardonnay vines began to produce, winemaker Peter Luthi decided to tweak them. He has introduced partial barrel-fermentation and limited malolactic, feeling that this adds elements of complexity that were missing in the young vine wines. Thankfully, there has been no change in the treatment of the Riesling, which is stainless steel all the way. The emphasis on the valley floor Cabernet is clearly on fruit.

Trefethen has one of the most extensive wine library operations in Napa, routinely holding back a fairly high percentage of each vintage for later release. This has proved to be a very popular move as Trefethen wines, at least the Chardonnay and Cabernet, do age very well, holding their structure and developing nicely in the bottle. I recently pulled out a 1997 Chardonnay, which is doddering old age for most California Chardonnay, and it was superb. This was one of the transition wines, moving from stainless steel to barrel-fermentation. Almost one-third of the wine had been barrel-fermented, none had undergone malolactic fermentation. It had been aged in oak for just over three months. It was that rare classic California Chardonnay that could be taken seriously. I also tasted, with winemaker Luthi, a 1989 Cabernet Sauvignon. Not a great year and Luthi jumped all over it because he tasted some "green elements". I found it an elegant wine, lean and bright. What Luthi called "herbal" I identified as tarragon with a surprising whisper of citrus. It worked. What seems to carry Trefethen wines into a satisfying old age is the bright acidity which characterizes both the red and white wines. Luthi says that quality, along with the marvellous cherry-berry fruit of the Cabernet, is a result of the cool climate, and the shallow infertile soils. And maybe the determination of the winemaking team, including the Trefethens, to leave well enough alone.

## Summing up

The Trefethens like to think of their impressive Cabernet Sauvignon as their flagship wine. But I suspect that most consumers think of Riesling when they think of Trefethen, and so they should. Trefethen Riesling is consistently at the head of the class for California. It has never been near any oak and is refreshingly crisp, with bright acidity and good varietal character. It is just on the cusp of dry, typically carrying about 0.6 per cent residual sugar. Most years Trefethen makes a botrytis late-harvest Riesling, which is delicious.

Trefethen's Cabernet Sauvignon is made from valley floor grapes, usually with a bit of Merlot and Cabernet Franc in the blend. The wine is aged in a mix of French and American oak for up to eighteen months. The tannins are soft and fruit flavours tend to be direct, focused on black cherry and plum, often with a hint of mint and chocolate. They are very good taken young, but have staying power as well, ageing in the fifteen to twenty year range. The Reserve Cabernets and Halo are made from the hillside vineyard. Halo is 100 per cent Cabernet and the Reserve is a blend of Cabernet Sauvignon and Merlot. It gets twenty-eight to thirty months in all French oak, as does the Halo.

The Trefethen Chardonnay has always been one of Napa Valley's jewels. Before the introduction of barrel-fermentation and malolactic fermentation it was a virtual homage to Chablis, and I mean that as a compliment. Short term, the changes have not taken anything away from the wine's integrity. I am not altogether convinced that the new style of Chardonnay will age as well as the traditional stainless-steel versions.

# 10

# Napa stars

These are other wineries that are worth checking out. They were not included in individual appellation listings because, for the most part, they make wine from several different appellations and are not closely associated with any particular district. Alternatively, for whatever reason, the wine does not seem typical of the appellation. In some cases, the winery may draw heavily on a single appellation but is not physically located in that appellation.

There are also several newcomers that show promise. Almost any of the wineries here, in any given vintage, could rise to A List status. The tasting notes here do not apply to any particular vintage, but are intended to represent the wine over a period of time. But at the same time, they are merely snapshots of my assessment of the wines at time of writing: five years ago they would not have been the same, and it is unlikely they will be the same five years hence.

## ANDERSON'S CONN CREEK VINEYARDS
680 Rossi Road, St Helena, CA 94574. Tel: 707 963 8600; Fax: 707 963 7818; Email: cvvinfo@connvalleyvineyards.com; Website: www.connvalleyvineyards.com
Vineyards: 39ha
Established in 1983, this underrated winery is a few minutes drive east of St Helena, at the foot of Howell Mountain where Conn Creek flows west toward the Napa River. The estate vineyard is on a ridge east of the river at an elevation of 121 metres (400 feet). The Cabernets, with some Merlot and Cabernet Franc blended in, have been outstanding since the first release in 1987. The flavour profile is tilted toward the Bordeaux style, offering elegance and finesse rather than power and concentration.

## ARAUJO ESTATE WINES

2155 Picket Road, Calistoga, CA 94515. Tel: 707 942 6061; Fax: 707 942
6471; Email: wine@araujoestate; Website: www.araujoestatewines.com
Vineyards: 14ha

The heart of Araujo's dense and tannic Cabernet Sauvignon comes from
the Eisele vineyard near Calistoga, which Joseph Phelps tapped for a series
of outstanding vineyard-designated Cabernets in the 1970s and 1980s.
The vineyard was bought by Bert Araujo in 1990. He replanted part of the
fourteen-hectare vineyard and also put in new plantings of Syrah and
Viognier. A small winery was built on the property. The wines are packed
with explosive flavours and have attracted favourable attention from the
wine press. There is some debate as to whether the Araujo Eisele Vineyard
Cabernet has the structure for ageing as did the Phelps.

## BELL WINE CELLARS

6200 Washington Street, Yountville, CA 94599. Tel: 707 944 1673; Fax: 707
944 1674; Email: info@bellwine.com; Website: www.bellwine.com
Vineyards: 4ha

Anthony Bell, a South African who originally came to the USA to study
winemaking in California, was head winemaker at Beaulieu Vineyards
when he established this winery in 1992. Bell makes dense, flavour-
packed Cabernet Sauvignon and Merlot from Rutherford, and from time
to time he also bottles other varieties from grapes sourced outside Napa.
He sold the winery in 2002 to a group of investors.

## BENESSERE VINEYARDS

1010 Big Tree Road, St Helena, CA 94574. Tel: 707 963 5853; Fax: 707 963
9546; Email: info@benesserevineyards.com; Website: www.benesserevineyards.com
Vineyards: 20ha

Breaking out of the Cabernet mode, Benessere makes remarkably good
Sangiovese from a revitalized 1970s vineyard near St Helena, as well as a
small amount of Zinfandel. The Sangiovese has delightful bright cherry
fruit with medium weight and finish. It is one of the best efforts in
California with that Italian varietal. It is all estate grown.

## BLANKIET ESTATE

PO Box 2100, Yountville, CA 94599. Tel: 707 963 2001; Fax: 707 963 2012;
Email: winery@blankiet.com; Website: www.blankiet.com
Vineyards: 6.5ha

The winery produces small amounts of Merlot and a proprietary red blend from Cabernet Sauvignon and Cabernet Franc from a 6.5-hectare vineyard west of Yountville in the foothills of the Mayacamas range. Helen Turley was the founding winemaker and her husband, John Wetlaufer is the vineyard manager.

## AUGUST BRIGGS WINES

333 Silverado Trail, Calistoga, CA 94515. Tel: 707 942 4912; Fax: 707 942 5854; Email: info@augustbriggswines.com; Website: www.augustbriggswines.com
Vineyards: n/a

After more than a decade making wine in California's Central Valley and in Oregon, August Briggs began to develop his own label in 1995. His small winery near Calistoga on the Silverado Trail opened in 2003. Briggs makes only about 5,000 cases of wine a year, but has attracted interest with his Pinot Noir from Carneros and the cool Coombsville area between the town of Napa and the Carneros AVA. He also makes a few other varieties, all from purchased grapes, including several bottlings of Pinot Noir and Chardonnay from outside Napa. Briggs is a name to watch in the future.

## BUEHLER VINEYARDS

820 Greenfield Road, St Helena, CA 94574. Tel: 707 963 2155; Fax: 707 963 3747; Website: www.buehlervineyards.com
Vineyards: 24ha

The Buehler family bought land in the eastern hills above Conn Valley in the early 1970s and planted about twenty-four hectares of Cabernet Sauvignon and Zinfandel, which they initially sold to other wineries, including Grgich Hills, Cuvaison, and Burgess Cellars. But realizing they had a good thing going, the family produced its first wine in 1978 and have made a fair success of estate-grown Cabernet Sauvignon and an excellent Zinfandel which shows great depth and complexity. In recent years, Buehler has produced Chardonnay from the Russian River Valley in Sonoma County and bottlings of Cabernet from other than estate grapes.

## BURGESS CELLARS

1108 Deer Park Road, St Helena, CA 94574. Tel: 707 963 4766; Fax: 707 963 8774; Website: www.burgesscellars.com
Vineyards: 42.4ha

Often included with Howell Mountain wineries, Burgess Cellars is actually just outside the appellation boundaries, although the Cabernet Sauvignon and Zinfandel are well within the parameters of the Howell Mountain style. The winery itself is on the site of an 1880 winery and was also the home of the original Souverain Cellars winery. The Burgess Cabernet is made from very low-yielding, dry-farmed vineyards. It can be muted when young but opens into a balanced and complex wine with five to eight years of bottle age, although it will keep much longer. The Zinfandel, also from estate vines, is made very much in the same style and ranks as one of the best Zins in California. Burgess also makes an exceptionally good, if somewhat oaky, Chardonnay from an estate vineyard near Yountville. Overall, Burgess ranks with the best in Napa year in and year out.

## CAFARO CELLARS

1550 Allyn Avenue, St Helena, CA 94574. Tel: 707 963 7181;
Fax: 707 963 8458; Email: info@cafaro.com; Website: www.cafaro.com
Vineyards: 6ha

Joe Cafaro, a consulting winemaker who has worked with Chappellet, Keenan, Acacia, and Sinskey, among others, started producing wine under his own label in the late 1980s. In the beginning, all the grapes were bought in, but he began developing his own Cabernet vineyard in the Stags Leap District in the mid-1990s. Cafaro Merlot and Cabernet are marked by deep fruit, rounded flavours, harmony, and balance. What's not to like? Production is limited, but worth looking for.

## CEJA VINEYARDS

PO Box 5957, Napa, CA 94581. Tel: 707 2553954; Fax: 707 253 7998;
Email: wine@cejavineyards.com; Website: www.cejavineyards.com
Vineyards: 45.5ha

The Ceja family came to Napa from Mexico to work in the vineyards. Now they own vineyards and a winery producing Chardonnay, Cabernet Sauvignon, and a red blend called Vino de Casa, a delicious "picnic" wine made from Pinot Noir with Merlot and Syrah. The Cabernet Sauvignon has soft, velvety tannins with a supple structure. The Chardonnay is one of the better new offerings from Carneros. It is barrel-fermented but does not undergo malolactic. It is typically bright and well balanced with minerally tones. Only a few years old, Ceja is a winery to watch.

## CHANDON

1 California Drive, Yountville, CA 94599. Tel: 707 944 8844;
Fax: 707 944 1123; Website: www.chandon.com
Vineyards: 445ha

Since its beginnings in 1977, Chandon has been producing remarkably consistent and often quite good sparkling wine. Chandon, which was the first of the French-owned sparkling wine houses in Napa, has chosen to offer only non-vintage bubbly, but with a high percentage of reserve wines, sometimes as much as thirty per cent. The Brut Reserve bottling is a complex wine with layers of flavour, always a winner. The top of the range étoile is a beauty as well, with mature flavours and good structure – it is always among California's top three or four sparkling wines. Chandon draws on vineyards on Mount Veeder, in Carneros, and its estate vineyards in Yountville.

## CHAPPELLET WINERY

1581 Sage Canyon Road, St Helena, CA 94574. Tel: 707 963 7136;
Fax: 707 963 7445. Email: info@chappellet.com; Website: www.chappellet.com
Vineyards: 44.5ha

Donn Chappellet established the winery in the Vaca hills east of the Silverado Trail in 1969. The Cabernet Sauvignon can be very good, with a firm structure and intense fruit. The Chardonnay is usually first rate with a rich depth and plenty of oak. Chappellet Winery also makes an exceptionally good Chenin Blanc in a dry style.

## CHATEAU MONTELENA

1429 Tubbs Lane, Calistoga, CA 94515. Tel: 707 942 5105; Fax: 707 942
4221; Email: customer-service@montelena.com; Website: www.montelena.com
Vineyards: 49ha

Tourists and wine buffs alike love Montelena. Tourists love the stone winery, built in 1882, and wine buffs love the Cabernet Sauvignon. The winery, just north of California, had been long abandoned when it was bought by the Barrett family in 1969. Mike Grgich (now the owner of Grgich Hills winery) came on as winemaker and it was his Chardonnay – a blend of Sonoma and Napa grapes – that won the Paris tasting in 1976 (*see* page 26). But it had never been Jim Barrett's intention to be known for Chardonnay. His goal from the beginning had been estate-bottled Cabernet Sauvignon and that is without doubt what Montelena is best known for. Jerry Luper followed Grgich and put the Cabernet programme on tracking, leaving in the early 1980s. Barrett's son, Bo, took over from Luper and is still the winemaker. The Cabernets are made for ageing. Powerful expressions of the varietal, they are loaded with concentrated black cherry fruit, creamy and rich in the centre. These are not Cabernets for the timid, but they do come around after a few years in bottle and can last twenty to twenty-five years.

## CLOS PEGASE

1060 Duinaweal Lane, Calsitoga, CA 94515. Tel: 707 942 4981;
Fax: 707 942 4994; Email: cp@clospegase.com; Website: www.clospegase.com
Vineyards: 182ha

Art collector and publisher Jan Shrem built an imposing winery just south of Calistoga (near Sterling Vineyards) in 1984. The winery, which holds part of Shrem's art collection, was very controversial when it was constructed. It does rather stand out. It was designed by post-modernist architect Michael Graves and local critics (who if they didn't know much about architecture, knew what they liked, or rather what they didn't like) held up construction for a time. It is a rather wonderful building which works well as a winery and also a roadside museum. Shrem also achieved a measure of notoriety when the Bureau of Alcohol, Tobacco, and Firearms rejected a Clos Pegase label in 1992 because it contained a painting of a female nude. Over the years, the wines have steadily improved, especially the Bordeaux blend called Hommage. In general, the Clos Pegase Cabernet Sauvignon and Merlot are medium weight wines with forward fruit and mild tannins with short-term ageing potential.

## CONN CREEK

8711 Silverado Trail, St Helena, CA 94574. Tel: 707 963 9100;
Fax: 707 963 7840; Email: info@conncreek.com; Website: www.conncreek.com
Vineyards: 1.2ha

Conn Creek is a neglected jewel. The winery itself was built in 1974, although the vineyard was planted by founder Bill Collins in the 1960s. The Zinfandel was first rate from the start and early Cabernets were also quite good. The winery expanded, but ran into marketing problems in the 1980s and was eventually sold to Chateau Ste Michelle of Washington state, which also owns Villa Mount Eden in Napa. Over the years production has been cut back until today there are about 5,000 cases of

Cabernet Sauvignon, Cabernet Franc, Merlot, and a Bordeaux-style blend called Anthology, which was launched in 1991. Anthology has received well-deserved high marks with each new release. It is an elegant and harmonious wine, capable of ageing in the ten to fifteen year range.

## COSENTINO VINEYARDS

7415 St Helena Highway, Yountville, CA 94599. Tel: 707 944 1220; Fax: 707 944 1254; Email: finewines@cosentinowinery.com; Website: www.cosentinowinery.com

Vineyards: 64.5ha

Mitch Cosentino began making wine in 1980 using rented warehouse space in Modesto in the Central Valley, better known as the home of E & J Gallo. But Cosentino soon began concentrating on red Bordeaux varieties and in 1990 he moved to Napa, building a winery on Highway 29 next door to a popular local restaurant called Mustards Grill. Most of his wines are made from purchased grapes, often from outside Napa. He makes a regular bottling of Cabernet Sauvignon and a reserve from Napa fruit; the reserve is a little riper, with a medium finish. The Cosentino is a lively wine with bright fruit. Top of the line is a sleek and silky red Meritage called M Coz.

## CRICHTON HALL VINEYARD

1150 Darms Lane, Napa, Ca 94558. Tel: 707 224 4200; Fax: 707 224 4218; Email: info@crichtonhall.com; Website: www.crichtonhall.com

Vineyards: 20ha

Richard and Judith Crichton settled in Napa in the late 1970s and planted Chardonnay on Darms Lane in southeast Napa. Their first release, in 1985, was well received. They have added Merlot and a Bordeaux blend called Reflexion as well as a very good Pinot Noir. The wines have an understated balance and focus that is very welcoming. The Pinot has a rich velvety texture that enriches the palate.

## CUVAISON WINERY

4550 Silverado Trail, Calistoga, CA 94515. Tel: 707 942 6266; Fax: 707 942 5732; Email: info@cuvaison.com; Website: www.cuvaison.com

Vineyards: 230.5ha

Founded in 1979, Cuvaison had some ups and downs early on, but has been at a high quality level over the past decade or so, with firm, tightly wound Cabernet Sauvignon capable of ageing up to fifteen years, and a silky Carneros Pinot Noir. The Chardonnay is a cut above average, crisp and fruity with deep pear and apple flavours.

## DARIOUSH WINERY

4240 Silverado Trail, Napa, CA 94558. Tel: 707 257 2345; Fax: 707 257 3132; Email: info@darioush.com; Website: www.darioush.com
Vineyards: 20ha

I could be jumping the starting line a bit on this one, but the early wines from this new winery on the Silverado Trail, just south of the Stags Leap District, show great promise. The owner, Darioush Khaledi, who grew up in the Shiraz region of Iran, founded the winery in 1997. The first wines will be Cabernet Sauvignon, Merlot, Shiraz (of course), Chardonnay, and Viognier. The first releases of all show a bold approach – there's nothing shy about these wines. At the time of writing, a spectacular winery is being constructed, the design inspired by the Persepolis, the city founded by Darius I, the first king of Persia. That's going to be a hard act to top, even in Napa.

## DOMAINE CHARBAY WINERY AND DISTILLERY

4001 Spring Mountain Road, St Helena, CA 94574. Tel: 707 963 9327; Fax: 707 963 3343; Email: info@charbay.com; Website: www.charbay.com
Vineyards: n/a

Miles and Susan Karakasevic and their family have way too much fun. They hang out near the top of Spring Mountain and think of wonderful spirits to distill and wines to make, including a smashing white port and some quite distinctive Cabernet from bought in fruit. The name comes from a drink they invented, a delicious combination of Chardonnay and alembic brandy from their own still. The Karakasevics also distill several different fruit-infused vodkas, pastis, and whisky. Too much fun.

## DUTCH HENRY WINERY

4310 Silverado Trail, Calistoga, CA 94515. Tel: 707 942 5771; Fax: 707 942 5512; Email: info@dutchhenry.com; Website: www.dutchhenry.com
Vineyards: 10ha

This small – just under 5,000 cases – family winery on the Silverado Trail is capable of making exceptional Cabernet Sauvignon from estate vineyards. There is also a good Napa Valley Merlot and an outstanding Napa Zinfandel made from purchased grapes. Most of the wine is sold at the cellar door, but it is worth seeking out.

## ELYSE WINERY

2100 Hoffman Lane, Napa, CA 94558. Tel: 707 944 2900; Fax: 707 945 0301;
Email: info@elysewinery.com; Website: www.elysewinery.com
Vineyards: 0.6ha

Good quality Zinfandel is the strong card at this small winery. Most of the production is sold through a mailing list, but the Zinfandel and Petite Sirah are worth a search. Most years, a Zinfandel is made from Rutherford grapes and a second bottling from Howell Mountain. They are both quite good and raise the question of why more Zinfandel isn't grown and made in Napa.

## ETUDE

PO Box 3382, Napa, CA 94558. Tel: 707 257 5300; Fax: 707 257 6022;
Website: www.etudewines.com
Vineyards: n/a

Tony Soter established étude by in the mid-1980s. As a consulting winemaker Soter's clients have included Chappellet and Spottswoode. For several years he made Carneros Pinot Noir in leased facilities. In 2002, he joined forces with Beringer Blass Wine Estates and that global giant bought a winery for him in Carneros, the old RMS brandy distillery, an aborted joint venture from the 1980s between Schramsberg and Rémy Martin. Soter's Pinots are sleek and powerful expressions of the varietal, made for ageing. The Heirloom Pinot, a limited production wine, is a good example of his approach.

## FAR NIENTE

1350 Acacia Drive, Oakville, CA 94562. Tel: 707 944 2861;
Fax: 707 944 2312; Email: info@farniente.com; Website: www.farniente.com
Vineyards: 101ha

Brothers Gil and John Nickel bought this abandoned nineteenth-century winery in 1978 and began restoring the building, which is next door to To Kalon. The only wines made at Far Niente are Cabernet Sauvignon and Chardonnay, which are sourced from several Napa Valley vineyards. The Chardonnay is one of Napa's best. It's a complex, almost baroque wine with a baseline minerally quality framing the dense fruit (*see* Appendix IV page 248). The wine does not go through malolactic. The Cabernet has always been in the shadow of the Chardonnay and was somewhat inconsistent in the past, but it has improved in recent vintages.

Dolce, an outstanding dessert wine, maybe the state's best, is also produced by Far Niente in a separate winery on the estate. Made from botrytis Sauvignon Blanc and Semillon, it is barrel-fermented and aged in new French oak for three years. The wine is absolutely delicious: it's sweet, sure, but with good acidity and a velvety mouthfeel.

## FIFE VINEYARDS

PO Box 553, St Helena, CA 94574. Tel: 707 963 1534; Fax: 707 963 8620; Email: info@fifevineyards.com; Website: www.fifevineyards.com
Vineyards: 14ha

Co-owner Dennis Fife started in the marketing side of the wine business. He worked at Beaulieu Vineyards and was the president of Inglenook at a time when efforts were being made to revive that historic estate. In 1991, he started his own winery, an idea he had been nursing for years. His partner in the winery (and in life) is Karen MacNeil, a widely published wine writer and wine educator. The couple own vineyards in Mendocino as well as on Spring Mountain. They specialize in single-vineyard wines, including Zinfandel and several Rhône varietals. For our purposes, Fife Spring Mountain Reserve Cabernet Sauvignon is the wine to go for.

## FLORA SPRINGS

1978 West Zinfandel Lane, St Helena, CA 94574. Tel: 707 963 4711; Fax: 707 963 7518. Email: greatwines@florasprings.com; Website: www.florasprings.com
Vineyards: 243ha

The Komes family, owners of Flora Springs, had not originally planned to make wine. They were interested in growing grapes and selling them to other Napa wineries. However, as more family members became involved in the business, they expanded the vineyards and began producing their own wine in the late 1970s. Flora Springs has vineyards in several Napa appellations and its various bottlings represent an interesting study of terroir. The best wine is Trilogy, a blend of Cabernet Sauvignon, Merlot, Cabernet Franc, and Malbec (the Malbec became part of the blend only recently). The grapes are all estate grown in the Rutherford appellation. Typically the wine is fruit-forward, but with the structure and balance for extended ageing. The Napa Valley Cabernet Sauvignon is a classic Cabernet. Grapes are from the Rutherford and Oakville appellations and reflect the rich intensity of mid-valley Cabernet fruit. Flora Springs Windfall Vineyard Merlot, made from Rutherford grapes, is an honest varietal, with hints of raspberry and black cherry. Most years a touch of Malbec is added which gives a subtle spin to the wine. There is ripe and fruity Sangiovese from the warmer Pope Valley. Among the whites, the Sauvignon Blanc-based Soliloquy is excellent.

## FOLIE A DEUX
PO Box 539, St Helena, CA 94574. Tel: 707 963 1160; Fax: 707 963 9223;
Email: fadinfo@folieadeux.com; Website: www.folieadeux.com
Vineyards: 4.8ha

Founded in the 1980s on Highway 29 just north of St Helena, the Folie à Deux winery is now owned by Richard Peterson and a group of investors. Peterson used to be winemaker at Beaulieu. The Napa Cabernet has good balance and structure. There is also an outstanding Zinfandel from Amador County in the Sierra foothills, as well as some interesting blends, such as Muscat and Chardonnay.

## FRANCISCAN
1178 Galleron Road, St Helena, CA 94574. Tel: 707 963 7111; Fax: 707 963
7867; Email: visitorcenter@franciscan.com; Website: www.franciscan.com
Vineyards: 104ha

Founded in 1971 just south of St Helena, Franciscan has seen many ups and downs. The winery went through a number of owners in its first few years, before landing on its feet as a partnership between Peter Eckes, the German company, and Agustin Huneeus, now the owner of Quintessa (*see* page 165). Huneeus, making full use of Franciscan's own vineyards as well as purchased grapes, restored the winery to respectability in the late 1980s and 1990s.

There were outstanding Cabernets coming out of the winery and the Cuvée Sauvage Chardonnay was one of the first in Napa to be fermented using native yeasts. The reds were never cutting-edge, but were solid expressions of variety and site. Huneeus, working with his wife Valeria, who handles the vineyard side of the partnership, developed the Franciscan Oakville Estate, an outstanding vineyard. A few years ago, the winery was sold to Canandaigua, the huge New York state wine, beer, and spirits conglomerate, which has vowed to maintain the high standards at Franciscan. Canandaigua also owns Ravenswood Vineyards and Simi Winery in Sonoma, and has set up a separate operating company to handle its premium California wineries.

## FREEMARK ABBEY

3022 St Helena Highway North, St Helena, CA 94574. Tel: 707 963 9694;
Fax: 707 963 0554; Email: wineinfo@freemarkabbey.com;
Website: www.freemarkabbey.com
Vineyards: 40.5ha

The first winery on this site at the northern edge of St Helena, just beyond Beringer, was built in 1886. It went out of production during Prohibition and was revived in 1940 by a partnership led by Albert Ahern. His nickname was Abbey and with bits picked from the names of other partners, the winery became Freemark Abbey. After Ahern's death in 1959, the winery went out of business. But it was brought to life again in 1967 by a new partnership. All through the 1970s the winery's vineyard-designated Cabernet Sauvignon, especially the Bosche Vineyard and the Sycamore Vineyard, were regarded as one of the best in Napa. The winemaker at the time was Bradford Webb, a much-respected figure in the California wine business. Freemark Abbey Cabernets can still reach outstanding levels and the Chardonnay has been much improved in recent years.

## GARGIULO VINEYARDS

575 Oakville Crossroad, Napa, CA 94558. Tel: 707 944 2770; Fax: 707 944 2780; Email: april@gargiulovineyards.com; Website: www.gargiulovineyards.com
Vineyards: 19.5ha

This "rising star" winery wasn't born yesterday. As it turns out, the family has been growing grapes for over a century and the wines are made in two small wineries in the Oakville region. The newer winery was built in 2003 on the Oakville Crossroad. The nearest neighbours are Rudd Winery, Screaming Eagle, and Dalle Valle. An impressive neighbourhood. The winery makes about 2,500 cases a year of Merlot, Cabernet Sauvignon, a Sangiovese/Cabernet blend called Aprile, and – bless their hearts – a Rosato di Sangiovese. Napa needs more pink wine! The Cabernet is supple and medium weight, with delicious cherry fruit. The Merlot is deep and lingering, with an edgy finish. Keep your eye on these guys.

## GRACE FAMILY VINEYARDS

1210 Rockland Road, St Helena, CA 94574. Tel: 707 965 0808;
Fax: 707 963 5271; Website: www.gracefamilyvineyards.com
Vineyards: 0.8ha

Grace Family Cabernet Sauvignon has a devoted following which is better deserved than many of the cult wine producers in Napa. The wine is sold almost entirely by mailing list.

## GRGICH HILLS CELLAR

1829 St Helena Highway, Rutherford, CA 94573. Tel: 707 963 2784;
Fax: 707 963 8725; Email: info@grgich.com; Website: www.grgich.com
Vineyards: 162ha

Mike Grgich and vineyard owner Austin Hills founded the winery in 1977. Grgich was fresh from making the Chardonnay that won the Paris tasting in 1976 (*see* page 26), so Chardonnay was the featured wine from the beginning. It is sourced from several Napa vineyards, including Carneros and is consistently among the best Napa Chardonnays, with good acidity balanced by a touch of oak. It does not go through malolactic fermentation. Grgich Hills also has a good Sauvignon Blanc – they call it Fumé Blanc – which can at times stray into oakiness. The regular bottling of Cabernet is often overlooked. It should not be. In good years it has a ripe fruity intensity, which is nicely rounded with oak. There is also a very good Yountville Estate Cabernet Sauvignon, concentrated and ripe.

## GUSTAVO THRACE WINERY

1146 First Street, Napa, CA 94559. Tel: 707 257 6796; Fax: 707 257 7001;
Email: gustavot@napanet.com; Website: www.gustavothrace.com
Vineyards: n/a

Gustavo Brambila, born in Jalisco, Mexico and Thrace Bromberger, of Greek descent, founded their winery in 1996 in downtown Napa. (Brambilia is a winemaker at Grgich Hills Cellars.) They make a good Chardonnay from Carneros fruit, but the powerful Zinfandel from Chiles Valley is nothing short of marvellous and an excellent example of Chiles Valley Zin, with dark opulent fruit and a long echoing finish. Viva!

## HAGAFEN WINERY

4160 Silverado Trail, Napa, CA 94558. Tel: 707 252 0781; Fax: 707 252 4562;
Email: info@hagafen.com; Website: www.hagafen.com
Vineyards: 5.2ha

Founded in 1979, Hagafen has carved a niche for itself as a producer of premium Kosher wines, chiefly Chardonnay and Cabernet Sauvignon. Early on, quality was shaky, but now the wines are often very good.

## HARRISON VINEYARD

1527 Sage Canyon Road, St Helena, CA 94574. Tel: 707 963 8271;
Fax: 707 963 4552; Email: info@harrisonvineyards.com;
Website: www.harrisonvineyards.com
Vineyards: 8.5ha

Established in the Vaca hills of east Napa, Harrison produces a very good mountain Cabernet Sauvignon, which is powerful and tannic but does age well. The excellent Chardonnay is bright and inviting in a rich style.

## HAVENS WINE CELLARS

2205 Hoffman Lane, Napa, CA 94558. Tel: 707 261 2000; Fax: 707 261 2043;
Email: info@havenswine.com; Website: www.havenswine.com
Vineyards: 8ha

Mike Havens, an English professor at the University of California at Los Angeles, developed a serious interest in wine and went back to school at UC Davis to learn more. He started making his own wines in the early 1980s, first in rented space, later on property next to Truchard in Carneros. Havens is a constant innovator, looking for new varietals as well as new winemaking techniques. He was one of the first in California to use the technique of micro-oxygenation, bubbling tiny amounts of oxygen through the wine to achieve greater complexity and, so it is hoped, create the flavour profile of an oak-aged wine without the oak. Havens was also a pioneer in showing what Merlot can do in Carneros. He also makes a rounded and harmonious Syrah, more in the style of the southern Rhône than the Australian Shiraz fruit sorbet treats. Indeed he has been quoted as saying that the Australians have made it difficult to sell real Syrah in the USA.

## HEITZ CELLARS

500 Taplin Road, St Helena, CA 94574. Tel: 707 953 3542;
Fax: 707 963 7454; Website: www.heitzcellar.com
Vineyards: 145.5ha

A legendary winery that, as good as it is, has never seemed to me to live up to its reputation. There have been occasional great Cabernets from Heitz, especially in the early years (the winery was founded by Joe Heitz in 1961) when it was one of the pioneers of single-vineyard wines. Heitz has a Napa Valley bottling but the stars of the show are the Martha's Vineyard and Bella Oaks. Martha's Vineyard was replanted in 1992, and quality has come back strongly in the late 1990s to approach the legendary vintages of the 1960s and 1970s. The wine is built for ageing, with a firm structure and deep fruit. The Bella Oaks is somewhat more accessible, with dark fruit and a rounded finish. In recent years, Heitz Chardonnay has been a treat, seeming to move towards a richer burgundian style. Heitz is one of the few producers of Grignolino, a light and fruity "picnic" wine.

## THE HESS COLLECTION
4411 Redwood Road, Napa, CA 94558; Tel: 707 255 1144;
Email: info@hesscollection.com; Website: www.hesscollection.com
Vineyards: 425ha

Located in the Mount Veeder appellation, Hess takes grapes from other Napa AVAs for its Napa Cabernet and Chardonnay, although there is a separate bottling of Mount Veeder Chardonnay. The wines are consistently first rate and often represent good value for money. The Cabernet is typically balanced and supple, and ages well for the medium term. Hess has a second label, Hess Select, which is blended from grapes outside Napa, for the most part. The "Collection" in the winery name refers to a museum-quality collection of modern paintings, owned by Swiss Donald Hess, which is open to the public daily.

## HONIG VINEYARD & WINERY
850 Rutherford Road, Rutherford CA 94573. Tel: 707 963 5618;
Fax: 707 963 5639; Email: info@honigwine.com; Website: www.honigwine.com
Vineyards: 27ha

The Honig family bought their vineyard in 1964 from Caymus Winery. For several years, the grapes were sold to neighbouring wineries. The first wine, a Sauvignon Blanc, was made in 1981, with an old tractor barn on the property serving as the winery. It won a gold medal at the Orange County Fair, and the Honigs have been making outstanding Sauvignon Blanc ever since. The Cabernet Sauvignon too, is always above average.

## KARL LAWRENCE CELLARS
PO Box 3598, Napa, CA 94559. Tel: 707 255 2843; Fax: 707 963 2703;
Email: info@karllawrence.com; Website: www.karllawrence.com
Vineyards: n/a

Michael Trujillo, the winemaker at Sequoia Grove, and partner Brian Henry, make only Cabernet Sauvignon from selected vineyards, including a section of To Kalon vineyard owned by Andy Beckstoffer. The wines are superb, typically with good balance and supple flavours, showing respect for the site. Although production is limited, this is a winery that bears watching. Karl and Lawrence are the middle names of Trujillo and Henry.

## KATHRYN HALL VINEYARDS

60 Auberge Road, Rutherford, CA 94573. Tel: 707 967 0700;
Fax: 707 963 8984; Email: info@kathrynhallvineyards.com;
Website: www.kathrynhallvineyards.com
Vineyards: 34.5ha

Craig and Kathryn Hall own vineyards in several areas of California. Hall's family are long-time grape-growers in Mendocino County. A few years ago, they bought the old Napa Valley Co-op winery with the intention of turning it into an ultra-premium Cabernet house for Napa estate-grown wines. The wines are sourced from vineyards in the St Helena AVA and the Vaca Mountains east of the Silverado Trail, and their quality is promising.

## KONGSGAARD WINE

PO Box 349, Oakville, CA 94582.
Tel: 707 963 1391; Fax: 707 963 4512; Email: jkwine@napanet.com
Vineyards: 4ha

For many years John Kongsgaard was winemaker at Newton Vineyards, where he consistently made outstanding Merlot. In his own small winery, where production is under 2,000 cases, Kongsgaard and his wife Maggy make excellent Chardonnay and a zesty Viognier and Roussanne blend from their rocky hillside vineyard. There is also a widely praised Syrah produced from grapes that are grown on the famed Hudson vineyard in Carneros-Napa.

## CHARLES KRUG WINERY

2800 St Helena Highway, St Helena, CA 94574. Tel: 707 967 2200;
Fax: 707 967 2291; Website: www.charleskrug.com;
Vineyards: 1,012ha

There were major improvements to this historic facility and a resultant increase in wine quality in the 1990s. The Cabernet Sauvignon, both the regular bottling and the Vintners Selection, can be quite good. The winery also makes a serviceable Merlot. Charles Krug does own, or control, some first-rate vineyards and quality should continue on an upward path.

## LANG & REED WINE COMPANY

PO Box 662, St Helena, CA 94574. Tel: 707 963 3758; Fax: 707 963 7333;
Email: john@langandreed.com; Website: www.langandreed.com
Vineyards: n/a

Owner John Skupny established his winery in 1992 to produce only Cabernet Franc. It has been a hard sell, but Skupny's background is wine marketing, so he was prepared for that. The wine is excellent, with attractive fruit and a firm structure. He also makes a delicious rosé from Cabernet Franc.

## LEWIS CELLARS

4101 Big Ranch Road, Napa, CA 94558. Tel: 707 255 3400; Fax: 707 255 3402; Email: wine@lewiscellars.com; Website: www.lewiscellars.com
Vineyards: n/a

The winery was founded in 1994 by racing car driver Randy Lewis. Production is limited, but early results have been impressive. The Cabernet Sauvignon is a rich wine, with bright black cherry fruit and enough structure and balance to age in the ten to fifteen year range. The Chardonnay is ripe and full-bodied with an inviting mouthfeel and a long finish. Both wines are made from Oakville appellation grapes. There is also an attractive Syrah.

## LIVINGSTON MOFFETT WINERY

1895 Cabernet Lane,St Helena, CA 94574. Tel: 707 963 2120; Fax: 707 963 9385; Email: info@livingstonwines.com; Website: www.livingstonwines.com
Vineyards: 4ha

A respected producer of Bordeaux blend reds, including the Rutherford Estate (a single-vineyard selection) and Stanley's Selection (a blend of several Napa Valley vineyards). The rich and intense Gemstone is a blend of Cabernet Sauvignon, Cabernet Franc, Merlot, and Petit Verdot made from a vineyard in the Yountville AVA. There is also a Chardonnay made from Carneros fruit and a Syrah.

## MARKHAM VINEYARDS

2812 St Helena Highway North, St Helena, CA 94574. Tel: 707 963 5292;
Fax: 707 963 4616; Email: admin@markhamvineyards.com;
Website: www.markhamvineyards.com
Vineyards: 91ha

Founded by Bruce Markham in 1978, Markham is now owned by the

Mercian Corp, a Japanese company. The Cabernet Sauvignon and Merlot were always good, but there was a great leap of quality, beginning in the early 1990s. The Merlot is the star of the show, with luscious cherry and black plum fruit and a soft mouthfeel. The Cabernet is more on the tannic side, but can be quite good if inconsistent. Chardonnay has also been much improved, showing bright, bold flavours in best years. Grapes come from vineyards located in several regions of Napa.

## LOUIS MARTINI WINERY

254 South St Helena Highway, St Helena, CA 94574.
Tel: 707 963 2736; Fax: 707 963 8750;
Email: info@louismartini.com; Website: www.louismartini.com
Vineyards: 364ha

Quality has been inconsistent for a number of years: sometimes quite good but on the whole rarely rising to average. The winery is now owned by E & J Gallo and the Modesto giant has spent several million dollars revamping the old facility, which was built at the end of Prohibition. Wine quality and consistency may well improve in the next few years.

## MASON CELLARS

3830 St Helena Highway, Oakville, CA 94562. Tel: 707 944 1710; Fax: 707 944
1293; Email: wine@masoncellars.com; Website: www.masoncellars.com
Vineyards: n/a

Veteran winemaker Randy Mason started his own winery in 1993, with the assistance of his wife Megan. Mason had been winemaker and consultant for Chappellet Winery for several years when that winery was forging a strong reputation. He released his first Cabernet Sauvignon in 2002 to critical acclaim. In general his wines always focus on expressing the variety through terroir: the Sauvignon Blanc is often spectacular and the Merlot is consistently good. All Mason Cellars wines are made at the Napa Wine Company (*see* page 211).

## MERRYVALE VINEYARDS

1000 Main Street, St Helena, CA94574. Tel: 707 963 2225;
Fax: 707 963 1949; Email: info@merryvale.com; Website: www.merryvale.com
Vineyards: 10ha

Established in 1983, Merryvale has always produced good to very good wines, including Cabernet Sauvignon, Merlot, Chardonnay, and Sauvignon Blanc. In the mid-1990s, quality went even higher when

Steven Test was hired as winemaker. Test has brought the wines to a level not seen before. Top of the line is Profile, a Meritage wine, with bright fruit and a long finish. The regular bottling of Cabernet Sauvignon also shows deep, rich fruit. Either wine will age for ten to fifteen years. The Merlot is typically on the cherry fruit side, a cut below the Cabernet. The Chardonnay strays rather far into oak from time to time

## MINER FAMILY VINEYARDS

7850 Silverado Trail, Oakville, CA 94562. Tel: 707 944 9500; Fax: 707 945 1280; Email: info@minerwines.com; Website: www.minerwines.com

Vineyards: 36.5ha

The Miner winery is on the Silverado Trail at the eastern edge of the Oakville AVA. Many of the wines are from Oakville vineyards, but others are sourced from other Napa AVAs. The winery, which was established in 1989 when it was known as Oakville Ranch Vineyards, has received well-deserved praise for silky, rich Cabernet Sauvignon.

## MONTICELLO VINEYARDS

4242 Big Ranch Road, Napa, CA 94558. Tel: 707 253 2802;
Fax: 707 253 1019; Email: wine@corleyfamilynapavalley.com;
Website: www.corleyfamilynapavalley.com

Vineyards: 48.5ha

Thomas Jefferson was one of Jay Corley's personal heroes, so when he got into the wine business in the early 1970s (first only as a grower) he named his company after the historic home of the second US president. After selling grapes for several years, Corley built his winery in 1982. Over the years, the Cabernet has shown grace and a supple elegance, both for short-term drinking and mid-term ageing. The Chardonnays have less to recommend them, but can be charming in good years. The Corley Family Reserve wines are built for long-term ageing and can be spectacular. Corley also makes a sparkling wine under the Domaine Montreaux label.

## MUMM NAPA

8445 Silverado Trail, Rutherford, CA 94573. Tel: 707 942 3400;
Fax: 707 942 3469; Email: mumm_info@mummcuveenapa.com;
Website: www.mummnapa.com

Vineyards: 45ha

From the first vintage of Mumm Napa in 1985, the quality level has been high, especially in the reserve wines. The base wines are made from up to sixty-five different vineyards in Napa, including quite a bit of Carneros fruit. The top of the line is the vintage DVX, named for Mumm Napa's founding winemaker Guy Devaux. The wine is complex and layered, yet with charming fruit that would keep anyone smiling. It ages fairly well, in the ten to fifteen year range. There is also a Carneros Chardonnay and a Pinot Noir, which are sold mostly in the winery tasting room and certainly worth looking for.

## NAPA WINE COMPANY
7830 St Helena Highway, Oakville, CA 94562. Tel: 707 944 8669; Fax: 707 944 9749; Email: retail@napawineco.com; Website: www.napawineco.com
Vineyards: 243ha
The Pelissa family have been grape-growers in Napa for more than a century. Today, with over 243 hectares of vines, they are the largest organic growers in the county. In 1993, the family bought a winery across the street from Opus One which was built in 1877. They remodelled the building, turning it into a modern custom crush winery for premium producers, such as Mason Cellars. They also make an elegant Cabernet Sauvignon with layers of flavour, great harmony, and balance.

## NEYERS VINEYARDS
2153 Sage Canyon Road, St Helena,CA 94574. Tel: 707 963 8840; Fax: 707 963 8894; Email: info@neyersvineyards.com; Website: www.neyersvineyards.com
Vineyards: n/a
Bruce Neyers began making his own Cabernet Sauvignon in a corner of the Joseph Phelps cellars, after a stint as winemaker at Mayacamas. In 1992, Neyers built his own winery in the Conn Valley region of Napa and continued to build his reputation for sound Cabernet Sauvignon. He also makes a rich Chardonnay from Carneros fruit.

## OAKVILLE RANCH VINEYARDS
7781 Silverado Trail, Napa, CA 94558. Tel: 707 963 2592; Fax: 707 963 5913; Email: paula@oakvilleranchvineyards.com; Website: www.oakvilleranchvineyards.com
Vineyards: 36.5ha
Excellent Cabernet and Merlot from hillside vineyards in the Oakville appellation. The wines are deep and intense, with a tight structure and are capable of extended ageing. There's also an interesting mix of

Zinfandel, Petite Sirah, and Carignane, a traditional field blend that packs a lot of power.

## PAHLMEYER WINERY

PO Box 2410, Napa CA 94558. Tel: 707 255 2321; Fax: 707 255 6786; Email: info@pahlmeyer.com; Website: www.pahlmeyer.com

Vineyards: n/a

Pahlmeyer has developed a devoted following for its dense super-ripe (and sometimes jammy) Cabernet Sauvignon.

## ROBERT PECOTA WINERY

3299 Bennett Lane, Calistoga, CA 94515. Tel: 707 942 6625; Fax: 707 942 6671; Email: bob@robertpecotawinery.com; Website: www.robertpecotawinery.com

Vineyards: 16ha

Located near Calistoga in the north of Napa Valley, Robert Pecota was working for Beringer when he bought this property in 1978. The vineyard was originally planted to Petite Sirah, which Pecota pulled out and replanted to Cabernet Sauvignon and Sauvignon Blanc: both earn very high marks. Typically, the Cabernet has delicious forward fruit and is drinkable young with some mid-term ageing possible. The Sauvignon Blanc can be quite good, as can an off-dry Muscat Blanc.

## PEJU PROVINCE

8466 St Helena Highway, Rutherford, CA 94573. Tel: 707 963 3600; Fax: 707 963 8860; Email: hb@peju.com; Website: www.peju.com

Vineyards: 61ha

An attractive winery located on Highway 29, Peju Province produces a pleasing Cabernet of medium intensity showcasing black cherry and cassis fruit. In good years, the wine has the structure and balance for ageing in the ten to fifteen year range. The Merlot is rarely up to the standards of the Cabernet.

## PLUMP JACK WINERY

620 Oakville Crossroad, Oakville, CA 94562. Tel: 707 945 1220; Fax: 707 944 0744; Email: winery@plumpjack.com; Website: www.plumpjack.com

Vineyards: 16ha

The wealthy Getty family of San Francisco founded Plump Jack in the mid-1990s in a good neighbourhood of Napa – Groth, Silver Oak, and

Saddleback Cellars are all nearby. The winemaker is Nils Venge, owner of Saddleback (*see* page 168). He makes only Cabernet, in a regular and reserve bottling. The wines are outstanding, deep and intense with a powerful structure and long finish. They should age into the fifteen year range. Plump Jack got a lot of press a few years ago when owner Gavin Newsom decided to bottle half of its wine using screwcap closures (*see* page 170).

## PORTFOLIO
PO Box 27, Napa,CA 94559. Tel: 707 265 6555; Fax: 707 265 6566;
Email: contact@portfoliowinery.com; Website: www.portfoliowinery.com
Vineyards: n/a

Genevieve Janssens, the director of winemaking at Robert Mondavi (*see* page 151), set up a tiny winery in her garage in the late 1990s, where she now makes a few hundred cases of Portfolio Limited Edition Cabernet Sauvignon every year. The 1999 was the first vintage. The wine is balanced and elegant, with luscious black cherry fruit and a wraparound finish. The grapes are sourced from a vineyard in the Mount Veeder AVA. The wine should age for up to twenty-five years. (*See* Appendix IV page 250.)

## PRAGER WINERY & PORT WORKS
1281 Lewelling Lane, St Helena, CA 94574. Tel: 707 963 7678;
Email: ahport@pragerport.com; Website: www.pragerport.com
Vineyards: 4ha

Located just south of the town of St Helena, Jim Prager makes varietal port-style wine from Cabernet Sauvignon and Petite Sirah. The wines are wildly inconsistent, but you have to admire anyone making "port" in Napa Valley for more than two decades.

## PROVENANCE VINEYARDS
1695 St Helena Highway, St Helena, CA 94574. Tel: 707 968 3633;
Fax: 707 968 3632; Email: info@provenancevineyards.com;
Website: www.provenancevineyards.com
Vineyards: 18ha

Provenance is off to a good start with bright and fruity Cabernet Sauvignon that shows potential for mid-term ageing. The idea behind the name is to make Cabernet and a little Merlot from various different AVAs in Napa. A former Chalone winery, it was bought by Constellation Brands in late 2004. Provenance is a property to watch in the future.

## KENT RASMUSSEN WINERY

1001 Silverado Trail, St Helena, CA 94574. Tel: 707 963 5667; Fax: 707 963 5664; Email: krwine@aol.com; Website: www.kentrasmussenwinery.com
Vineyards: 5.6ha

Rasmussen makes Pinot Noir and Chardonnay from Carneros District grapes. The Chardonnay is top-notch, with a buttery edge spread over lively fruit. When it's on form, the Pinot Noir is very good. However, the little treasures to look for from Rasmussen are special bottlings released under the Ramsey label. You might find a Syrah or a Sangiovese or, really, just about anything. They are always worth a look.

## RAYMOND VINEYARD

849 Zinfandel Lane, St Helena,CA 94574. Tel: 707 963 3141;
Email: hospitality@raymondwine.com; Website: www.raymondwine.com
Vineyards: 182ha

The Raymond family have been grape-growers in Napa since Prohibition. It was not until 1974, however, that they turned to making wine. Most of their wines are a blend of estate grapes and grapes from other Napa vineyards. Over the years, Raymond Cabernets have ranged from very good to just average quality. The Napa Valley Reserve typically features bright black cherry fruit with medium tannins. The Private Reserve is a riper, richer wine with deep layers of flavour and the potential for extended ageing past ten years. The winery also makes attractive Chardonnay for early drinking. The second label, Amberhill, is a good-value range mostly sourced from grapes grown outside Napa. Kirin Brewery Company of Japan owns a majority interest in the winery.

## RENTERIA WINES

6236 Silverado Trail, Napa, Ca 94558. Tel: 707 944 1382; Fax: 707 945 0395;
Website: www.renteriawines.com
Vineyards: n/a

Founded in 1997, Renteria has made a very good start with Cabernet Sauvignon featuring silky tannins and a firm structure. One to watch.

## PARTRIDGE CELLARS

451 Sanitarium Road, St Helena, CA 94574. Tel: 707 963 0551; Fax: 562 802 3186; Email: info@richardpartridge.com; Website: www.richardpartridge.com
Vineyards: n/a

Another new winery, producing small amounts of Cabernet Sauvignon and Chardonnay from selected Napa vineyards. The first vintages of Cabernet Sauvignon have been impressive, marked by black cherry fruit and a trace of anise.

## ROBERT BIALE VINEYARDS

2040 Brown Street, Napa, CA 94559. Tel: 707 257 7555; Fax: 707 257 0105; Email: info@robertbialevineyards.com; Website: www.robertbialevineyards.com
Vineyards: 12ha

The Biale family are growers turned winemakers. They offer rich and intense Zinfandel, capable of some ageing. The Petite Sirah and Syrah are often outstanding. Hard to find, but worth seeking out.

## ROBERT CRAIG

2475 Summit Lake Drive, Angwin, CA 94509; Tel: 707 252 2250; Fax: 707 252 2639; Email: lynn@robertcraigwine.com; Website: www.robertcraig.com
Vineyards: 10ha

This limited production winery, located on Howell Mountain, makes small amounts of Cabernet Sauvignon from vineyards on Howell Mountain, Mount Veeder, and the valley floor. The wines are outstanding: big and intense, yet stylish and with a true sense of place. Robert Craig also makes Chardonnay, Zinfandel, and Syrah from non-Napa grapes.

## ROBERT SINSKEY

6320 Silverado Trail, Napa, CA 94558. Tel: 707 944 9090; Email: rsv@robertsinskey.com; Website: www.robertsinskey.com
Vineyards: 65ha

The winery, which was founded in 1988, is in the Stags Leap District, but most of Robert Sinskey's vineyards are in Carneros. His Carneros Merlot is outstanding. His best Stags Leap wine is a red Bordeaux blend called RSV, made from a small vineyard near the winery.

## ROCCA FAMILY VINEYARDS

1500 Yountville Crossroad, Yountville, CA 94599. Tel: 707 944 9022; Fax: 707 944 8376; Email: sales@roccawines.com; Website: www.roccawines.com

Vineyards: 12.5ha

Another rising star, Rocca was established in 1999 by business and life partners Eric Grigsby and Mary Fran Rocca, when they bought a vineyard in the Yountville appellation in benchland at the foot of the Vaca range. The following year, they bought a vineyard in the Coombsville area, a cool region between the Carneros and Yountville appellations. The stated goal of the winery is to produce estate red wines that are "full-flavoured and expressive, yet velvety smooth and elegant". On the basis of early returns with the Syrah and Cabernet, they are meeting that goal very well. The winemaker is the very talented Celia Welch Masyczek, who has also made wine at Staglin Family, Hartwell, and elsewhere. Rocca could well turn into one of Napa's best in another decade.

## ROMBAUER VINEYARDS

3522 Silverado Trail, St Helena, CA 94574. Tel: 707 963 5170;
Fax: 707 963 5752; Email: sheanar@rombauervineyards.com;
Website: www.rombauervineyards.com
Vineyards: n/a

Rombaur's sturdy Cabernet Sauvignon, which is usually blended with a bit of Merlot and Cabernet Franc, tends towards oaky tannins that are occasionally matched by ripe fruit, with medium ageing potential. The Merlot can also be quite good, with red cherry fruit and a medium finish.

## ST CLEMENT VINEYARDS

2867 St Helena Highway North, St Helena, CA 94574. Tel: 707 967 3033;
Fax: 707 251 3350; Email: info@stclement.com; Website: www.stclement.com
Vineyards: 8ha

Some of Napa's most consistently drinkable, balanced, and supple Cabernet Sauvignon comes out of this winery. The wines have a firm structure with inviting underlying fruit that makes them drinkable when young, but also honestly age-worthy. The Merlot is ripe and deeply flavoured, again one of the best in the valley, year in and year out. Oroppas, a red Meritage blend of Cabernet, Merlot, and Cabernet Franc has been somewhat inconsistent, but in most years is quite good. St Clement is owned by Beringer Blass.

## ST SUPERY VINEYARD & WINERY

8440 St Helena Highway, Rutherford, CA 94573.

Tel: 707 963 4507; Fax: 707 963 4526;

Email: divinecab@stsupery.com; Website: www.stsupery.com

Vineyards: 275ha

St Supéry makes classic Napa Cabernet Sauvignon from estate grapes on the valley floor and sometimes rough and tumble Cabernet from the Dollarhide vineyards in Pope Valley. The Merlot has pleasing forward fruit and a supple, balanced finish. The white Meritage is routinely superb, with rich and intense flavours. You will look in vain in your handy "saint reference book" for Supéry; he is just a charming invention. St Supéry is owned by Skalli, the large French wine company.

## V SATTUI WINERY

1111 White Lane, St Helena, CA 94574. Tel: 707 963 7774;

Fax: 707 963 4324; Email: info@vsattui.com; Website: www.vsattui.com

Vineyards: 91ha

This is the winery to keep in mind only if you are on the ground in Napa. Good picnic facilities and a well-stocked deli is what V Sattui is all about. This is one of the wineries that sparked the debate in the 1970s about defining a Napa winery (see page 30), because for several years, there were no winemaking facilities on the property. Since then, owner Daryl Sattui has bought vineyards and installed a working winery. Here's the catch: except for a handful of restaurants, the only place you can buy the wines are on the property. They are, in a rustic kind of way, surprisingly good. Especially the Zinfandel.

## SAWYER CELLARS

8350 St Helena Highway, Rutherford, CA 94573. Tel: 707 963 1980;

Fax: 707 963 3410; Website: www.sawyercellars.com

Vineyards: 20ha

A Napa newcomer which was founded in 1998 by the Sawyer family. Early wines have been very good, especially the Cabernet Sauvignon, which shows intense blackberry fruit, coupled with a tightly wound structure. It should age for at least a decade. Sawyer also produces a Merlot, a Sauvignon Blanc, and the Bradford Meritage blend with fifty-nine per cent Cabernet.

## SCHUETZ OLES

PO Box 834, St Helena, CA 94574. Tel: 707 963 5121; Fax: 707 963 9431

Vineyards: 24ha

Founded in 1991 by winemaker Rick Schuetz and viticulturist Lore Oles, this small winery specializes in ripe and simply delicious Zinfandel. There is also a bit of Petite Sirah to try.

## SELENE WINES

60 Juniper Drive, Napa, CA 94559. Tel: 707 258 8199; Fax: 707 258 8132; Email: mia@selenewines.com; Website: www.selenewines.com

Vineyards: n/a

Winemaker Mia Klein makes only about 2,000 cases a year at this small production winery. Merlot and Sauvignon Blanc are the only wines and both are made from Carneros District grapes. Both are very good, but the edge goes to the multi-layered and complex Hyde Vineyard Sauvignon Blanc. There are plans to release tiny amounts of Cabernet Sauvignon and Cabernet Franc in the future.

## SEQUOIA GROVE WINERY

8338 St Helena Highway, Napa, CA 94558. Tel: 707 963 5107; Fax: 707 963 9411; Email: info@sequoiagrove.com; Website: www.sequoiagrove.com

Vineyards: n/a

Brothers Jim and Steve Allen established Sequoia Grove in 1980 on the site of a pre-Prohibition winery. There is a small estate vineyard which supplies part of the Cabernet Sauvignon for the regular and reserve bottlings. They also own a vineyard in Carneros from which they make a Chardonnay, and one in Rutherford, which is planted to Cabernet. The Cabernet is excellent with medium tannins and a ripe consistency of flavour with good fruit. The reserve bottling tends toward more oak than the regular Cabernet. The Carneros Chardonnay is bright and focused with lively acidity.

## SIGNORELLO VINEYARDS

4500 Silverado Trail, Napa, CA 94558. Tel: 707 255 5990; Fax: 707 255 5999; Email: info@signorellovineyards.com; Website: www.signorellovineyards.com

Vineyards: 40.5ha

Signorello produces some seriously impressive wines from grapes grown on an estate vineyard in the eastern hills of Napa on the Silverado Trail.

There are a variety of slopes, giving different exposures during the day and depending on the time of year. The Cabernet Sauvignon is intense and rich, with big extracted flavours. Signorello also bottles several proprietary wines, including my favourite, Padrone, which is a blend of Cabernet Sauvignon, Merlot, and Cabernet Franc. It's an intense wine with layers of fruit and tremendous complexity. The winery also makes a rich and intense Semillon which is almost always first class.

## SILVER OAK WINE CELLARS
915 Oakville Crossroad, Oakville, CA 94562; Tel: 707 944 8808;
Fax: 707 944 2817; Email: info@silveroak.com; Website: www.silveroak.com
Vineyards: 141.5ha
Typically, Silver Oak Cabernet Sauvignon is widely praised, but for my taste the wine is sometimes off the mark. Having said that, I must say that when it is on, it can be very good, with bright, distinctive fruit and rich layers of flavour. Silver Oak makes three Cabernets, one from Alexander Valley in Sonoma County, a Napa Valley, and Bonny's Vineyard, also Napa Valley. All are more or less fruit-forward wines, capable of ageing in the ten to twelve year range.

## STERLING VINEYARDS
1111 Dunaweal Lane, Calistoga, CA 94515. Tel: 707 942 3300;
Fax: 707 942 3466; Website: www.sterlingvineyards.com
Vineyards: 300ha
Sterling, once a jewel in Napa Valley's crown, is struggling to regain some measure of its former glory. The wines are not at all bad, it's just hard to place them in the front rank these days. The slide has been going on for some time, despite the fact that this Diageo-owned winery has some magnificent vineyards. Still, the Merlot is worth a second look. It is often quite pleasing, with bright cherry fruit, and is capable of ageing in the eight to ten year range. The Three Palms Vineyard Merlot/Cabernet blend can be a stunning wine, with deep wraparound flavours. Cabernet, made in both regular and the reserve bottlings, has been on the up-swing in recent years, especially the Sterling Reserve. The Sauvignon Blanc is also a cut above average.

## SULLIVAN VINEYARDS

1090 Galleron Road, Rutherford, CA 94573. Tel: 707 963 9646; Fax: 707 963 0377; Email: sean@sullivanwine.com; Website: www.sullivanwine.com

Vineyards: n/a

Based in Rutherford bench, Sullivan produces quite good Cabernet Sauvignon and Merlot, showing a bold "take no prisoners" approach. There is also a special barrel reserve select bottling of Cabernet Sauvignon called Coeur de Vigne, which is considerably more elegant and supple, for those of us who prefer to be gently stroked. Sullivan's only white wine is a private reserve Chardonnay.

## TOM EDDY WINERY

3870 Highway 128, Calistoga, CA 94515. Tel: 707 942 4267; Fax: 707 942 4246; Email: tomeddy@tomeddywines.com; Website: www.tomeddywines.com

Vineyards: 1.2ha

Over the years, Tom Eddy has made some of Napa's best Caberent, but always working for other people. Now he has his own winery and is producing elegant hillside Cabernet Sauvignon with intense fruit and complexity, but also harmony and balance. He makes several Cabernets as well as a Petit Verdot from a handful of Napa vineyards. They are all worth looking for.

## TRINCHERO FAMILY ESTATES

100 St Helena Highway South, St Helena, CA 94574. Tel: 707 963 3104; Website: www.sutterhome.com

Vineyards: 2,428ha (most outside Napa)

This is the new up-market corporate name of Sutter Home Winery. (It looks as if the Trincheros might be trying to distance themselves from White Zinfandel.) The new Trinchero Family wines are off to a reasonably good start, especially the Cabernet Sauvignon. If you like to slurp down a chilled White Zin with your hot dog, Trinchero has a good one. Sutter Home has a long and honourable history of Zinfandel made from grapes grown in the Sierra foothills.

## TURLEY WINE CELLARS

3358 St Helena Highway, St Helena, CA 94574. Tel: 707 964 0949; Fax: 707 963 8683; Website: turleywinecellars.com

Vineyards: 28ha

Larry Turley, a co-founder with John Williams of Frog's Leap winery (*see* page 148), founded his own winery in 1993. Helen Turley, his sister, helped out the first few years and established the "in your face" style, building on the premise that bigger is better. If you are a fan of super-ripe, over-extracted Zinfandel – and many are – this is the wine for you.

## TURNBULL WINE CELLAR

8210 St Helena Highway, Oakville, CA 94562. Tel: 707 963 5839;
Fax: 707 963 4407; Website: www.turnbullwines.com
Vineyards: 65ha

The Cabernet Sauvignon from Turnbull can be quite good, often showing a minty edge that goes well with the bright fruit and chocolate elements commonly found in the wine. In good years, the wine is balanced and supple, with long layers of flavour on the finish.

## VIADER VINEYARDS

1120 Deer Park Road, Deer Park, CA 94576. Tel: 707 963 3816;
Fax: 707 963 3817; Email: delia@viader.com; Website: www.viader.com
Vineyards: 37ha

Viader's stylish wine, a Bordeaux-inspired Cabernet Sauvignon and Cabernet Franc blend, comes from a vineyard situated at the 396-metre (1,300-feet) level on Howell Mountain, just below the 427-metre (1,400-feet) appellation line. Delia Viader also grows Petit Verdot and Syrah. The Cabernet blend typically has bold fruit and intense flavours, with the structure for long ageing, perhaps up to twenty years. Viader has flirted with cult status for years, but I believe the wines are too elegant and supple for that.

## VINE CLIFF WINERY

7400 Silverado Trail, Napa, CA 94558. Tel: 707 944 2388;
Fax: 707 944 2399; Email: info@vinecliff.com; Website: www.vinecliff.com
Vineyards: 16ha

Located in the hills just off the Silverado Trail, Vine Cliff established a sound reputation for ripe and intense Cabernet Sauvignon from its first vintage in the early 1990s. The wines have a firm structure and benefit from ten years or more in the cellar. The hillside vineyard is planted to Cabernet Sauvignon, Merlot, and Cabernet Franc. Vine Cliff also makes a separate bottling of Merlot, which can be quite good, as well as a Chardonnay.

## VINEYARD 29

2929 St Helena Highway North, St Helen a, CA 94574. Tel: 707 963 9292;
Fax: 707 963 7848; Email: info@vineyard29.com; Website: www.vineyard29.com
Vineyards: 16ha

This small winery north of St Helena offers an extraordinary Cabernet Sauvignon, sleek and powerful with rich earthy aromas, capable of extended ageing. The Zinfandel is spicy and pleasantly jammy, with layers of fruit on the finish. There is also an elegant, supple Merlot with bright fruit. The grapes are from the Aida Vineyard in the St Helena AVA.

## WHITE ROCK VINEYARDS

1115 Loma Vista Drive, Napa, CA 94558. Tel: 707 257 7922;
Fax: 707 257 7922; Email: caves@whiterockvineyards.com;
Website: www.whiterockvineyards.com
Vineyards: 14ha

White Rock is on the site of a vineyard and winery dating back to 1870, in the hills south of the Stags Leap AVA. The modern hillside vineyard was planted in the 1970s to Bordeaux varieties, with Chardonnay in the coolest part of the vineyard. The red wine, which is called Claret, is a blend of Cabernet Sauvignon, typically about sixty per cent, Cabernet Franc, Merlot, and Petit Verdot. It's a dense wine, featuring dark fruit with touches of anise and blueberry.

## WHITEHALL LANE

1563 St Helena Highway, St Helena, CA 94574. Tel: 707 963 9454; Fax: 707 963 7035; Email: greatwine@whitehalllane.com; Website: www.whitehalllane.com
Vineyards: 40.5ha

There is a small estate vineyard at the winery (just south of St Helena) but the Sauvignon Blanc, Merlot, and Cabernet Sauvignon are blended from vineyards in several parts of Napa Valley. The Sauvignon Blanc is highly recommended. The Merlot can be quite good, with juicy fruit and supple balance. The Cabernet Sauvignon, both the regular bottling and the reserve, is made in a ripe, fruit-forward style, but with the structure for mid-term ageing.

## WILLIAM HILL WINERY

1761 Atlas Peak Road, Napa, CA 94558. Tel: 707 224 5424; Fax: 707 224 4484; Email: whw_info@williamhillwinery.com; Website: www.williamhill.com
Vineyards: 48.5ha

A reliable producer of Cabernet Sauvignon and a Carneros-based Chardonnay. The winery, which is owned by Allied Domecq, has lately added some interesting single-vineyard Chardonnays to its list.

## ZD WINES

8383 Silverado Trail, Napa, CA 94558. Tel: 707 963 5188; Fax: 707 963 2640; Email: info@zdwines.com; Website: www.zdwines.com
Vineyards: 14ha

This winery located on the Silverado Trail sources Pinot Noir and some Chardonnay from Carneros. ZD has built a good reputation for both wines, although on occasion the Chardonnay can be a little oaky and unbalanced. The Cabernet from estate grapes is age-worthy if sometimes a bit tannic.

## ZAHTILA VINEYARDS

2250 Lake County Highway, Calistoga, CA 94515. Tel: 707 942 9251; Fax: 707 942 9241; Email: sales@zahtilavineyards.com;
Website: www.zahtilavineyards.com
Vineyards: 1.2ha

Laura Zahtila specializes in Cabernet Sauvignon and Zinfandel. The Cabernets are from Napa Valley vineyards, including a sensational Beckstoffer vineyard bottling from the Rutherford AVA. Zins come from the estate vineyard near Calistoga, as well as Dry Creek and Russian River in Sonoma County. Zahtila was only founded in 1999 but is off to a very good start. Clearly this is a winery to watch.

# 11

# Last words

What is a classic Napa wine? Perhaps it is now time to deal with that question. Napa wines were thrust onto the world scene quite young, really. They are growing up, making mistakes, learning, and maturing in the spotlight of the trend-chasing global wine market. Not a happy experience in some cases. Napa wines, and I'm talking chiefly of the Bordeaux red varietals with a nod toward Carneros for Pinot Noir and Chardonnay, are wines in transition: a work in progress.

Napa wines have always been fruit-forward and more up-front than European wines. It's all that sunshine and good weather. But there should be more to a classic Napa wine than fruit, however attractive that may be. Beyond or backing up the fruit, the best Napa wines typically, or historically at any rate, have offered soft tannins and a supple and silky mouthfeel that can be quite inviting.

## THE ROLE OF TECHNOLOGY
Today, it seems that the profile of a Napa wine is changing, or at least being tugged in two directions. There is a growing tension between the classic Napa and the new techno-Napa. Rapid advances in viticultural technology make it possible to precision-grow grapes to match whatever the winemaker wants, from easy-drinking elbow benders for the budget buyer (though that doesn't happen often in Napa) to huge, concentrated wines for the macho-minded. That supple Napa classic is being squeezed somewhere in the centre. This new vineyard technology combined with information technology is now making it possible for growers to micro-manage the vines in ways that would have been impossible, indeed not even imagined, more than ten years ago.

Andy Beckstoffer farms more than 1,200 hecatres of vines in Napa, Mendocino, and Lake Counties. Several Napa wineries are happy to make single-vineyard wines from Beckstoffer vineyards scattered throughout Napa, including a portion of the To Kolon vineyard. He is a strong supporter of the new vineyard technology, arguing with some justice that vineyards are much healthier now. He believes that changes in trellis systems, increased knowledge of clones and rootstocks, and water management, which is now carried out virtually on a vine by vine basis, have all led to better wines. Beckstoffer says:

> When we first started talking about microclimates, people like André Tchelistcheff would mention the differences between Carneros and Rutherford. After a while, we began to talk about differences within the district. Today, we are dealing with the microclimate of the grape cluster. We are looking at how many leaves are shading the cluster, whether one cluster is touching another, what is the humidity around the cluster. We are farming by the cluster.

Information technology has enabled growers like Beckstoffer to build a database that can be applied with precision to one row of a vineyard – or even part of a row. Growers are making harvest decisions based on which side of the row gets the most sun. Information from moisture sensors, heat sensors, wind sensors, and dozens of other devices are read and sent to laptops twenty-four hours a day. According to Beckstoffer, the next big step will be applying that information to custom-design the grapes, isolating the elements within the grape that are related to flavour profile.

This new technology is a marvellous tool for growers and winemakers alike. Wine quality, in a technical sense, has never been higher. The vineyards are healthy, grape quality is superb. Bear in mind, however, that this amazing technology is in the end only a tool, or rather an entire tool kit. If all that was needed to make great wine was the right technology, why aren't there more great wines? Why do I open so many bottles of wine, try a glass, and say "ho-hum"?

Dave Michul, who manages Beckstoffer's To Kolon vineyard, explains there are many elements that go into the wines from To Kolon. "But in the end, it all comes down to the dirt," he says. All those shiny hi-tech toys can't replace having the right grapes in the right place. At the risk of sounding like a Luddite, I would venture to ask, where was the new technology when Warren Winiarski's 1973 Cabernet took top marks at the Paris tasting in 1976?

I bring up Winiarski not primarily because of the Paris tasting – as indicated elsewhere I have reservations about that event – but because the new precision technology can be used to undermine the very element in Napa wine that Winiarski has focused on with such passion: terroir. At a time when Napa wine-growers are just beginning to understand the relationship of the soil, the terroir, to the wine in the bottle – and some of that understanding it is true is based on the new technology – that same technology can be used to mute that relationship, especially when it is used to play the numbers game. There is not a winemaker or winery owner in Napa who doesn't keep an eye on the scorecard – how many points out of 100 did his or her wine get from those publications that present such rankings. Vintners know that a ninety-seven- or ninety-eight-point rating gives them extra clout in the market, not only for that single vintage but for several vintages to come if the marketing department plays its cards right.

Ten or fifteen years ago, grapes were rather routinely harvested based on sugar levels. When a reading of twenty-four Brix (a measurement of the sugar level in the grape) was reached, the grapes were picked. Winemakers calculated that the alcohol level of the wine would be about half of the Brix level and most aimed for an alcohol reading of about twelve per cent, give or take 0.5 per cent. It didn't take long to realize that higher alcohol levels were often translating into higher numbers on the 100-point scale. Not only that, modern trellis systems increasingly exposed the grapes to more sunshine, thus more ripeness, thus more sugar, thus still higher alcohols. Add to that mix the improvement in modern yeasts, which do a superior job of converting sugar to alcohol, and you begin to see alcohol levels of Napa Cabernets (as well as wines elsewhere) creep up to fifteen per cent, sometimes higher.

Next, winemakers saw that the influential critics seemed to like big fat wines with low acidity, lots of jammy fruit and with luck a scoop of chocolate. Do it right and you've got yourself ninety-eight points and a nice bonus from the owner. (Given all that, I was not surprised at a recent tasting to hear a winemaker from quite a well-known Napa house say, in regard to his 2001 Cabernet, that he was not concerned about acid levels nor, apparently, was he concerned about what would happen to his wines in four or five years. "I'll let the consumer decide when to drink the wine after he or she buys it. That isn't my job," he asserted. If it isn't his job, whose is it, I wondered?)

## ACID AND ALCOHOL
Acidity is a key factor in the ability of a wine to age and improve in bottle. As grapes stay on the vine longer and the sugar level rises, acidity falls. One measure of this is called pH, which is a number measuring the hydrogen ion concentration of a liquid. A pH of 7.0 is considered neutral. Wines generally range between 3.1 and 4.0, although 4.0 would be rather high. As acidity falls, wine pH rises. It has been demonstrated that a wine with a pH of above 3.5 is unlikely to age beyond a few years. The structure and balance of the wine is skewed, the wine falls apart in the bottle. Even when young, it may taste flabby and dull. Today, wines with a pH above 3.5 are common. High pH wines also seem to be more susceptible to microbiological spoilage activity, such as *Brettanomyces*. (Not that Brett is all bad. I'm actually a major fan of a pinch of Brett in my red wine.)

Of course, the riper the grape in terms of sugar level, the lower the acidity – acids fall as sugar levels rise. Some winemakers like to leave the grapes on the vine as long as possible to promote phenolic or physiological ripeness. (Phenols are those compounds in the grape that control colour, tannins, and flavours.) The longer the grapes hang on the vine, the greater the concentration and intensity of flavour in the wine. The problem is that because of warmer weather around the globe, combined with precision grape-growing, sugar levels are going way too high before phenolic ripeness is reached. Before the introduction of the new virus-free clones (vineyard technology at work) the vines were mostly too racked with various diseases (fan leaf virus, etc.) to benefit from hang time. Growers were happy if the vine made it to twenty-four Brix before taking to its sick bed and curling up for a long winter rest.

I can't remember when I first heard the words "hang time" used in connection with wine grapes. It must have been in the early 1990s and, at the time, I thought it seemed like a good idea. Well, I was wrong and so were a great many winemakers, not just in Napa and California but around the world. What was overlooked all around was that the end product in terms of a concentrated grape is the raisin. It's virtually pure sugar. Do we really want that sort of extraction in a wine? I don't. Not unless I'm indulging in a glass of *vin santo*.

I begin to come to my senses in the mid-1990s. About that time I had a conversation with wine importer Kermit Lynch, who has a superb retail shop in Berkeley and imports French wines (and a few Italian) for national distribution. When, Lynch asked, did wine become all about concentration? What happened, he went on, to elegance and balance? What happened to truth and beauty he might well have asked. Elegance and balance, not to mention harmony, don't get you many ninety-five-point ratings nor a stash of gold medals in wine competitions.

A by-product of hang time (collateral damage in military terms) was the rapid increase in alcohol content of table wine throughout the 1990s. When I first started writing about wine, an alcohol range of 10.5 per cent to 12.5 per cent was fairly normal, although even then California wines might run a half-point higher by virtue of all that lovely California sunshine. By the mid-1990s, alcohol by volume was generally two points or more higher; and that was the official for-the-record reading. In many cases, the alcohol content of California table wines must have been fifteen per cent by volume by the end of the century.

What does two or three more percentage points mean? Think about it. A wine that is fifteen per cent alcohol contains twenty-five per cent more alcohol than a twelve per cent alcohol wine. That's significant, not only in terms of how much alcohol you are asking your liver to process, but what kind of impact it is having on the flavour of the wine. High alcohol, super-concentrated wines tend to lose the mid-palate; the flavour is all up-front or at the finish.

Another factor in the development of these super-concentrated wines could be the trend toward smaller and smaller crop levels. Yes, a smaller crop means more concentration in the wine, but how low can you go? In the end, wine is supposed to taste good, isn't it? Whatever happened to that plan? Concentration may be a good thing up to a point, but if the wine becomes out of balance, what is the point?

The question comes up: if the wine drinking public wants overripe super-concentrated wines, what's wrong with that? Why can't we just let them eat cake if they have a taste for cake? I don't happen to think the public does want those kind of wines. I think the public wants the assurance of the numbers, at least the American public does. Buying and serving a wine that received a ninety-seven-point rating is like a seal of approval. It's a way of being an insider and displaying that knowledge.

Finally, as a kind of last word, let's get back to terroir. Winiarski contends that the international emphasis on big, overripe and over-extracted wines wipes out terroir. "If you pick an underripe grape, the wine is going to taste the same, no matter where the grape was grown. The same thing happens with an overripe grape. It obliterates terroir, any sense of place. It could be from anywhere or nowhere."

And there, exactly is my concern. Wine that can be from "anywhere or nowhere" is an industrial product. In creating techno-wines to try to catch the 100-point gold, winemakers have come full circle to the UC Davis model of the mid-twentieth century. The vineyard is once more regarded as a grape factory to produce model wines for the global market and those wines become creatures of that market.

## CHAMPIONS OF TERROIR

Thankfully, it isn't all going the way of the numbers players. Andrew Hoxsey is the third generation of the Pelissa family, who have been farming in Napa for more than a century. He grows over 200 hectares of organic grapes and also operates Napa Wine Company (*see* page 211), a custom crush facility for fine wine production and makes his own wine under the Napa Wine Co label. He puts if flatly: "The only reason for a high alcohol wine is to get a high point score." Hoxsey believes that the trendy wines, the wines which are often in the news, do seem to be highly extracted with over-the-top flavour profiles:

*I feel that one is not allowed to have a mood. I like to experience slightly different nuances with each sip of a great wine. So often these wines slap you on the face with a sort of one dimensional quality and are often much too high in alcohol.*

Michael Trujillo, the winemaker at Sequoia Grove, a respected producer of elegant, sometimes understated Cabernet Sauvignon, admits that he is looking for ways to get more recognition for the wines, but he intends to do that by seeking better vineyard sources. He insists that he would not play the numbers game. "Absolutely not. My best wine education was working with André Tchelistcheff when he consulted at Sequoia Grove in the 1980s. Wine is about balance. André said wine is about texture, complexity, and balance. That is what you strive for," explains Trujillo. It's not a bad idea to have Tchelistcheff on your team when you are making Napa Cabernet Sauvignon.

Taking an optimistic view for the long run, the tension between the techno-wines and the terroir-based wines could be a good thing for Napa. Winemakers are popping up out of the cellar to join the debate, discussing and analyzing the wines in new ways, for them. This should lead to even better wines for although Napa wines are very good, there is always the possibility of being even better and this clash of ideas and styles could bring that about.

Perhaps the makers of techno-wines will find a way to include the voice of the terroir in the wines, will learn how to craft powerful and concentrated wines that still speak of a place. After all, the technology is neutral, it is the application of the technology that can screw up good grapes. So perhaps the terroirists will continue to use the new technology to make Napa wines even better in the future. As it stands, they are already very good, although perhaps not quite as good as many in Napa think they are.

In truth, Napa now stands at yet another defining crossroads. Its wines are in danger of becoming polished, perfectly formed expressions of technical and marketing expertise; wines that can be admired and lavishly praised, but never hedonistically enjoyed, seldom drunk for pleasure. I would argue that the crisis facing Napa today is far more serious than phylloxera, more serious than urban sprawl or even Prohibition: it's a crisis of vision. It's necessary to look into the heart of the wine, look to its origin and respect it. At that point, Napa wines will truly join the ranks of the world's best.

# Appendices

# *I*

# Napa vintages

Because of differences in microclimates (and in overall climate pattern as well), elevation, and other factors, it is difficult if not virtually impossible to make a one-size-fits-all vintage description make any sense for Napa. What may be true at the 609-metre (2,000-feet) elevation on Howell Mountain is not true in Oakville on the banks of the Napa River. Not only does the jumbled geography and weather of Napa's appellations affect vintage quality, the vineyards themselves have to be considered.

This has become especially true in the last decade or so as vineyards replanted because of the phylloxera plague of the late 1980s and early 1990s, have come into maturity. These new vineyards are micro-managed in ways that no one would have dreamed of twenty years ago. Take an obvious factor like row orientation: today, walking through a vineyard, you are suddenly aware that one vineyard block is planted north-south, another east-west; one follows the contour of a hillside, another might march straight up the hill. Fine, but so what? What does row orientation have to do with vintage quality? Plenty.

Grapes growing on vines planted east-west are going to catch more intense afternoon heat, especially those on the east side of the Napa Valley, such as in the Stags Leap District. That means that in an intense heat spike, those grapes are more likely to sunburn and dry out, raising sugar levels while acidity falls. That's just the beginning. You also have to take into account shoot position, trellis system, leaf pulling, not to mention root and clonal selection. The best vineyards in Napa are no longer a monoculture, either in terms of the vines themselves or how the vines are farmed. All those variables have an impact on the quality of grapes at harvest.

Then there's the human factor, which begins, again, in the vineyard. The best growers and wineries now have full-time vineyard crews, employed year around, hiring extra crew only at harvest. These full-timers are not just passing through Napa on the way to harvest apples in Washington. They are in the vineyards just about every day of the year. They know the vines probably better than the man with the title of vineyard manager. They also know that their work is appreciated and they take pride in what they do.

In the winery, the sorting table has become standard equipment. Underripe, overripe or mouldy grapes are discarded. At many wineries, vineyard workers are brought in after early morning picking to staff the sorting tables. At the best wineries, fermentation is in small tanks. If a problem develops in fermenting must, that lot can be cut out of the production process with no harm done to the final blend.

Many of these things are done elsewhere, of course. Napa doesn't have an exclusive on sorting tables. That isn't the point. The point is that vintage commentary and analysis should be made, most years, on a vineyard-by-vineyard basis. Sweeping statements of the old school like, "Year X was a terrible vintage for Pinot Noir in Carneros", are worse than meaningless – they do harm to winemakers and vineyard staff who have paid attention and done a good job and they mislead the consumer who, blindly following such advice, may miss out on some delightful wines or on the other hand, invest in wines that are not worthwhile.

Obviously, then, the vintage commentary that follows is meant to be taken in a very general way, not as the final word on any particular wine. The commentary is for Bordeaux varietals only and for Cabernet Sauvignon in particular. I have begun with the 1973 vintage as this was the vintage of Stag's Leap Cabernet Sauvignon that won the Paris tasting in 1976 and, in many ways, marks the beginning of the modern era in Napa. The entries can stand, if you will, only as an introduction to a particular year. In the end, they merely supply an outline for the consumer to fill in. Have fun.

**1973:** After a wet winter, good weather in the spring continued through most of the growing season. There were no heat spikes and the weather continued mild, even on the cool side right through harvest, which was large. Wines developed with good structure and have aged well, although even the best probably reached their peak in the mid-1990s.

**1974:** A splendid year. Spring was cool, followed by a moderate summer. The grapes ripened slowly and evenly, leading to good tannic structure. Even the run-of-the-press Cabernets were good for eight to twelve years of bottle age, with some of the better bottlings still at a plateau as the twenty-first century opened. However, drink any remainders now.

**1975:** A vintage that most Napa winemakers would like to forget. Frosts, rains, and a very cool growing season made it a quirky year at best. For the most part, the wines were thin with little structure and no staying power. However, the rare exception – Caymus was one – achieved a balance and elegance that led to superb wines ten to fifteen years out.

**1976:** This was the first year of a four-year drought, although there were some rains during harvest. Spring was early and warm and the summer was hot. Grapes were small with low acidity, high sugars, and therefore high alcohol, at least for the time. The wines tend to lack balance and structure. If you have any wines left from this vintage, drink them immediately or replenish your vinegar barrel.

**1977:** The second year of the drought. Quality was average at best, following a cool spring and summer with scattered rains at harvest. Anything left from this vintage is dead on arrival.

**1978:** The drought lives on. Unlike '77, this was a warm vintage, leading in many cases to wines that seemed lovely early on, but soon faded, lost in a kind of lush limbo of jammy fruit and soft tannins. The best, Stag's Leap being one, held well into the 1990s, but there were few of those. In general, a forgettable year.

**1979:** One of those years that if you know the producer, you can still find wines worth the trouble of pulling the cork. There were frequent heat spikes during the harvest with the temperature topping 37°C (100°F) for days, followed by rains that were too late to do any good for the grapes. Now, the lesson here for those considering California vintages, is that those who picked before the rains – Shafer and Clos du Val for example– came in with a very pleasing vintage, at least for short-term ageing.

**1980:** The drought ended during the winter of 1979–80 with heavy rains that didn't let up until late spring. The summer was warm and there were high hopes for the harvest, which was short and warm. In general, the wines had good up-front fruit, but lacked the structure for serious ageing. If you have any left in your cellar, give them to your Cousin Bert for his birthday. You could tell him about the warm summer of '80 in California.

**1981:** A much better vintage than it seemed right off the mark. There was intense heat during the summer, leading to an early harvest. Wines were soft with abundant fruit and many thought they would lack staying power. However, by the late 1980s, it was clear that the best wines of the vintage were balanced and were improving in the bottle. Through the 1990s, the vintage was delightful, but was just about dead in the bottle by the turn of the century.

**1982:** Although there are a few outstanding wines from this vintage – Randy Dunn again and the Mondavi Reserve – for the most part it was a forgettable year. It was a cool summer with more rain than usual in California at harvest. Many wines were thin and weedy.

**1983:** Another dismal year for Napa Cabernet. The growing season was mild, but heavy rains set in and persisted during harvest, leading to wines very similar to the '82s. There were a few exceptions, including Forman and, need I say, Randy Dunn.

**1984:** This was perhaps the best vintage in at least ten years, although some would rate the 1978 higher. The growing season was warm with an early and fast harvest. Wines were powerful with good tannic structure and abundant fruit, if sometimes slightly jammy. Most had passed their peak by the year 2000, but many, especially those made in reserve style, should hold longer, up to twenty-five years from harvest.

**1985**: Many believed this to have been the best vintage in Napa in fifty years. It was an amazing growing season, with warm weather right into harvest. The growing season was long and even, with virtually no heat spikes and a dry harvest. It was the longest season in memory for many growers. (Could it be that this vintage gave rise to the over-emphasis on hang time?) Grapes had good acidity to balance the sugars, producing wines of great depth and complexity. Many of them will last twenty-five to thirty years.

**1986**: There were winter floods on the Napa River, followed by warm rains in early spring, leading to early bud break. Temperatures in early summer were high, but a cooling trend in mid-summer slowed grape development, leading to even maturity and wines of some grace and power. I find the '86s more interesting, more nuanced than the '85s. There were some questions regarding ageability, but I find them ageing beautifully well into the twenty-first century.

**1987**: Winter was dry and the spring was cool. A heat spike in May during bloom caused considerable loss of crop, as much as twenty to twenty-five per cent in some cases. The summer growing season was moderate with grapes developing good flavour intensity. There was a rush to harvest because of extreme heat in September, but overall, the season was average to good, with a few wineries, Caymus for one, producing outstanding wines capable of ageing up to twenty years.

**1988**: The vintage pattern was almost identical to 1987, lacking only the September heat. Harvest was spread out over four to five weeks, with most vineyards picked by mid-October when heavy rains set in. There was much excitement early on about this vintage. Although the wines are balanced, they are not really built for long-term ageing, with few lasting more than ten years, although the occasional reserve bottling should hold for about twenty years.

**1989**: This vintage was damned by the trade even before the grapes were picked. The growing season had been ideal, with warm spring weather and even development through the summer. It was looking like a perfect vintage until heavy rains hit in mid-September. Hardly any Cabernet had been harvested at that point. A few days later, another storm system swept through the North Coast off the Pacific. Grape sugar levels plunged. However, the rains were over by the end of September and a period of warm dry days and cool nights set in. Those who waited out the storm picked in the third and fourth weeks of October, with some reasonably good wines being made. Some, despite all expectations, were drinking well right into the new century.

**1990:** A very good vintage with wines of intensity and power, perhaps helped by heavy rains during bloom in May, which was nature's way of "pruning" the crop back by thirty per cent or more. The summer growing season was mild with grapes developing evenly with a good balance of acids and sugar. Scattered rain in late September didn't cause any harvest problems, for the most part. The vintage is keeping exceptionally well.

**1991:** This proved to be a somewhat controversial vintage. Those who like the jammy fruit-bomb style of Cabernet will be disappointed. But if you go for finesse, elegance, and harmony, this should suit you well. After heavy rains in March, breaking a mini-drought, the growing season was cool and exceptionally long. Many growers were still picking Cabernet well into November, at least a month later than normal. Those who waited for the grapes to mature came up with wines that should age gracefully for fifteen to twenty years.

**1992:** Another good vintage, although perhaps a little weaker than the 1991. The summer was cool with a hot spell in mid-August followed by a textbook perfect end to the season, with warm days and cool nights building well-balanced wines. Just looking at the numbers, acids, sugar levels, tannins, etc., one would expect the '92s to age as well as the '90s or '91s, but they haven't. Most wines were at their peak by 2002 and are starting to slide downhill.

**1993:** An average, if mostly forgettable, vintage – at least in terms of ageing. The growing season was weird, with cool streaks and heat spikes alternating throughout the summer and into September, when hot weather arrived in earnest. Most growers had finished the harvest at an absurdly early date, mid-September in many cases, and the wines are out of balance and awkward. Those who waited for the heat spell to break, in late September, produced reasonable wines, but nothing worth seeking out ten years later.

**1994:** Overall, one of the best Napa Cabernet vintages in twenty years. It was another season featuring light May rains during bloom which cut the crop size, followed by a long, cool growing season. There were light rains in September, but nothing of any real concern. Harvest continued into early November. Wines are balanced and long-lasting with superb fruit and focused acidity. Hold on to the '94s until 2008 or 2010.

**1995:** Incredibly, an even better vintage than the previous year. Spring temperatures were below normal with winter rains continuing into May, resulting in a light fruit set. The summer continued cool with even development of the fruit. The weather turned warm at harvest, bringing the fruit to quick maturity, leading many to fear uneven and unbalanced wines. However, they were – and very much continue to be – splendid. The tannic structure and acidity are in perfect balance and while the wines are certainly accessible young, this is a vintage to keep for up to two decades.

**1996:** Not a great year by any means, although it is developing somewhat better than critics expected. The growing season was very difficult with a warm summer following extensive rains in May and early June. The weather at harvest continued hot, forcing sugar levels up while acid fell. As is often the case in a difficult year, those winemakers who paid attention made wines of at least average to sometimes above average quality – Spottswoode and Beringer to name only two – while most of the vintage fell short of the mark. Pass on this one.

**1997:** This was the vintage when winemakers stopped taking baths because they needed all possible storage space to hold the new wine. Yes, it was a heavy harvest, but a surprisingly good one, as it turned out. Spring was warm, leading to an abundant set of crop. The summer was warm, but not exceptionally so. There were showers in mid-August and again in mid-September, but the grapes developed evenly leading to wine with lush forward flavours, yet having the structure to develop and last for a decade or more. Not a great vintage, perhaps, but an excellent year for early to mid-range drinking.

**1998:** When wine-growers describe a vintage as "challenging" you can take that as an indicator not to fill your cellar. Grower Andy Beckstoffer, trying to put a good spin on the vintage, called it a "European" year. There were heavy rains through the spring and right into May. Cool weather persisted into the summer. Clusters ripened unevenly and there were problems with mildew and rot in many vineyards. Finally, as harvest arrived, a string of warm days and cool nights restored some balance to the grapes. In some cases, however, grapes didn't ripen until November. There is the occasional bright spot, again from winemakers who paid attention, but overall, forget the '98s.

**1999:** The last vintage of the twentieth century was excellent. Spring and summer were cool with frequent heavy morning fog, leading to even ripening and good acidity levels but leaving sugars lagging behind. However, in the last week of September, warmer weather set in, bringing up sugars and leading to superb natural balance in the grapes. The good weather held well into October, leading to wines of great intensity and superb balance. This may well turn out to be the best vintage of the 1990s, with wines capable of ageing two-plus decades. Stock up.

**2000:** The new century got off to a good start in Napa, with an unusually trouble-free growing season. The weather was mild and dry through late spring and into summer except for one brief heat spike in June. Grape maturity was even and balanced leading to exceptional wine quality with deep, concentrated flavours and some complexity. If ever it could be said wines are made in the vineyard, it is true of this vintage. Expect big, inky Cabernets, with the structure to mature slowly in bottle and age well past two decades.

**2001:** Another "big wine" year with Cabernet of great concentration, intensity, and richness. There were light rains during the winter, followed by the hottest May on record in Napa. It continued warm in June, but a long-range cooling trend set in that continued throughout July and August. The heat in May, which spiked during bloom, resulted in a twenty to twenty-five per cent lower crop on average and pushed the grape growth cycle ahead, meaning that most of the harvest was finished by October. Wines tend to be focused on fruit, but in most cases there is the right structure for moderate ageing in the ten-year range.

**2002:** A long and fairly mild growing season has produced wines of average to just above average quality. April was chilly, with frosts in some vineyards, and rains came in May. However, the summer was unexceptional with warm days and good nightime cooling. Heat picked up again in September, leading to a harvest rush that might have been too hasty in some cases in terms of acidity and balance. It's a little early to be sure about ageing (as I write, some of the wines are just being bottled) but prospects appear moderate on that count.

**2003:** This is a vintage that most wine-growers would like to delete from the books, no matter how they try to spin it. Vines received an unusually early wake-up call from early heat spikes in March, then had to shiver through a cool April which was also the wettest on record in Napa. Essentially, vines were in stall patterns, waiting for someone to turn on the heat. When it was turned on, it may have been set too high as a warm to hot June was followed by more heat spikes in July and August and again in mid-September. Then, as harvest got underway in earnest, cool weather returned and grapes hung on the vine until November in many cases. The easy way out here is to call this an "average" vintage, but in fact, some wineries made great wine, some made awful wine. This is truly a vintage that is going to have to be judged on a vineyard-by-vineyard basis.

**2004:** Scant winter rains and a warm spring led to bud break and bloom at least three weeks early. Grapes developed evenly through the summer and it was looking like smooth sailing until a prolonged heat wave hit the North Coast in late August. Grapes ripened quickly. In some cases, late varieties were being picked at the same time as early varieties. Most vineyards were bare of grapes by October. At time of writing, it looks like, at best, an average year.

# *II*
# Being there

Napa can be a charming place to visit, or a nightmare traffic jam. The good news is that it isn't all that hard to avoid the crowds. Plan to visit in the late winter or early spring: February, March, April. There will be plenty of other visitors, to be sure, but you stand a better chance of some quality time in the tasting room rather than being trampled by a tour bus filled with day trippers. Do remember to bring your umbrella, as rains sometimes continue right into May.

The valley is also at its best in spring. Winter rains leave the Vaca and Mayacamas Mountains a brilliant green and wild flowers are everywhere, even in the vineyards, where yellow displays of wild mustard will have you reaching for the camera. There is an annual Mustard Festival, which is generally held in mid-February, when the flowers are at peak display. During the Festival week there are various music events, special wine tastings, and other roadside attractions.

The other major Napa event is the Napa Valley Charity Wine Auction, held in early June. This has become an over-the-top extravaganza with bidders offering huge sums for Napa's ever popular cult wines and other excesses. But it is all for a good cause, there's a lot of good wine and food on offer, and you don't have to bid if you don't want.

Napa is compact enough that even in a short visit, it's possible to see a great many wineries. For the larger wineries, there is no need to make an appointment, but it could help for smaller producers. Some are not permitted to have visitors except by appointment and even though in some cases you can call from your cell phone as you arrive, if you give them a little more time, you will have a better tasting experience. Most of the wineries now charge for tastings, but the fee is usually waived if you buy a bottle of wine. Many wineries have a two-tier tasting arrangement, with a tasting of the reserve or library wines offered at a higher fee. One of the best general winery tours is offered at Robert Mondavi. St Supéry also has an excellent educational tour, with exhibits to help keep children happy as well.

There is no lack of places to stay in Napa, ranging from moderate motels on Highway 29 in the city of Napa, to luxury quarters up and down the valley. And you don't need to bring lunch, either. Restaurants range from inexpensive Mexican restaurants to world class, such as the French Laundry in Yountville, which some critics say is the best restaurant in the world.

Not so long ago, the town of Napa was just a place you hurried through to get to the up-valley wineries. But now downtown Napa is one of the highlights of a visit to Napa Valley. The area along the Napa River has been tastefully redeveloped, with a river-front pedestrian walkway. There are good restaurants, hotels, and art galleries featuring local artists. Copia, the food and wine centre, is only a few blocks away. It offers food and wine classes, special tastings, and art exhibits related to food and wine. It was inspired by Robert Mondavi and his second wife Margrit, who led the drive to establish the centre. The gardens, which fall away toward the river, are delightful. Inside, Julia's Kitchen (named after Julia Child) offers a changing menu of California cuisine.

St Helena, in the mid valley, was once a dusty commercial village. With the Napa wine boom, it has blossomed into a tourist mecca, with half a dozen good restaurants, art galleries, wine shops, and speciality shops, all within a three or four block stretch of Main Street, which is Highway 29. Chances are you'll find the locals playing pool at Ana's Cantina, where the margaritas sometimes make a refreshing change from Cabernet.

Further up the valley, Calistoga is known for its spas built around hot springs. There is a curious spa tradition called the mud bath. Bathers soak in tubs filled with hot mud spewed from mineral springs. Apparently, it was a popular ritual among Native Americans, which is no excuse.

One option worth considering is to use San Francisco as a base. It's not much more than one hour's drive (unless traffic is heavy) from San Francisco to the town of Napa. If you stay in San Francisco, it opens up a much wider range of hotels, as well as an amazing selection of ethnic cuisine, featuring restaurants from all over Asia and Latin America.

# III

# Contacts

## WHERE TO EAT

An excellent source of information for restaurants and events in Napa and San Francisco is the website www.sfgate.com, an online version of the *San Francisco Chronicle*. The following restaurants are my recommendations:

**All Seasons Café & Wine Shop:** Casual wine country menu. Buy a bottle of wine in the shop and take it to your table. 1400 Lincoln Avenue, Calistoga. Tel: 707 942 9111.

**Auberge du Soleil:** An up-market restaurant and inn situated on the east side of the Silverado Trail, overlooking the valley. 180 Rutherford Hill Road. Tel: 707 963 1211; Website: www.aubergedusoleil.com

**Bistro Don Giovanni:** A favourite in the wine industry, with an eclectic Ital-Cal menu and an extensive wine list. 4110 Howard Lane, Napa. Tel: 707 224 3300; Website: www.bistrogiovanni.com

**Bistro Jeanty:** Philippe Jeanty, who put the restaurant at Domaine Chandon on the culinary map, offers a menu inspired by French country cooking. There is also Jeanty at Jack's in San Francisco. 6510 Washington Street, Yountville. Tel: 707 944 0103; Website: www.bistrojeanty.com

**Bouchon:** Thomas Keller, the owner and chef at the French Laundry (*see* below), opened this Napa rendition of a Paris bistro. It has become a favourite haunt for those who don't want to get on the three-month waiting list for the Laundry. 6534 Washington Street, Yountville. Tel: 707 944 8037.

**Chandon:** The restaurant at the winery features a California menu with a French accent, plus an outstanding California wine list. It's worth a trip from San Francisco. 1 California Drive, Yountville. Tel: 707 944 2892; Website: www.chandon.com

**Cindy's Backstreet Kitchen:** Cindy Pawlcyn, who was one of the first people to bring good food to Napa with her Mustards Grill in the 1970s (*see* below), has opened a shrine to comfort food just off Main Street in St Helena. The food here is delicious and there's a good wine list including an extensive wine by the glass selection. 1327 Railroad Avenue, St Helena. Tel: 707 963

1200; Website: www.cindysbackstreetkitchen.com

**The French Laundry:** Yes, it's worth it. Worth the wait for reservations, worth the price. Thomas Keller's food is not only good, it is witty and artful. Book months ahead. 6640 Washington Street, Yountville. Tel: 707 944 2380; Website: www.frenchlaundry.com

**Market:** A delightful restaurant on Main Street in St Helena, featuring a casual all-American menu with dozens of wines by the glass. Great place for a quick lunch in between wine tastings. 1347 Main Street, St Helena. Tel: 707 963 3799.

**Martini House:** A gorgeous restaurant in an historic St Helena Victorian. Perhaps the best service in Napa, a California bistro menu and, for sure, the best wine list in Napa. Downstairs bar for casual lunches. 1245 Spring Street, St Helena. Tel: 707 963 2233; Website: www.martinihouse.com

**Mustards Grill:** Always reliable and sometimes brilliant, the menu is California bistro with some fascinating twists. 7399 Highway 29, Napa. Tel: 707 944 2424; Website: www.mustardsgrill.com

**Pilar:** A small plates restaurant in downtown Napa across the street from the river. The food is delicious and varied with a good wine selection. 807 Main Street, Napa. Tel: 707 255 0110.

**Tra Vigne:** Tuscany comes to Napa in a stunning setting, with a dreamy courtyard for warm summer nights. 1050 Charter Oak Avenue, St Helena. Tel: 707 963 4444; Website: www.travignerestaurant.com

## WHERE TO STAY

Except during summer weekends and holidays, it isn't hard to find a room in Napa. But it's always a good idea to at least nail down the first night. Check with the Napa Valley Conference and Visitors Bureau website at www.napavalley.com, for a list of hotels and motels. If you are a fan of quaint inns and bed and breakfasts, Napa is awash with them. Check www.bbonline.com for more details.

## WHAT TO DO

There's plenty to do in Napa! Recommended events and places to visit:

**Di Rosa Art and Nature Preserve:** This delightful destination, right across the road from Domaine Carneros, is fun to visit. The idea is to create and place art in unexpected settings. By appointment only. 5200 Carneros Highway, Napa. Tel: 707 226 5991; Website: www.dirosapreserve.com.

**Napa Valley Mustard Festival:** A week-long series of events, including the blessing of the balloons (*see* page 242). Tel: 707 529 9020; Website: www.mustardfestival.com.

**Napa Valley Vintners Association:** A one-shop stop for all your winery questions. There are maps, phone numbers, information on tasting room hours, almost anything you'd like to know. The Napa Vintners sponsor the annual Napa Valley Charity Wine Auction. A good place to start planning for your Napa trip. PO Box 141, St Helena, CA 94574. Tel: 707 963 3388; Website: www.napavintners.com

**Napa Valley Wine Train:** What a hokey treat, especially for train buffs. You can roll through Napa vineyards, sipping wine and having an adequate lunch. Best bet is Friday, when there's a regular vintner's lunch with plenty of free wine to sample. 275 McKinstry Street, Napa, CA 94559. Tel: 800 427 4124; Website: www.winetrain.com

# *IV*
# Sitelines

## HAVE ANOTHER CIGARETTE, ANDRÉ?

André Tchelistcheff probably did more than any other single person to establish the Napa Cabernet style. He seemed to have the ability to do the right thing, always. Tchelistcheff died in 1994 at the age of ninety-three. He had been a cigarette smoker from an early age. When he was in his late seventies, a well-meaning doctor told him he should stop smoking. Tchelistcheff rarely seemed to do what anyone told him to do, but in this case, he followed the doctor's orders and quit cold. Only to discover he had lost his palate. For decades, he had tasted wine through a fine fuzz of tobacco, and without tobacco, he no longer trusted his taste buds. Of course, he began smoking again. I've never had any inclination to check out the truth of this story, one of many Tchelistcheff legends. I wouldn't want facts to spoil it.

## CRANE ON CARNEROS

Eileen Crane from Domaine Carneros says:

> *Carneros growers and vintners were very open; we could go to Francis Mahoney and taste his array of clones. There was immediate kinship between the Napa and Sonoma sides. Our small vines were easier to keep in balance, our shallow soils produced great intensity, the climate ensured more hang time, and our wines showed incredible balance of acidity, flavour and body. In the early 1980s, virtually no wines carried Carneros labels, but the French said the soils in Carneros would produce great sparkling wine because they were so "lousy". By 1985, sparkling wine was where it was happening, and I was privileged to make the first one with a Carneros label from that vintage.*

## OYSTER SURPRISE

Napa is not about Chardonnay. If all the Chardonnay in Napa were to disappear tomorrow in some great Dionysian rapture it would not lower Napa's world reputation one point on the Parker scale. That's true, notwithstanding the occasional quite wonderful Napa Chardonnay. And there's always the huge exception of Carneros.

Nevertheless. Each year on the day after Thanksgiving, a group of folk of my kin and acquaintance traditionally gather at Tomales Bay on the coast north of San Francisco to celebrate surviving one more day of turkey and to eat oysters. Tomales Bay is best known as a kind of nursery for the great white shark, long may it roam, and several oyster farms. I'll be the first to admit that California does not produce great oysters. At least, not any more. During Gold Rush days the San Francisco Bay oyster was highly praised and much enjoyed. So much enjoyed, in fact, that it pretty much ceased to exist on site.

On one particular day-after-Thanksgiving several years past, my co-padre (my son's father-in-law) was in the Tomales Bay party. He is a fool for Chardonnay. Because my cellar was bare of Sancerre, I brought along four bottles of Far Niente Chardonnay, a vertical selection from the early 1990s – 1990 through 1993 as I recall. I had not seriously tasted Far Niente Chardonnay in years. In my memory, it was an awkward, over-oaked wine, somewhat heavy on the palate. I thought it would go over well with a group of hungover Californians who had been drinking sparkling wine for the last hour. After all, it had a pretty label.

I was amazed. Not only was the wine good, with crisp bright flavours and biting acidity, it even went well with raw oysters. Rarely have I known such an improvement in a wine in such a short time. After that, I tasted the wine on a regular basis and it has kept improving. So I would be sorry if all Far Niente Chardonnay were to disappear.

## FIRST CRUSH AT SCHRAMSBERG

In 1969, Jack and Jamie Davies were planning their first crush at the then partially restored, nineteenth-century winery on Diamond Mountain. They had bought the estate, which had first been planted by Napa pioneer Jacob Schram in 1863. During the first four years, the base wines had been made at Charles Krug. They decided to put on a bit of a party and invited friends and neighbours who had helped them to get started. And, being the Davies, they didn't forget to ask a few key members of the wine media to stop by.

However, at the critical time with grapes, friends, and media standing by, the crusher refused to work. What to do? Finally, a gruff voice called out from the crowd, almost certainly through a veil of cigarette smoke as it was André Tchelistcheff: "Jamie, your duty is clear". Without hesitating, Jamie took off her shoes and started crushing by foot. Others in the crowd joined her and the first crush at Schramsberg was a real crowd-pleaser. Over the years, many have accused the always media-hip Davies of planning the whole thing. They have steadfastly denied it.

## HOT GRAPES

Genevieve Janssens, director of winemaking at Robert Mondavi Winery, is seeing evidence of global warming in Napa vineyards and it has led her to suggest changes in the trellising system and canopy management system in Mondavi's vineyards. What Janssens has found in the last few years is an increased problem with dehydration and raisining of grape clusters due to low humidity. "That's always been a problem," she explains, "but until recently there would be a few days of hot, dry weather, then it would cool and we would get more humidity. Now it lasts for several days."

Traditionally, vine treatment has been to open up the vine canopy by various techniques, such as leaf pulling and shoot positioning, to allow more sunshine to reach the grapes. However, Janssens thinks this might have to change if the weather pattern of the first few years of the twenty-first century continues. "Now we are looking for ways to leave the grapes in partial shade to conserve humidity around the clusters," she says.

It is interesting to speculate that global warming may be contributing to the over-concentration of some Napa wines. If so, not only will viticultural practices need to be changed in future, but winemaking techniques will need to be altered as well.

## THE GREEN HUNGARIAN PUZZLE

Green Hungarian is California's "other" mystery grape. Unlike Zinfandel, it has virtually disappeared, and a good thing, too. Nothing exactly like Green Hungarian has ever been found in Europe, although some authorities say is the Putzscheere, once grown in Alsace. How and when it arrived in California is not known. It produces, at best, a fairly neutral white wine, of medium acidity.

Something called Green Hungarian first turned up in California in the 1870s in the Sierra foothills where it was used to make the ubiquitous dessert wine, Angelica. That particular sighting may actually have been Sylvaner. However, Green Hungarian was fairly widely planted in the 1890s and the variety somehow survived Prohibition. Green Hungarian wines were made at Lee Stewart's Souverain Cellars in Napa in the 1940s and early 1950s and won all sorts of gold medals. The suspicion has always been that Stewart perked up the usually bland Green Hungarian with ten to fifteen per cent Muscat, which would have given it a little life. Green Hungarian lingered on into the 1970s but has now virtually disappeared, and about time, too.

## BOXING THE OWLS

Huichica (wee-CHEEK-ka) Hills vineyard in the Napa Carneros AVA takes its name from the Miwok Native American name for the small burrowing owl, commonly found near creeks and on hillsides in the Carneros District. The Miwok believed the owl to have supernatural powers, no doubt because it was equally at home on the ground, under the ground, and in the air. Unlike other owls, it was also seen in the daytime as well as night, adding to its mystery. Huichica Hills is owned by Robert Mondavi and is farmed using environmentally friendly practices, including the placing of owl boxes in the vineyard for rodent control. No one could say whether the burrowing owl has taken to the boxes or not.

## A GARAGE WINE IN NAPA

Genevieve Janssens hasn't given up her day job, despite rave reviews for Portfolio, a limited production wine she makes in the garage of her Napa home. Her day job happens to be director of winemaking for Robert Mondavi's Napa wines. At Mondavi in Oakville, she is responsible for about 350,000 cases of wine annually and two dozen different wines. She and her husband Luc Janssens, an artist and photographer, work together on Portfolio and make about 225 cases of wine a year. It sells for $100 a bottle and, naturally, there is a waiting list to buy it.

Unlike many of the expensive Napa cult wines, Janssens has the street credentials to back-up the price. She is from a family that has made wine for five generations, in Algeria, Corsica, and France. She has consulted in Bordeaux and run a wine laboratory in Provence. She first came to Mondavi in 1979, following a chance meeting (while on the standard tour) with Mondavi winemaker Zelma Long. In 1989 she became production director at Opus One, where she stayed for nine years and oversaw production of the winery before returning to Mondavi as director of winemaking in 1997.

Doesn't she have enough to do at Mondavi? "Luc and I wanted to do something we could work on together, at home. It is a very different experience. I wanted to create something very different than what we do at Mondavi," she says. The wine is a blend of Cabernet Sauvignon, Cabernet Franc, and Petit Verdot and its first vintage was 1999. Portfolio is superb: elegant, supple, and balanced, yet with in inner power that echoes through the palate.

Grapes for Portfolio come from two vineyards, the Hendry Ranch vineyard, which is planted on an alluvial fan or terrace east of Napa in the lower reaches of the Mount Veeder appellation, and the Weitz vineyard on the east end of the Oakville appellation on volcanic soils in the Vaca range. Janssens first worked with Hendry grapes as part of the Opus One blend. At Opus, the grapes had to fit into the framework of Opus One. For Portfolio, she lets the terroir speak.

## KING OF THE MOUNTAIN
Some of his neighbours refer to Fritz Maytag, in a friendly fashion, as the "Lord of Spring Mountain". Maytag doesn't have star attraction to the general public like Robert Mondavi, but he is well known and respected by industry insiders. His family founded the Maytag appliance company in Iowa, building the first washing machine that actually got clothes clean, according to family history.

Having no interest in home appliances, Maytag went to California, as many of the restless younger generation were doing in the 1960s. He became interested in Japanese literature and poetry and was studying at Stanford in 1963 when President John F Kennedy was assassinated. He says that the impact of Kennedy's murder brought him back to the real world, out of academia.

For a few years, the real world turned out to be North Beach, the old Italian neighbourhood in San Francisco that was the birthplace of the Beat Movement. When Maytag learned that the Anchor Steam Brewery was about to go out of business, he bought the brewery rather than facing life without his favorite beer. The decrepit brewery dated back to California Gold Rush days, and Maytag spent several years refurbishing the old building and improving the quality of the beer. His work at Anchor Steam kicked off the microbrew revolution in California. He is also distilling rye whisky and gin in part of the San Francisco plant and has plans for making an apple brandy.

In the late 1960s, Maytag was looking for a place where he and his family could go camping that was close to San Francisco. He found and bought a stunning property on top of Spring Mountain, with sweeping views east over Napa and west over Sonoma. The property had been planted to grapes in the nineteenth century and became the Spring Mountain Vineyard Company in 1903. Grapes from the property went into the nearby La Perla winery, now part of Spring Mountain Vineyards. Maytag renamed the property York Creek Vineyards, for the creek that flowed through the estate. Maytag was no stranger to the wine business. He and Paul Draper had been classmates at Stanford and they worked together on a long-forgotten winery project in Chile in the early 1960s, before Draper founded Ridge Vineyards. Draper bought grapes from York Creek and made a vineyard-designated Cabernet Sauvignon, Petite Sirah, and Zinfandel as early as 1971 from old vines.

In the mid-1990s, Maytag started releasing his own York Creek wines, made by Cathy Corison in leased space in Napa. The wines are now made in a building across the street from his San Francisco brewery, the only winery in San Francisco. The York Creek label shows twenty-four native California trees that he has found on the property. Maytag still sells most of his grapes to other wineries, including Ridge, Cain Cellars, and Pride Mountain. He has about fifty hectares of grapes. His best foot forward wine is a Meritage red blend, but he also makes Petit Verdot, Cabernet Franc, Pinot Blanc, and a blend called MXB, or mixed black, made from Zinfandel, Petite Sirah, Carignane, and Alicante Bouschet. He makes about 2,400 cases a year.

Maytag likes to call York Creek a grower's winery. He has fourteen different varieties now and is open to planting more. It gives him plenty of chance to mix and match. Maytag wines are, in some ways, an expression of his personality; quirky perhaps, but always interesting and worth trying.

## THE MONDAVIS PERFORM

It was a very Napa experience. My wife, Ann, and I had stopped at Bouchon Restaurant in Yountville for an early dinner, after an afternoon appointment on Spring Mountain had unexpectedly (but delightfully) lasted almost four hours. Bouchon is owned by Thomas Keller of French Laundry fame, but is a California casual sort of place with decent food. They always keep a few tables for drop-ins, even drop-ins dressed for tramping through the vineyards. We were tucked away in a cosy corner and were well into a reviving glass of local bubbly when a well-dressed older gentleman, walking with the aid of a cane, accompanied by a fashionable looking woman of a similar age leading a small and neatly turned out white dog on a leash entered the restaurant.

Now, dogs are simply not accepted in restaurants in the USA. Should a health inspector have been present (and what a curious job title that is) citations would have been issued at once. However, it was out of working hours for health inspectors and the dog happened to be accompanied by Robert and Margrit Mondavi. The Robert was fussed over by the staff and Margrit was kissed on both cheeks at least three times. She flashed her painted on, yet very genuine, smile all around. We all beamed, I'm sure. The dog looked around for a few moments, then hopped into a canvas pet carrier beside The Robert's chair. In short order, the Mondavis were presented with a bottle of wine – Robert Mondavi Fumé Blanc from the look of the bottle – and a waiter offered dog biscuits to their canine pal.

In a few minutes, a small group of obviously wine trade people (who were English, if I caught the accent properly) all very badly dressed and looking like they had been out in the sun too long while drinking Napa Cabernet, arrived and joined the Mondavis. So there was The Robert, well into his nineties, in the company of wife and dog, hosting dinner in the hopes of hustling a few cases of wine, just as he has been doing for more than seventy years. "Poor bastard," I said to Ann, imagining the table talk he was enduring. "Not at all," she said. "It's better than sitting at home watching the tube and besides, he is stone deaf. He doesn't have to listen to a word they say." The dog was sleeping soundly.

## MOUNTAIN RIESLING

Standing in the middle of a dry, rocky vineyard at an elevation of just under 610 metres (2,000 feet) on Spring Mountain, one would assume the surrounding vines were Cabernet or Merlot. That would be an error. The vineyard is farmed by Stuart and Charles Smith, co-owners of Smith-Madrone winery and the vines are Riesling.

Riesling, which I happen to believe may well be the world's greatest white wine grape, is not the first nor even the fifth wine to spring to mind in connection with Napa. But it did play a larger role historically. Joseph Phelps winery, now near the top of the list for Cabernet Sauvignon, was perhaps better known in the 1970s for its Rieslings. However, it would be unusual to have a winemaker today bet the ranch on Riesling.

Yet the Smith brothers are doing just that. They make the obligatory Chardonnay and a very nice Cabernet Sauvignon, but Riesling is their pride and joy. Not just young, fruity Riesling, buy this morning and drink this afternoon, but older Riesling as well. The brothers have received good press for their Riesling since their first vintage in 1977. A bottle of that wine, left over from a trade tasting, was entered, almost as an after thought in the Gault-Millau Wine Olympics competition held in Paris in 1979. It took top honors as "Best Riesling" out of a field of Rieslings from around the world.

"We have always had a great respect for Riesling," Stuart Smith says. "We believe a hectare of Riesling is as important as a hectare of Cabernet or a hectare of Chardonnay. I think one problem with Riesling in California is that it ripens the same time as Chardonnay. Faced with a choice, most winemakers would say, 'Screw the Riesling. We'll get to it when we can, let's pick the Chardonnay.' You can't make good wine when you have separate priorities. We love Riesling."

From time to time, Smith-Madrone re-releases a limited amount of older Riesling from the winery library, just to make the point that California Riesling is capable of ageing. "I know that our Rieslings age with beauty and grace and become magnificent wines, every bit the rival of great Cabernets and Pinot Noirs. Americans have been misled to believe that red wines age and white wines don't. That's rubbish. Great Rieslings and Gewurztraminers only get better with age."

Smith-Madrone Riesling is grown on a steep hillside with slopes of up to thirty-five per cent. The vines are dry-farmed on red volcanic soils and were planted on their own rootstock in 1972. Inevitably, phylloxera has come into the vineyard and the Smiths are replanting a few vines at a time. The vines yield about six tons per hectare. "We are putting drip irrigation on the young vines but will dry-farm them when they are ready," Smith said. "My goal is to dry-farm all the vines."

Charles Smith, who handles the winemaking, understands that the process of making a wine really begins with deciding when to pick. "The most important decision you can make is when the grapes are ready. We used to pick at 21.5 Brix but we have crept up a little to twenty-two-plus, maybe 22.5. We are not afraid of alcohol with Riesling. You have to get away from the idea that we need to keep alcohol down just because German wines have low alcohol. We learned to make it the way we want – ripe, dryer, full-bodied, and that comes from higher maturity. However, our alcohols are usually in the low-to-mid twelves." He aims at a stylistic point somewhere between the German and Alsace styles of Riesling. "I like the mineral middle of Alsatian but not the tart finish. Wine is supposed to be hedonistic and give pleasure, so we like a little residual sugar to sweeten the finish."

In the market, Stu is seeing younger people in the trade and younger consumers discovering Riesling. He believes there was a perception in the past that Riesling was perhaps a little old-fashioned and even boring. "But people in their thirties are coming along and they are not burdened by old attitudes. They are tasting and buying what they like. All people have to do is open their eyes and taste Riesling. They will love it."

## PLEASE BE SEATED

When the creation of the Oakville and Rutherford AVAs was being discussed in the late 1980s, a small group of vintners also petitioned the Bureau of Alcohol, Tobacco, and Firearms (BATF) to create two sub-divisions within the proposed AVAs to be called the Rutherford Bench and the Oakville Bench. It was argued that the slightly elevated slice of land at the foot of the Mayacamas range, sloping down almost to Highway 29, was distinct from the valley floor and deserved its own appellation. There is some truth in that claim. The soils are much more gravelly and well drained than the deeper purely alluvial soils closer to the Napa River. It could be that supporters of the "benchland" appellations might have been successful had they not used the word benchland. It was argued, successfully, that the area in question was not actually true river-carved benchland, which can be seen along the Russian River in Mendocino and Sonoma Counties, but merely eroded soils from Mayacamas range.

The bench petition met with universal opposition from those outside the proposed AVA and became something of a joke. Agustin Huneeus, who then owned Franciscan Vineyards, set up a huge bench outside the winery with a sign reading "Rutherford Bench". The petition was finally dropped before the BATF could act on it and the original Rutherford and Oakville AVAs were approved. Unfortunately, this has left the term undefined and some growers have used it (although not on labels as an official site descriptor) as a claim to quality vineyards when the vineyards are actually on the valley floor.

## IF YOU PLEASE, SIR

Petty Sir. That's what the old time growers in California called, and still call for that matter, Petite Sirah. That name will work as well as any, because one man's Petite Sirah is another man's Durif when it comes to California vineyards. Or maybe some other obscure southern French grape. According to wine historian Charles Sullivan, who has a habit of being right, in the nineteenth century the true Syrah, what they call in the Rhône Valley Petite Syrah because it is low-yielding to distinguish it from the grosse Syrah, a high-yielding and undesirable grape, was introduced in California. It was cultivated in Napa, at Charles Krug among other places, but growers never took to it precisely because it was low-yielding.

The Durif grape, which is a cross between Peloursin and true Syrah, was introduced to California in the 1880s and was also called Petite Sirah. Durif was popular because it yielded wines of deep colour that could stand up to shipping because of its tough skin. It became even more popular, just for those reasons, during Prohibition, when it was shipped to home winemakers.

After Prohibition, Petite Sirah made a useful contribution to many California red "burgundies" and just before World War II there were about 1,200 hectares planted in Napa, more than forty per cent of the total state crop. By that time, no one really knew if what they were growing was Petite Sirah, Durif or what we in California have taken to calling "true" Syrah. A few wineries, such as Stags' Leap in Napa, made some decent wines from the grape, whatever it was. It is also common in the popular California Rhône blends, and is sometimes blended with Zinfandel. A study by UC Davis in 1992 concluded that there are at least three different grapes called Petite Sirah in California: Durif, Peloursin, and Béclan.

## VERMOUTH

Vermouth is one of those things that keeps civilization as we know it moving on. It is not just another drink. Vermouth marks the pause between the work day and the rest of life – talking with friends, fixing dinner, maybe just letting the busy daytime mind shut down before the pleasures of the evening. The word "aperitif" comes from the Latin *aperite*, which roughly translated means "to open the appetite". Not only the appetite for food but also the appetite of the mind. I found my favourite vermouth years ago at a small bar just off the Plaza Mayor in Madrid. It comes straight from the barrel, a golden life-enhancing liquid.

However, there is a Napa vermouth that can also work. It's called King Eider and is made by the Duckhorn Vineyards (*see* page 139). Correct: another feathered friend from Duckhorn. I have to start by saying that most California vermouth is utterly without merit. You shouldn't even cook with the stuff. It's generally made from inferior – let's be honest, awful – wine using no doubt artificial flavours.

King Eider is made from Duckhorn Sauvignon Blanc, triple distilled brandy, and a blend of chamomile, star anise, cinnamon, bitter orange rind, and Moroccan rose buds. A portion is aged briefly in barrel. Why King Eider? According to the Duckhorns, the King Eider duck lives and breeds farther north than any other waterfowl. They can often be found floating about on drift ice, on the rocks, as it were. The way civilized people order their vermouth. Twist of lemon optional.

# Bibliography

**Adams, Leon,** *The Wines of America*, New York, McGraw Hill Publishing, Fourth Edition, 1990.

**Bettiga, Larry; Golino, Deborah; McGourty, Glenn; Smith, Rhonda; Verdegaal, Paul; Weber, Edward,***Wine Grape Varieties in California*, Oakland, University of California Press, 2003.

**Cass, Bruce,** *The Oxford Companion to the Wines of North America*, Oxford University Press, 2000.

**Mondavi, Robert,** *Harvests of Joy*, New York, Harcourt Brace & Co, 1998.

**Muscatine, Doris; Amerine, Maynard; Thompson, Bob,** *The University of California/Sotheby Book of California Wine*, Los Angeles, London, University of California Press, Sotheby Publications, 1984.

**Roby, Norman and Olken, Charles,** *The Connoisseurs' Handbook of the Wines of California and the Pacific Northwest*, New York, Alfred Knopf, Fourth Edition, 1998.

**Sullivan, Charles,** *Napa Wine: A History from Mission Days to Present*, San Francisco, The Wine Appreciation Guild, 1994.
*A Companion to California Wine*, Berkeley, University of California Press, 1998.

The Sullivan books are invaluable, especially for the early history of Napa.

# Index